Q & A SERIES
ENGLISH
LEGAL SYSTEM

FOURTH EDITION

With best wishes TOM

All best wishes & Success

from Dr. V.N.SASTR

02.9.11.

Cavendish
Publishing
Limited

London • Sydney

TITLES IN THE Q&A SERIES

'A' LEVEL LAW

BUSINESS LAW

CIVIL LIBERTIES AND HUMAN RIGHTS

COMMERCIAL LAW

COMPANY LAW

CONFLICT OF LAWS

CONSTITUTIONAL & ADMINISTRATIVE LAW

CONTRACT LAW

CRIMINAL LAW

EMPLOYMENT LAW

ENGLISH LEGAL SYSTEM

EQUITY & TRUSTS

EUROPEAN UNION LAW

EVIDENCE

FAMILY LAW

INTELLECTUAL PROPERTY LAW

INTERNATIONAL TRADE LAW

JURISPRUDENCE

LAND LAW

PUBLIC INTERNATIONAL LAW

REVENUE LAW

SUCCESSION

TORTS LAW

Q & A SERIES
ENGLISH
LEGAL SYSTEM

FOURTH EDITION

Gary Slapper, LLB, LLM, PhD, PGCE
Director of the Law Programme
The Open University
and

David Kelly, BA, BA (Law), PhD
Principal Lecturer
The Law School
Staffordshire University

Cavendish
Publishing
Limited

London • Sydney

Fourth edition first published in Great Britain 2001 by Cavendish
Publishing Limited, The Glass House, Wharton Street, London
WC1X 9PX, United Kingdom
Telephone: +44 (0)20 7278 8000   Facsimile: +44 (0)20 7278 8080
Email: info@cavendishpublishing.com
Website: www.cavendishpublishing.com

© Slapper, G and Kelly, D   2001

First edition   1993
Second edition   1995
Third edition   1999
Fourth edition   2001

British Library Cataloguing in Publication Data

Slapper, Gary
English legal system – 4th ed – (The Cavendish Q & A series)
1. Law – England 2. Law – Wales
I. Title II. Kelly, David, 1950 Aug 16–
349.4'2
ISBN 1 85941 626 8

Printed and bound in Great Britain

CONTENTS

INTRODUCTION

This book has been written to assist students in their study of the English legal system. It has been composed for students of this subject, in general, and for undergraduates and those studying for professional examinations, in particular. The text is not a substitute for course books, law reports and legal journals, but aims to complement them by showing how typical examination and assignment questions can be answered.

The subject matter of the English legal system requires students to be familiar with our legal institutions and procedures, the criminal and civil processes, some substantive law, legal theories and debates in the realms of morals and politics. One thread running through all these topics is the requirement that students be evaluative and critical in their approach to the issues. It is also essential that answers take account of recent developments. Our answers in this book aim to show examples of such technique.

These answers will, perhaps, be most appreciated by students who have already acquired a good working knowledge of the relevant issues, principles and law and who desire clarification on the techniques that can be used to best present their knowledge in response to typical questions. The questions are modelled on those from a variety of English legal system courses, including the University of London (External) LLB. We have chosen a mix of essay and 'problem' questions and concentrated on issues which have current significance.

There have been seismic changes within the English legal system since the third edition of this book was published in 1999. There have been more major miscarriage of justice cases, like those involving the release of the Bridgewater Three, and the posthumous quashing of Derek Bentley's conviction for murder. There have been major changes to the criminal appeal system, and the establishment of the Criminal Cases Review Commission. We have seen with the new Civil Procedure Rules the most fundamental changes to the civil process for over a century, the Bowman Report on the Court of Appeal (Civil Division), and major consultation papers from the Lord Chancellor on conditional fees and rights of audience.

The Access to Justice Act 1999 has led to the establishment of the Legal Services Commission and the Community Legal Service and has redrawn the legal landscape. The 1998 Civil Procedure Rules came into force in 1999 and have been amended and updated 21 times since – the rules revolutionise the way people make civil claims and the way in which the courts deal with them. The Human Rights Act 1998 came into force in October 2000, and has already begun to ramify into virtually all aspects of law and, thus, how the legal system operates. To prepare for its implementation, the judiciary underwent the most comprehensive and detailed formal training in its entire 1,000 year history. The Auld Committee has undertaken a root and branch review of the criminal justice system. The Crown Prosecution Service has been re-organised, the nature of judicial impartiality has been authoritatively defined, the role of the jury has been exposed to intense public and legal debate, liability of advocates for courtroom negligence has been established, the appeals system has been altered, Alternative Dispute Resolution has become a major feature of British life and European law has continued to widen and deepen its application.

As a result of these profound changes, we have re-designed the structure of the book and offered an almost completely new range of questions and answers.

We are very grateful to Marilyn Lannigan for her fastidious and expert research assistance. We are also very grateful to our families for their forbearance in not asking too many questions while we were answering those in this book.

We have endeavoured to state the law as of 2001.

Gary Slapper
David Kelly
March 2001

TABLE OF CASES

TABLE OF STATUTES

TABLE OF STATUTORY INSTRUMENTS

TABLE OF EUROPEAN LEGISLATION

CHAPTER 1

SOURCES OF LAW AND LEGAL REFORM

Introduction

There are different interpretations of the phrase 'source of law'. It can, in jurisprudence, refer to what it is in our nature or society that necessitates law. More generally, however, the expression refers to the procedural origin of the law which is applied in the courts. There are three main sources, parliamentary legislation, delegated legislation and the common law. Used in this sense, the latter phrase, 'common law', connotes all judge made law and therefore includes equity.

If you are covering this theme, you should be very familiar with the origins and modern role of both common law and equity. You should also understand the details of the process of enacting legislation from the stage before the publication of Green Papers to the final stage, the Royal Assent. However, the English legal system cannot be treated as static; it is continuously responding to changes that take place in society as a whole. To deny the relevance of European law in an English legal system course would not only be restrictive, it would be wrong to the extent that it ignored an increasingly important factor in the formation and determination of UK law

You should also have a good knowledge of the different bodies associated with reform; permanent institutions, that is, the Law Reform Committee, the Criminal Law Revision Committee, the Law Commission and *ad hoc* bodies, such as Royal Commissions. You should, also, understand how the system resolves the interplay of several competing interest groups in order to produce legislation. This is a subject area where it is especially useful to have a sound knowledge of recent examples.

Checklist

You should be familiar with:

- the origin and modern operation of the common law;
- the origin and modern operation of equity;
- the stages of promulgation of legislation;
- parliamentary sovereignty and types of legislation;
- the types of delegated legislation and its advantages and disadvantages;
  the major institutions of the European Union (EU), particularly the European Court of Justice (ECJ);
- the institutions of law reform, Law Commission, *ad hoc* bodies, etc.

Question 1

What are the main sources of law today?

Answer plan

This is an, apparently, very straightforward question, but the temptation is to ignore the European Community (EC) as a source of law and to over emphasise custom as a source. The following structure does not make these mistakes:

- in the contemporary situation, it would not be improper to start with the EC as a source of UK law;
- then attention should be moved on to domestic sources of law: statute and common law;
- the increased use of delegated legislation should be emphasised;
- custom should be referred to, but its extremely limited operation must be emphasised.

Answer

European law

Since the UK joined the European Economic Community (EEC), now the EC, it has progressively, but effectively, passed the power to create laws which are operative in this country to the wider European institutions. The UK is now subject to Community law, not just as a direct consequence of the various treaties of accession passed by the UK Parliament, but, increasingly, it is subject to the secondary legislation generated by the various institutions of the EC.

European law takes three distinct forms; regulations, directives and decisions. Regulations are immediately effective without the need for the UK Parliament to produce its own legislation. Directives, on the other hand, require specific legislation to implement their proposals but the UK Parliament is under an obligation to enact such legislation as will give effect to the implementation of the directive. Decisions of the ECJ are binding throughout the Community and take precedence over any domestic law.

Parliamentary legislation

If the institutions of the EC are sovereign within its boundaries, then, within the more limited boundaries of the UK, the sovereign power to make law lies with Parliament. Under UK constitutional law, it is recognised that Parliament has the power to enact, revoke or alter such, and any, law it sees fit to deal with and no one Parliament can bind its successors. The extent of the ambit of this sovereignty may be brought into question with respect to the EC for such time as the UK remains a member, but, within the UK, Parliament's power is absolute. This absolute power is a consequence of the historical struggle between Parliament and the Stuart monarchy in the 18th century. Parliament arrogated to itself absolute law making power; a power not challenged by the courts, which were, in turn, granted an independent sphere of operation. It should be remembered, however, that the Human Rights Act (HRA) 1998 has, for the first time, given the courts the power to question, although not strike down, primary legislation

3

as being incompatible with the rights protected under European Convention on Human Rights (ECHR). It also allows the courts to declare secondary legislation to be invalid for the same reason.

Parliament makes law in the form of legislation, that is, Acts of Parliament. There are various types of legislation. Whereas public Acts affect the public generally, private acts only affect a limited sector of the populace, either particular people or people within a particular locality. Within the category of public Acts, a further distinction can be made between Government Bills and Private Members' Bills. The former are, usually, introduced by the Government, whilst the latter are the product of individual initiative on the part of particular MPs.

Before enactment, the future Act is referred to as a Bill and many Bills are the product of independent commissions, such as the Law Commission, or committees, such as the Law Reform Committee and the Criminal Law Revision Committee. Without going into the details of the procedure, Bills have to be considered by both Houses of Parliament and have to receive Royal Assent before they are actually enacted.

Delegated legislation has to be considered as a source of law, in addition, but subordinate, to general Acts of Parliament. Generally speaking, delegated legislation is law made by some person or body to whom Parliament has delegated its general law making power. In statistical terms, it is arguable that, at present, delegated legislation is actually more significant than primary Acts of Parliament. The output of delegated legislation in any year greatly exceeds the output of Acts of Parliament and, each year, there are over 3,000 sets of rules and regulations made in the form of delegated legislation, compared to fewer than 100 public Acts of Parliament. Delegated legislation can take the form of Orders in Council, which permit the Government to make law through the Privy Council. This power is usually considered in relation to impending emergencies but, perhaps, its widest effect is to be found in relation to EC law, for, under s 2(2) of the European Communities Act 1972, ministers can give effect to provisions of the Community which do not have direct effect. Most delegated legislation, however, takes the form of statutory instruments, through which government ministers exercise the powers given to them by general enabling legislation to make the particular rules which are to apply to any given situation within its ambit. A third type of delegated legislation is the bylaw, through which local authorities and public bodies are able to make legally binding rules within their area of competence or authority.

Delegated legislation has developed for a number of reasons. One such is the increased pressure on parliamentary time, with the consequent hiving off of detailed and time consuming work to ministers and their specialist departments. Another reason for the growth in the output of delegated legislation, is the highly technical nature of the subject matter to which it tends to be addressed and the concomitant need for such rules themselves to be highly technical. Any piece of delegated legislation is only valid if it is within the ambit of the powers actually delegated by Parliament. Any law made outside that restricted ambit of authority is void, as being *ultra vires,* and is open to challenge in the courts under the process of judicial review.

Common law

The next source of law that has to be considered is case law; the effective creation and refinement of law in the course of judicial decisions. It should be remembered that the UK's law is still a common law system and, even if legislation in its various guises is of ever increasing importance, the significance and effectiveness of judicial creativity should not be discounted. Judicial decisions are a source of law, through the operation of the doctrine of judicial precedent. This process depends on the established hierarchy of the courts and operates in such a way that, generally, a court is bound by the *ratio decidendi,* or rule of law implicit in the decision of a court above it in the hierarchy and, usually, by a court of equal standing in that hierarchy. Where statute law does not cover a particular area, or where the law is silent, generally, it will be necessary for a court deciding cases relating to such an area to determine what the law is and, in so doing, that court will inescapably and unarguably be creating law. The scope for judicial creativity should not be underestimated and, it should be remembered, that the task of interpreting the actual meaning of legislation in particular cases also falls to the judiciary and provides it with a further important area of discretionary creativity. As the highest court in the land, the House of Lords has particular scope for creating or extending the common law, and a relatively contemporary example of its adopting such a active stance can be seen in the way in which it overruled the long standing presumption that a man could not be guilty of the crime of rape against his wife (see *R* (1991)). It should, of course, always be remembered that Parliament remains sovereign as regards the creation of law and any aspect of the judicially created common law is subject to direct alteration by statute.

An extension of the doctrine of judicial precedent leads to a consideration of a further possible source of law; for, when the court is unable to locate a precise or analogous precedent, it may refer to legal textbooks for guidance and assistance. Such books are sub-divided, depending on when they were written. In strict terms, only certain venerable works of antiquity are actually treated as authoritative sources of law. Amongst the most important of these works are those by Glanvill from the 12th century, Bracton from the 13th century, Coke from the 17th century and Blackstone from the 18th century. Legal works produced after *Blackstone's Commentaries* of 1765 are considered to be of recent origin, but, although they cannot be treated as authoritative sources, the courts, on occasion, will look at the most eminent works by accepted experts in particular fields in order to help determine what the law is or should be.

Custom

The final source of law that remains to be considered is custom. The romantic view of the common law is that it represented a crystallisation of common customs, distilled by the judiciary in the course of its travels round the land. Although some of the common law may have had its basis in general custom, as Professor Zander points out, a large proportion of these so called customs were invented by the judges themselves and represented what they wanted the law to be, rather than what people, generally, thought it was.

There is, however, a second possible customary source of law and that is, rules derived from *specific* local customs. Here, there is the possibility that the local custom might differ from the common law and, thus, limit its operation. Even in this respect, however, reliance on customary law as opposed to common law, although not impossible, is made unlikely by the stringent test that any appeal to it has to satisfy. Amongst these requirements are that the custom must have existed from 'time immemorial' (that is, 1189) and must have been exercised continuously, within that period, and without opposition. The custom must also have been felt as obligatory, have been consistent with other customs and, in the final analysis, must be reasonable. Given this list of requirements, it can be seen why local custom does not loom large as an important source of law.

Question 2

How far would you agree with the contention that King Henry II deserves to be called 'the father of the common law'?

Answer plan

A suggested plan for answering this question is as follows:
- introduction – the range of contributory factors;
- 'tradition expressed in action' (Simpson);
- the role of Henry II's clerics – itinerant royal justice;
- royal justice in competition with other sorts of justice;
- Pollock and Maitland's six principles;
- conclusion – evaluating the role of an individual in legal history.

Answer

Before the Norman conquest in 1066, the English legal system involved a mass of oral customary rules, which varied according to region. Most writers agree with Pollock and Maitland's view that the common law had been largely established by the accession to the throne of Edward I in 1272. Certainly, the three courts of King's Bench, Common Pleas and Exchequer were operational by this time. It is true that Henry II, who reigned 1154–89, did much of significance to enhance the development of the common law, for instance, by popularising the King's court with the introduction of the Petty Assizes. We are, however, not really familiar with how the *Curia Regis* acted during the Norman period before Henry II, because the earliest plea rolls date from his reign, so it would perhaps be overpresumptuous to credit too much to Henry II. In any event, the development of the common law was contributed to by many factors of a general historical nature and it might be more meaningful to speak of the various parties which helped nurture the common law from its first green shoots to its full bloom rather than to try and find a 'father'.

Unlike continental civil law, the English system does not originate from any particular set of texts or digests but from what Simpson has called 'tradition expressed in action'. It began as customary law used in the King's court to settle disputes and conflicts which touched the monarch directly. To begin with, these only included the graver crimes which became Pleas of the Crown. After the Norman invasion, there were still many different types of court apart from the royal court: the stannary courts of Devon and Cornwall, the courts of the royal hunting forests but, principally, in potential rivalry with the royal court, were the feudal and manorial courts. It was during Henry II's reign (but, clearly, not wholly attributable to this one man), that the clerics in his court (that is, his royal entourage) began specialising in legal business and acting in a judicial capacity.

In the jurisdictional expansion considered presently, an important role was played by the clerics who developed a range of writs and establishing procedures which, perhaps very significantly, afforded themselves greater importance and provided themselves with a generous income. These practices developed into the common law of England, the law which was available throughout the realm. In Simpson's words: 'It was common as a prostitute is common: available to all.' On this point, it is, perhaps, the most convincing of the reasons why Henry should be regarded as the 'father of the common law', that he was largely responsible for the regional and itinerant royal justice, through which (by sending his judges up and down the country) the law truly became common.

Henry sent officials from the royal household to the counties and the travelling judges formed a nucleus of *iusticiarii totius Angliae* who had no local roots. They were, thus, much less susceptible to the corruption which had spoilt a similar attempt, earlier in the 12th century, in which the royal judges had actually been based in the local communities. It was under Henry II that judges were, for the first time, sent on 'circuits', hearing pleas in the major places they visited and taking over the work of the local courts. In this travelling mode, the royal representatives were *iusticiae errantes* (wandering justices) or *iusticiarii in itinere* (justices in *eyre*, that is, law French for journey). The judges were, periodically, sent on a 'general *eyre*', which included the whole country. Baker has argued, though, that it was the smaller circuit which was to prove 'the essence of the common law system', by bringing royal justice regularly to the counties.

The era, running from the Norman invasion to the accession of Edward I, saw the important struggle to administer justice between the royal judges and the tribunals of feudal lords, the shires and the hundreds which had survived from Anglo-Saxon times. The efforts of the royal judges were significantly assisted by the works of the text writers Glanvill and Bracton. Glanvill's *Tractatus de Legibus Angliae* (published under Henry II) was the first clear statement of the law, administered throughout the procedure of the royal courts. Glanvill was a senior royal judge. The writer's preface (it was, probably, not actually written by Glanvill, but by Hubert Walter or by Henry II's Chief Justiciary) divides the pleas into criminal and civil and the body of the work is mostly practical.

With only a few principles of general application before them and, by virtue, of some particular advantages of the evolving system, the royal judges had established the supremacy of their courts over all competing jurisdictions by the time of Edward's reign. Pollock and Maitland formulated six principles upon which were founded the usurpation of general jurisdiction by the *Curia Regis*. These principles show that, while much was done by Henry II to promote the common law, there were several other factors which engendered it, some of which were effective only after Henry II's reign.

First, the King's court was a court to go to in default of justice. Under the Norman kings, the litigant who wished to proceed in the ordinary court obtained the King's 'Writ of Right Patent' which contained the threat *quod nisi feceris vicecomes meus faciet* (if you do not do this, my sheriff will). Complaints and petitions for justice were numerous and these cases formed the basis of the growth of the common law throughout the development of the Register of Writs (added to each time a judge accepted a new writ as suitable to be used again in similar cases).

Secondly, the Writ of Right issued by the Royal Chancery became compulsory for all pleas relating to freehold land, according to an apparently lost ordinance of Henry II. This was so, even where the case was to be tried in the seigniorial court and, so, gave the King power over manorial courts.

Thirdly, was the introduction by Henry II of the Grand Assize, as an alternative to trial by battle in the proceedings on the Writ of Right. As these cases were decided by impartial neighbours, it became much more popular than trial by battle and was only available in the royal court.

Fourthly, was Henry II's introduction of the Petty Assizes, also only obtainable in the King's court. These assizes were for trying disputes concerning *disseisin* of land. They did not actually infringe the feudal rights of the lord to try actions relating to the title to the freeholds of his tenants. They did, though, become very popular because of their summary nature and were frequently used by dispossessed owners to recover *seisin*, since the opponent rarely took any further action if his claim was weak.

The fifth factor accounting for the usurpation of jurisdiction by the King's court was the expansion of the 'King's Peace' (the monarch's as opposed to a lord's right to deal with any local disorder, crime, etc). Pleas of the Crown increased rapidly at this time and included many claims that would, eventually, evolve into torts.

Finally, Pollock and Maitland mention the important series of writs which began with the word *praecipe*, where the sheriff was commanded to investigate a matter and give any wrongdoer the right to give satisfaction, or else face the royal judges for their judgment. This was among the Pleas of the Crown and, again, quickly became quite popular on account of its efficiency.

Kiralfy has advanced another factor significant in the acquisition of jurisdiction by the royal courts, namely the construction given to the Statute of Gloucester 1278 by the royal judges. This statute provided that no cases involving an amount of less than 40 shillings should be brought in the royal courts, but that they should be tried before local tribunals. The judges interpreted this to mean that no personal actions to recover a sum greater than 40 shillings could be commenced in the local courts, thus, reserving all important legislation for themselves. It is relevant here that the judges were anxious to attract litigants because their fees varied with the amount of business done.

Apart from the advantageous nature of the remedy in the recovery of land provided by the Petty Assizes, the growth in popularity of the royal courts is connected with the progressive move towards strong, centralised government and its accompanying ability to compel attendance at court and enforce execution of its judgments. By contrast, we can look at the diminution in power of the feudal lords, their dilatory procedures and the inadequate powers to make defendants appear in their courts and to enforce judgments. Additionally, only the royal courts could give litigants the novel and desirable method of proof, the *recognitio* or jury, as it came to be called.

In conclusion, it can be seen that, although Henry II was instrumental in making a number of important innovations which promoted the development of the common law, these policies were part of a wide and complex struggle for the power and revenue to be enjoyed by whoever controlled and administered justice. There were many other important figures involved, such as the clerics, the judges and the writers, whose own behaviour and interests it is important to appreciate in developing a proper understanding of the origins of the common law.

Question 3

Why was the development of equity necessary? Did equity satisfy those needs?

Answer plan

In response to this question, you should:
- define concept of equity;
- outline the origins of the system of equity;

- examine defects in the common law: expense, delay, corruption, single remedy, etc;
- note trusts;
- note the advantages of equity – no formality, enforceable judgments, mobility of court, varied remedies, etc;
- include some mention of the 1873–75 legislation;
- comment on the irony of modern equity being slow and rule bound.

Answer

In his *Nichomachean Ethics*, Aristotle argued that law operates through general rules in the pursuit of justice and is, thus, imperfect because it will fail to deal fairly with all eventualities. It is impossible for those who draft law to anticipate the infinite variety of circumstances which could arise in the future. Thus, if we are to have justice, we must use not simply a system of rules but, also, a power to depart from the rules in certain cases. Aristotle referred to *epieikia*, 'equity', as it was later known in its English form, as the absolute justice which corrects law in particular cases. In the light of the many problems encountered by litigants at common law, and the concerns of many Chancery personalities, equity developed to 'soften and mollify the extremity of the law': *per* Lord Ellesmere in *The Earl of Oxford's Case* (1615).

The establishment of the common law courts, in the early medieval period, did not represent the full extent of the Crown's jurisdiction. The monarch as the 'fountain of justice' retained a residuary power 'to do equal and right justice and discretion in mercy and truth' (Coronation Oath). The King received many petitions for justice from dissatisfied litigants and, by the 14th century, there were so many that they were being dealt with by the King's Council. By the end of the century, most were being sent directly to the Chancellor, the most senior officer of the Council.

The Chancery originated as the royal secretariat (its name comes from the chancel or latticed screen behind which the clerks worked) and the Chancellor was responsible for authenticating writs in ordinary cases. The earliest judicial work in Chancery was concerned with settling disputes within the department. Petitions to the King for legal redress against the Crown also began here. These proceedings were recorded in Latin, but it was the so called 'English side' of Chancery which grew to meet the more mundane needs of litigants, that hatched the Court of Chancery.

By the late 14th century, the Chancellor was dealing with a high number of petitions which could not properly be heard 'on the Latin side' of Chancery. By 1460, the Court of Chancery was as established as the common law courts. The ordinary ways of obtaining justice were not feasible options for many prospective litigants because they were too poor to afford the expensive process entailed in an action through the Court of Common Pleas. The plaintiff had to take care that the writ he chose was the appropriate one and that all the particulars were correct, otherwise the case might be lost as a result of the procedural defect.

A greater problem was that the common law only provided the remedy of damages, whereas a claimant might really wish for the defendant to desist from carrying out some activity (for example, a nuisance) or force him to carry out an obligation (for example, to sell a particular area of land). Additionally, the common law did not recognise simple breaches of common law as actionable. Actions for breaches of agreement could only be brought if they could be framed as writs for debt or detinue (wrongful detention of another's goods). The common law courts did not recognise actions for breaches of contract *per se*.

Local corruption also thwarted many claims. There is even evidence, mentioned by Baker, that some supplicants complained of witchcraft.

The common law had been quite well developed and was, as Simpson has argued, passed down as an essentially oral tradition amongst a very small legal profession (not many more than 50 judges and important lawyers, in about 1450). This group, however, had a very conservative conception of law. The response of the common law to the development of trusts, for example, illustrates how its conservatism led to the need for equity. The practice of making trusts (for example, a father giving property to two trusted friends to hold, on trust, for his son until the son reached a certain age) was becoming more popular by the end of the 14th century, especially amongst those who were going off to battle and were uncertain whether they would return. The common law courts, though, did not recognise such an arrangement. The property had been given to the trustees and it was theirs, thought the common law, to do with as they pleased. The intended beneficiary, the son, could have no legal remedy if the trustees abused their position. The Chancellor could, and did, act in such circumstances to order the trustees to fulfil the trust reposed in them.

The law was no respecter of persons and afforded no justice to those who came a cropper of a technicality. By contrast, equity acts *in personam*, that is, it is concerned with the conscience of the individual. In one 15th century case, Fortescue CJ rebuked counsel for advancing a legal point: 'We are here to argue conscience not the law!'

There were, principally, two theoretical justifications used by the Chancellors who developed the doctrines of equity. The first was that they were administering not law, but *conscience*. Thus, those who abused their position as trustee, or who sought to take an unconscionable advantage of another's mistake in a contract were corrected by equity. In the 15th century, the Chancellor's court was called a court of conscience. The use of the term 'equity' in this context, and its Aristotelian meaning, became more popular in the 16th century.

There were great advantages in the early forms of Chancery action. Unlike the actions at common law, the petition required no formality and the *subpoena* which was issued was much more effective than the common law *capias*. The former commanded the respondent to appear in Chancery and answer the petition under a fixed pain, often 100. There were none of the sort of problems involved at common law, where litigants were defeated by errors on the face of the writ because no cause of *subpoena* was stated on the petition. The hearings were not hampered by rules of evidence like those which required debts to be proven with deeds, and the Chancellor – who acted without a jury – could take evidence from the parties themselves. Unlike the common law courts, Chancery was not in a fixed place and followed the Chancellor. The court could even convene in his private house. A number of discretionary remedies were developed by Chancery. Specific performance was an order to compel a defendant to perform a specified activity, usually involving the sale of land. The injunction was an order used to prevent defendants from taking some specified action.

By the 16th century, the distinct approaches and procedures of law and equity had become clear. Law was concerned with a body of rules applicable to certain facts, whereas the Chancellor was concerned with individual cases which were dealt with according to the dictates of 'conscience'. Equity was consolidated during the 17th and 18th centuries, but difficulties were still experienced by litigants who had to seek legal and equitable remedies in separate courts. This could be problematic (slow and expensive) where a case required consideration from both legal and equitable perspectives. The administration of law and equity was achieved through the Judicature Acts 1873–75 after which, equity could be obtained in any division of the High Court.

It was a problem for equity that, on the one hand, its justice flowed from it not being a rule bound system, but one operating on discretion whilst, on the other hand, uncontrolled discretion could itself become oppressive by its unpredictability. Conscience varied from man to man. It was Selden who remarked that, if the measure of equity was the Chancellor's conscience, then one might as well make the standard measure of one foot the Chancellor's foot. Chancellors began to give reasons for their decisions in the 17th century and these were reported and gradually formed into a set of rules. Some maxims of equity were published in 1727 by Richard Francis, and have been relied on by courts ever since. They include the propositions: 'he who comes to equity must have clean hands'; 'equity is equality'; 'equity does nothing in vain'; and 'equity regards the substance not the form'. However, the improved system of reporting during the 18th century helped a system of equity precedents to develop and by then, as Baker puts it, *rigor aequitatis* had set in.

It is an irony of legal history that, as equity developed, it became less discretionary and was often as rigid as law.

Not long after its emergence, the Court of Chancery with its cheap, quick and effective procedures, became attractive to the wealthy as well as the poor. Avery has shown that, between 1452–50, the total number of petitions to the court increased sixfold and over 90% of the cases were, by this time, disputes about land.

From the 17th century, Chancery became notorious for delay and expense, a theme given a wonderfully biting and humourous exposure in Dickens' *Bleak House*. The court was insufficiently staffed with judges and had no effective appeal system. Estimates of cases pending in Chancery at this time went as high as 20,000. Some cases were still pending after 30 years. The court was also plagued with corruption. Gifts of gold or silver to court officials could often expedite proceedings and, by long usage, many of the gifts became 'fees' which could be demanded as of right. Fees could be demanded at each distinct stage of the proceedings, so Masters procured rules of court which extended court cases beyond any reasonable length.

What had begun as a system based on speed, cheapness, informality and a concern to assist the poor had collapsed by the 19th century into an incredibly protracted, rule bound, expensive system for the wealthy.

This irony can, however, be overstated. There were several more positive contributions made by equity to the legal system. Its discretionary remedies of the injunction and specific performance; the law of trusts; and the equity of redemption should all be cited in this regard.

Question 4

What is legislation? Where does it come from, how is it produced, and what does it do?

Answer plan

This is a wide ranging question that requires a fairly close knowledge of the workings of Parliament. A suggested structure is:

- distinguish statute law from judge made common law;
- consider where the actual proposals for legislation come from – for example, government policy, Green Papers, White Papers;
- mention the limited scope for individual MPs to generate legislation;
- set out the actual process that legislation has to pass through to be enacted;
- reference should be made to the various types of legislation, emphasising the role of delegated legislation; mention should also be made of the potential impact of the HRA 1998.

Answer

Although the courts retain an essential function in the interpretation of statutes, it has to be be recognised that legislation is the predominant form of law making in contemporary times. The process through which an Act is passed by Parliament is itself a long one, but, before concentrating on that process, some attention should be focused on the pre-parliamentary process through which the substantive content of the Act is generated.

Sources of legislation

There are various sources of legislative proposals.

The majority arise from government departments, in pursuit of their policies in relation to their allocated area of responsibility. Actual policy will, of course, be a consequence of the political persuasion and imperatives of the Government of the day and as, by convention, the Government is drawn from the majority party, it can effectively decide what legislation is to be enacted through its control over the day to day procedure of the House of Commons, backed by its majority voting power. The decision as

17

to which Bills are to be placed before Parliament in any session is under the effective control of a cabinet committee known as the Legislation Committee, which draws up the legislative programme announced in the Queen's Speech, delivered at the opening of the parliamentary session.

In some cases, the Government will set out its tentative plans for legislation in the form of a Green Paper and will invite interested parties to comment on the proposals. After considering any response, the Government may publish a second document, in the form of a White Paper, in which it sets out its firm proposals for legislation.

If the Government is the source of most legislation, the role of the individual MP, acting through the process for the enactment of Private Members Bills, should not be forgotten. There are, in fact, three ways in which an individual MP can propose legislation. These are through the ballot procedure, by means of which backbench MPs get the right to propose legislation on the 10, or so, Fridays specifically set aside to consider such proposals; under Standing Order 39 and, under the 10 minute rule procedure. Of these procedures, however, only the first has any great chance of success and, even then, success will depend on securing a high place in the ballot and, in practice, must not incur government disapproval. If such a proposal is looked upon with favour by the Government, it has an especially good chance of being enacted, since the Government may provide additional time to allow it to complete its passage. Perhaps the most famous Private Members Bills have related to the provision of abortion. The original Abortion Act 1967 was introduced by the Liberal MP, David Steel, and has been subject to numerous attempts to amend it by further Private Members' Bills.

Alternative sources for proposed legislation are the recommendations of independent commissions and committees, such as the Law Commission, or the Law Reform Committee, which considers alterations in the civil law, and the Criminal Law Reform Committee, which performs similar functions in relation to the criminal law.

It is always open to pressure groups to lobby political parties and individual MPs in an attempt to have their particular interests made concrete in legislation. However, some concern has been expressed at the growing number of professional lobbyists who are paid to make sure that their clients' cases are prominently placed before the appropriate people within the legislature.

The legislative process

Before any legislative proposal, known at that stage as a Bill, can become an Act of Parliament, it must proceed through, and be approved by, both Houses of Parliament and must receive the Royal Assent. A Bill must be given three readings in both the House of Commons and the House of Lords before it can be presented for the Royal Assent. It is possible to commence the procedure in either House, although money Bills must be placed before the Commons, in the first instance.

When a Bill is introduced in the Commons, it undergoes five distinct procedures:

(a) it receives its first reading. This is purely a formal procedure in which its title is read and a date set for its second reading;

(b) after this comes the second reading of the Bill and this is the time when its general principles are subject to extensive debate. The second reading is the critical point in the process of a Bill. At the end, a vote may be taken on its merits and, if it is approved, it is likely that it will, eventually, find a place in the statute book;

(c) if the Bill passes its second reading it is sent for consideration by a standing committee which will consider its provisions in detail. The function of the standing committee, which, if it is successfully proposed, may be replaced by a Select Committee or committee of the whole House, is to go through the Bill clause by clause and to amend it to bring it into line with the general approval given by the House at its second reading;

(d) the next stage is the report stage, at which the standing committee reports the Bill back to the House for the consideration of any amendments made by it;

(e) the final stage in the process is the third reading, during which further debate may take place; although, on this occasion, it is restricted strictly to matters relating to the content; matters relating to general principles cannot be raised.

When a Bill has passed all these stages, it is passed to the House of Lords for its consideration, which is essentially similar, if less constrained by the pressures of time. After consideration by the Lords, the Bill is passed back, with any amendments, to the Commons which must then consider such amendments. Where one House refuses to agree to the amendments made by the other, Bills can be repeatedly passed between them, but, it must be remembered, that Bills must complete their passage within the life of a particular parliamentary session and that a failure to reach agreement within that period might lead to the total loss of the Bill. Given the fact that the House of Lords is a non-elected institution and that the Members of the House of Commons are the democratically elected representatives of the voters, it has been apparent since 1911 that the House of Lords should not be in a position to block the clearly expressed wishes of the Commons. The Parliament Acts of that year, and of 1949, restricted the blocking power of the Lords. The situation now is that a 'money Bill', containing only financial provisions, can be enacted, without the approval of the House of Lords, after only one month's delay and any other Bill can only be delayed by one year by the House of Lords' recalcitrance. For the moment, the House of Lords has twice rejected attempts to pass Acts of Parliament to withdraw an accused person's right to elect for jury trial in relation to 'either way' offences. The Government, however, remains committed to the measure and insists that, if necessary, it will use the Parliament Acts to force the legislation through Parliament.

No statute becomes law unless it has received the Royal Assent and, although, in the unwritten Constitution of the UK, no specific rule expressly states that the monarch has to assent to any Act passed by Parliament, there is, by now, a convention to that effect and any monarch would place their constitutional status in extreme jeopardy by a refusal to grant the Royal Assent to legislation passed by Parliament. The procedural nature of the Royal Assent was highlighted the Royal Assent Act 1967, which reduced the process of acquiring Royal Assent to a formal reading out of the short titles of any Act in both Houses of Parliament.

An Act of Parliament comes into effect on the date of the Royal Assent, unless there is any provision to the contrary in the Act itself. It is, perhaps, necessary – given the regulatory purpose and form of modern legislation – and it is increasingly common for newly enacted statutes to contain commencements which provide for the Act to become operational at some date in the future. Difficulty and an inevitable lack of certainty is produced, however, by the, now common, occurrence of passing general enabling Acts which delegate powers to a government minister to introduce specific parts of the Acts in question at some later date, through the means of statutory instruments.

Types of legislation

There are two distinct types of legislation; the Public Act and the Private Act. The former relates to questions which affect the general public, whereas the latter relates to the powers and interests of particular individuals or institutions, although, it has to be remembered, that the provision of statutory powers to particular institutions can have a major effect on the general public. Public Bills can be further categorised into Government Bills and Private Members' Bills, to which reference has already been made.

Acts of Parliament can also be distinguished on the basis of their function. Some are designed to initiate new legislation to cover new areas of activity, previously not governed by legal rules; but, other Acts are aimed at rationalising or amending existing legislative provisions. Examples of the latter type of legislation are the consolidating Act and the codifying Act. The purpose of any consolidating Act is to bring together the various statutory provisions contained in a number of discrete pieces of legislation, without altering them, for the main part. Company law is a classic example of this procedure, in that, it has evolved through the enactment of numerous Acts of Parliament which have, every so often, been brought together under one large consolidating Act. The Companies Act of 1985 is just such an Act; although it is arguable that a new consolidation Act is due in the light of the subsequent changes that (the 1985) Act has undergone since was passed.

Codifying Acts seek, not just to bring existing statutory provisions under one Act, but also look to give statutory expression to common law rules. The classic examples of such legislation are to be found in the commercial sector; amongst them are the Partnership Act of 1890 and the Sale of Goods Act 1893.

21

The HRA 1998

Traditionally, by virtue of the operation of the doctrine of parliamentary sovereignty, Parliament could pass whatever laws it though proper, without the courts being able to challenge the legality of such legislation. Although the HRA 1998 has not directly changed this relationship, it has, nonetheless, altered it significantly. Even where a court holds that a piece of primary legislation does not comply with the provisions of the ECHR, that court cannot declare the legislation invalid: the court has no such power to strike down primary legislation. However, the court can issue a declaration of incompatibility stating that the Act breaches the provisions of the Convention. Although changing the incompatible Act remains solely the power of Parliament, it is highly likely that a judicial declaration of incompatibility would lead to an alteration of the Act in question. The HRA 1998 provides for a fast track procedure for changing any Act subsequently found to be in breach of the Convention.

Question 5

What do you understand by 'delegated legislation'? Consider its advantages and disadvantages and explain how it is controlled by Parliament and the courts.

Answer plan

This question focuses more closely than the previous one on delegated legislation. It is suggested that the increased importance of delegated legislation makes it a likely question topic. An good plan might take the following form:

- an explanation of what is meant by delegated legislation;
- it is important to emphasise the large amount of delegated legislation that is produced annually;
- examples of the various types of delegated legislation should be provided;
- the various advantages and disadvantages should be listed and considered in some detail;

- mention should be made of parliamentary scrutiny of delegated legislation;
- the powers of the courts to control delegated legislation, through judicial review and under the HRA 1998, should be considered;
- it would be appropriate to weigh the advantages and disadvantages and offer a conclusion in favour or against its use.

Answer

It is apparent that, in the course of the last 100 years, as the State has, increasingly, become involved in regulating society in general and the economy in particular, the actual form of legislation has altered. Instead of general and definitive Acts of Parliament which attempt to lay down detailed provisions, the modern form of legislation tends to be of the enabling type, which simply states the general purpose and aims of the Act and lays down a broad framework, whilst delegating to ministers of the State the power to produce detailed provisions in pursuit of those general aims.

Generally speaking, delegated legislation is law made by some person or body to whom Parliament has delegated its general law making power. In statistical terms, it is arguable that, at present, delegated legislation is, actually, more significant than primary Acts of Parliament. The output of delegated legislation in any year greatly exceeds the output of Acts of Parliament and, each year, there are over 3,000 sets of rules and regulations made in the form of delegated legislation, compared to fewer than 100 public Acts of Parliament.

Any piece of delegated legislation has the same legal force and effect as the Act of Parliament under which it is enacted, but, equally, only has effect to the extent that it is authorised by its enabling Act.

Delegated legislation can take the form of Orders in Council which permit the Government, through the Privy Council, to make law. The Privy Council is, nominally, a non-party political body of eminent parliamentarians, but, in effect, it is simply a means through which the Government, in the form of a committee of ministers, can introduce legislation without the need to go through the full parliamentary process. Although legal textbooks tend to use situations of State emergency as exemplifying occasions when the Government will resort to the use of Orders in Council, in actual fact, a great number of Acts are brought into operation through these provisions. Perhaps the widest scope for Orders in Council is to be found in relation to EC law, for, under s 2(2) of the European Communities Act 1972, ministers can give effect to provisions of the Community which do not have direct effect.

Statutory instruments are the means through which Government ministers introduce particular regulations under powers delegated to them by Parliament by enabling legislation. As with Orders in Council, such provisions do not have to undergo the full rigour of parliamentary procedure involved in the passing of Acts of Parliament. The relative and, indeed, the absolute importance of statutory instruments can be seen by the fact that, in 1998, parliament enacted 3,321 statutory instruments, as compared to only 49 general public Acts. There is such a range of powers delegated to ministers and such a range of Acts of Parliament which are given practical effect by statutory instruments, that it is almost pointless to give examples of statutory instruments; but, it is certainly worth pointing out that such regulations tend to be of a highly specific and technical nature. One example of the way in which statutory instruments are used, if not abused, may be found in the Limited Liability Partnership Act 2000. Although the Act establishes this new form of legal entity, it says very little about how it is to operate and be regulated. Sections 14 and 15 of the Act simply state that appropriate regulations will be made in the future and introduced through statutory instruments.

Bylaws are the third type of delegated legislation; by means of which, local authorities and public bodies are empowered by Parliament to make legally binding rules within their area of competence or authority. Bylaws may be made by local authorities under such enabling legislation as the Local Government Act 1972.

In addition to the foregoing, the various Court Rule Committees are empowered to make the rules which govern procedure in the particular courts over which they have delegated authority, under such Acts as the Supreme Court Act 1981, the County Courts Act 1984, and the Magistrates' Courts Act 1980.

The final source of delegated legislation is to be found in the power given to certain professional bodies to regulate the conduct of their members. An example of this type of delegated legislation is the power that the Law Society has been granted under the Solicitors' Act 1974 to control the conduct of practising solicitors.

The very fact that modern law tends to be the means through which an interventionist state, actually and actively, participates in civil society has had the effect that the very form of law has had to change. Rather than simply establishing a legal framework of general abstract rules, modern legal regulation requires that legal rules be both specific in their aims and particular in their application.

Parliament delegates its law making powers for a number of reasons. Amongst these are the fact that it simply does not have the time to consider every detail that might be required to fill out the framework of enabling legislation. A related point is the fact that, given the highly specialised and extremely technical nature of many of the regulations that are introduced through delegated legislation, the majority of MPs simply do not have sufficient expertise or the technical knowledge to consider such provisions effectively.

These reasons why there has been a increased reliance on delegated legislation also suggest its potential advantages over the more traditional set-piece public Acts. For example, the fact that Parliament does not have to spend its time considering the minutiae of specific regulations, permits it to focus its attention more closely, and at greater length, on the broader, but no less important matters of principle in relation to the enactment of general enabling legislation. The use of delegated legislation also permits far greater flexibility in regulation, permitting rules to be changed quickly in response to changes in the situations they are aimed at regulating. It can also be appreciated that, the use of delegated legislation not only permits an *ad hoc* response, but also a quicker response to emergencies or unforeseen problems. With regard to bylaws, it practically goes without saying that local and specialist knowledge should give rise to more appropriate rules than reliance on the general enactments of Parliament.

There are, however, distinct disadvantages in the prevalence of delegated legislation as a means of making legal rules. The most important of these relates to a perceived erosion in the constitutional role of Parliament to the extent that it does not actually consider provisions made in this way. To the extent that Parliament, as a body, is disempowered, other people, notably government ministers and the civil servants who work under them, in order to produce the detailed provisions of delegated legislation, are given more power than might be thought constitutionally correct. The foregoing, which inevitably involves the question of general accountability and the need for effective scrutiny, is compounded by the difficulty which ordinary MPs face in keeping abreast of the sheer mass of technically detailed legislation that is enacted in this form. Also, the point must be raised that, if parliamentarians cannot keep up with the flow of delegated legislation, how can the general public be expected so to do?

These difficulties and potential shortcomings in the use of delegated legislation are, at least to a degree, mitigated by the fact that specific controls exist in relation to it. These controls are twofold; parliamentary and judicial. Parliament exercises general control, to the extent that ministers are always responsible to Parliament for the regulations they actually make within the powers delegated to them by Parliament. Additionally, it is a usual requirement that such regulations be laid before Parliament. This laying before Parliament can take two forms, depending on the provision of the enabling legislation. The majority of Acts simply require that regulations made under their auspices be placed before Parliament and automatically become law after a period of 40 days, *unless a resolution to annul them is passed*. Other regulations, on the other hand, require a positive resolution of one or both of the Houses of Parliament before they become law. Also, since 1973, there has been a Joint Select Committee on Statutory Instruments, whose function is to consider statutory instruments. It has to be remembered, however, that this committee merely scrutinises statutory instruments from a technical point of view, as regards drafting, and, therefore, has no power as regards any question of policy in the regulation. Its effectiveness as a general control is, therefore, limited. EC legislation is overseen by a specific committee and local authority bylaws are usually subject to the approval of the Department of the Environment.

Previously, judicial control of delegated legislation was limited, but not unimportant. It was always possible for delegated legislation to be challenged, through the procedure of judicial review, on the basis that the person or body to whom Parliament has delegated its authority has acted in a way that exceeds the limited powers delegated to them. Any provision found to be outside this authority was *ultra vires* and, consequently, void. Additionally, there is a presumption that any power delegated by Parliament is to be used in a reasonable manner and the courts may, on occasion, hold particular delegated legislation to be void on the basis that it is unreasonable. It should be noted that this latter judicial power has been exercised more often in relation to local authorities than government ministers. The HRA 1998 fundamentally alters the courts' power over delegated legislation. As secondary legislation, rather than primary legislation such as Acts of Parliament, delegated legislation may be declared ineffective by the courts where it is found not to comply with the provisions of the HRA 1998, so ministers must be extremely careful to ensure that any delegated legislation does, in fact, comply with the ECHR.

In conclusion, it may be suggested that the use of delegated legislation is now typical of modern law making. Even if it does involve considerable problems in relation to its control, it is unlikely to diminish as the modern State increasingly adopts an active role in society and uses law as simply a mechanism through which to exercise that role. However, the courts have a potentially very significant means of controlling its misuse under the HRA 1998, although it remains to be seen how such powers will be used.

Question 6

The English legal system can no longer be considered on its own, but has to be understood within the context of the EC and its institutions.

What are the institutions referred to and what is their impact on the English legal system?

Answer plan

Again, it has to emphasised that the English legal system can only be understood in the context of the EC. This straightforward question ensures that a candidate is at least aware of that context. Such an awareness can be shown by covering the following points:

- a short history of the EC – consideration of its present status and, perhaps, its future;
- a detailed account of the various types of EC legislation, that is, treaties, regulations and directives and how they are each brought into effect;
- the essential institutions of the EC and their relationships and particular roles and functions;
- particular attention to the relationship between the ECJ and the domestic courts of the UK, with examples where possible.

Answer

The EC was set up by the Treaty of Rome in 1957, and the UK joined the Community in 1973.

Before the UK joined, Community law was just as foreign as law made under any other jurisdiction and it only affected those UK citizens who had dealings with its Members. On joining the Community, however, the UK and its citizens accepted, and became subject to, the EC law. This subjection to European law remains the case, even where the parties to any transaction are themselves both UK subjects. In other words, in areas where it is applicable, European law supersedes any existing UK law to the contrary.

Community law consists primarily of the Treaty of Rome and any amending legislation such as the Single European Act (SEA) to which the UK acceded in 1986; or the Maastricht Treaty.

The Treaty of Rome, as subsequently amended, provides for two types of legislation: regulations and directives:

(a) regulations: regulations, under Art 189 of the Treaty of Rome, apply to, and within, Member States generally without the need for those States to pass their own legislation. They are binding and enforceable, therefore, from the time of their creation within the European context and need no further validation by national Parliaments;

(b) directives: directives, on the other hand, are, in theory, supposed to state general goals and leave the precise implementation to individual Member States in the form that they consider appropriate. In practice, however, directives tend to state the means, as well as the ends, to which they are aimed and the ECJ will give direct effect to directives which are sufficiently clear and complete.

The major institutions of the EC are: the Council; the European Parliament; the Economic and Social Committee; the Commission; the ECJ.

The Council

The Council is made up of ministerial representatives of each of the 15 Member States of the Community. Thus, when considering economic matters, the various States will be represented by their finance ministers or, if the matter relates to agriculture, the various agricultural ministers will attend. The Council of Ministers is, in essence, the supreme organ of the EC and, as such, it has the final say in deciding upon Community legislation. Although it acts on recommendations and proposals made to it by the Commission, it does have the power to instruct the Commission to undertake particular investigations and to submit detailed proposals for its consideration.

As the format of particular council fluctuates, much of its day to day work is delegated to a committee of permanent representatives which operates under the title of COREPER.

The European Parliament

The European Parliament is the directly elected European institution and, to that extent, it can be seen as the body which exercises democratic control over the operation on the EC. As in national Parliaments, Members are elected to represent constituencies, the elections being held every five years. Membership is divided amongst the 15 Member States in proportion to the size of their various populations. The Parliament's general secretariat is based in Luxembourg and, although the Parliament sits in plenary session in Strasbourg for one week in each month, its detailed and preparatory work is carried out through 18 permanent committees which usually meet in Brussels.

The powers of the European Parliament, however, should not be confused with those of national Parliaments, for the European Parliament is not a legislative institution and, in that respect, it plays a subsidiary role to the Council of Ministers. Originally, its powers were merely advisory and supervisory.

In pursuance of its advisory function, the Parliament always had the right to comment on the proposals of the Commission and, since 1980, the Council has been required to wait for the Parliament's opinion before adopting any law. In its supervisory role, the Parliament scrutinises the activities of the Commission and has the power to remove the Commission by passing a motion of censure against it by a two-thirds majority.

The legislative powers of the Parliament were substantially enhanced by the SEA 1986. Since that enactment, it has had a more influential role to play, particularly in relation to the completion of the internal market. For one thing, it can now negotiate directly with the Council as to any alterations or amendments it wishes to see in proposed legislation. It can also intervene to question and, indeed, to alter any 'joint position' adopted by the Council on proposals put to it by the Commission. If the Council then insists on pursuing its original 'joint position', it can only do so on the basis of unanimity.

The SEA 1986 also requires Parliament's assent to any international agreements to be entered into by the Community. As a consequence, it has ultimate control, not just in relation to trade treaties, but also as regards any future expansion of the Community's membership.

The European Parliament is, together with the Council of Ministers, the budgetary authority of the EC. The budget is drawn up by the Commission and is presented to both the Council and the Parliament. As regards what is known as 'obligatory' expenditure, the Council has the final say, but in relation to 'non-obligatory' expenditure, Parliament has the final decision whether or not to approve the budget. Such budgetary control places the Parliament in an extremely powerful position to influence Community policy and it has not failed to make use of such power. Indeed, in 1979 and 1984, it rejected the proposed budgets, which had to be redrafted.

The Economic and Social Committee

If the Parliament represents the directly elected arm of the Community, then the Economic and Social Committee represents a collection of unelected but, nonetheless, influential interest groups throughout the Community. This committee is a consultative institution and its opinion must be sought prior to the adoption of any Commission proposal by the Council. The Economic and Social Committee represents the underlying 'corporatist' nature of the Community to the extent that it seeks to locate and express a commonality of view and opinion on proposals from such divergent interests groups as employers, trade unions and consumers. It is, perhaps, symptomatic of the attitude of recent British Governments to this underlying corporatist, essentially Christian Democratic, strand within the EC, that it dispensed with its own similar internal grouping, the National Economic Development Council, in 1992.

The Commission

The Commission is the executive of the EC, but it also has a vital part to play in the legislative process. To the extent that the Council can only act on proposals put before it by the Commission, the latter institution has a duty to propose to the Council measures that will advance the achievement of the Community's general policies.

Another of the key functions of the Commission is the implementation of the policies of the Community and, to that end, it controls the allocation of funds to the various common programmes within the Community. It also acts, under instructions from the Council, as negotiator between the Community and external countries.

A further executive role of the Commission is to be found in the manner in which it operates to ensures that Treaty obligations between States are met and that Community laws relating to individuals are enforced. In order to fulfil these functions, the Commission has been provided with extensive powers, both in relation to the investigation of potential breaches of Community law and the subsequent punishment of offenders. The classic area in which these powers can be seen in operation is in the area of competition law. Under Arts 85 and 86 of the Treaty of Rome, the Commission has substantial powers to investigate and control potential monopolies and anti-competitive behaviour and it has used these powers to levy what, in the case of private individuals, would amount to huge fines where breaches of Community competition law has been discovered. If the individual against whom a finding has been made objects to either the result of the investigation or the penalty imposed, the course of appeal is to the ECJ.

The Court of Justice

The ECJ is the judicial arm of the EC and, in the field of Community law, its judgments overrule those of national courts. It consists of 13 judges, assisted by six advocates general, and the Court sits in Luxembourg. The role of the advocates general is to investigate the matter submitted to the Court and to produce a report, together with a recommendation for the consideration of the court. The actual court is free to accept the report, or not, as it sees fit.

The jurisdiction of the ECJ involves it in two key areas in particular:

(a) determining whether any measures adopted, or rights denied, by the Commission, Council or any national government are compatible with treaty obligations. Such actions may be raised by any Community institution, government or individual. A Member State may fail to comply with its Treaty obligations in a number of ways. It might fail or indeed refuse to comply with a provision of the Treaty or a regulation; or, alternatively, it might refuse to implement a directive within the allotted time provided. Under such circumstances, the State in question will be brought before the ECJ, either by the Commission or another Member State or, indeed, individuals within the State, as being in dereliction of its responsibility;

(b) determining, at the request of national courts, the interpretation of points of Community law. This procedure can take the form of a preliminary ruling where the request precedes the actual determination of a case by the national court. The point that has to be remembered, however, is that it is the Court of Justice's role to determine such issues and, in relation to those issues, it is superior to any national court.

The Court of First Instance

The SEA 1986 was not without effect on the operation of the justice system in the Community, in that it provided for a new Court of First Instance to be attached to the existing Court of Justice. The jurisdiction of the Court of First Instance is limited mainly to internal claims by employees of the Community and to claims against fines made by the Commission under Community competition law. The aim is to reduce the burden of work on the Court of Justice, but there is a right of appeal, on points of law only, to the full Court of Justice.

Question 7

Explain the powers of the ECJ, paying particular regard to its relationship with UK courts.

Answer plan

This question focuses in more detail on the role of the ECJ within the EC and requires some particular attention to be paid to the relationship of that court to the domestic courts within the UK. In answering it, students could usefully apply the following structure:

- detail the role and powers of the ECJ;
- describe its structure and how it operates, making some mention of the Court of First Instance;
- explain the way in which references can be made to the ECJ from domestic courts under Art 234 (formerly Art 177);
- provide some examples of cases decoded by the ECJ that have had particular impact on the UK.

Answer

The ECJ is the judicial arm of the EU and, in the field of Community law, its judgments overrule those of national courts. It consists of 15 judges, assisted by nine advocates general, and sits in Luxembourg. The role of the advocates general is to investigate the matter submitted to the Court and to produce a report, together with a recommendation for the consideration of the Court. The actual Court is free to accept the report, or not, as it sees fit.

The SEA 1986 provided for a new Court of First Instance to be attached to the existing ECJ. The jurisdiction of the Court of First Instance is limited mainly to internal claims by employees of the Community and to claims against fines made by the Commission under Community competition law. The aim is to reduce the burden of work on the ECJ but there is a right of appeal, on points of law only, to the full ECJ.

The ECJ performs two key functions:

(a) it decides whether any measures adopted, or rights denied, by the Commission, Council or any national government are compatible with treaty obligations. Such actions may be raised by any EU institution, government or individual. A Member State may fail to comply with its Treaty obligations in a number of ways. It might fail or, indeed, refuse to comply with a provision of the Treaty or a regulation; or, alternatively, it might refuse to implement a directive within the allotted time provided for. Under such circumstances, the State in question will be brought before the ECJ, either by the Commission or another Member State, or, indeed, individuals within the State concerned;

(b) it provides authoritative rulings, at the request of national courts under Art 234 (formerly Art 177) of the Treaty of Rome, on the interpretation of points of Community law. When an application is made under Art 234, the national proceedings are suspended, until such time as the determination of the point in question is delivered by the ECJ. Whilst the case is being decided by the ECJ, the national court is expected to provide appropriate interim relief, even if this involves going against a domestic legal provision, as in *Factortame Ltd v Secretary of State for Transport (No 1)* (1989). The Common Fishing Policy established by the EEC had placed limits on the amount of fish that any Member country's fishing fleet was permitted to catch. In order to gain access to British fish stocks and quotas, Spanish fishing boat owners formed British companies and reregistered their boats as British. In order to prevent what it saw as an abuse and an encroachment on the rights of indigenous fishermen, the British Government introduced the Merchant Shipping Act 1988, which provided that any fishing company seeking to register as British would have to have its principal place of business in the UK and at least 75% of its shareholders would have to be British nationals. This, effectively, debarred the Spanish boats from taking up any of the British fishing quota. Some 95 Spanish boat owners applied to the British courts for judicial review of the Merchant Shipping Act 1988, on the basis that it was contrary to Community law. The case went from the High Court, through the Court of Appeal, to the House of Lords who referred the case to the ECJ. There, it was decided that the Treaty of Rome required domestic courts to give effect to the directly enforceable provisions of Community law and, in doing so, such courts are required to ignore any national law that runs counter to Community law.

This procedure can take the form of a preliminary ruling where the request precedes the actual determination of a case by the national court.

Article 234 (formerly Art 177) provides that:

The Court of Justice shall have jurisdiction to give preliminary rulings concerning:

(a) the interpretation of treaties;

(b) the validity and interpretation of acts of the institutions of the Union and of the European Central Bank;

(c) the interpretation of the statutes of bodies established by an act of the Council, where those statutes so provide.

Where such a question is raised before any court or tribunal of a Member State, that court or tribunal may, if it considers that a decision on the question is necessary to enable it to give judgment, request the Court of Justice to give a ruling thereon.

Where any such question is raised in a case pending before a court or tribunal of a Member State against whose decision there is no judicial remedy under national law, that court or tribunal shall bring the matter before the Court of Justice.

It is clear that it is for the national court, and not the individual parties concerned, to make the reference. Where the national court or tribunal is not the 'final' court or tribunal, the reference to the ECJ is discretionary. Where the national court or tribunal is the 'final' court, then reference is obligatory. However, there are circumstances under which a 'final' court need not make a reference under Art 234 (formerly Art 177). These are:

(a) where the question of Community law is not truly relevant to the decision to be made by the national court;

(b) where there has been a previous interpretation of the provision in question by the ECJ, so that its meaning has been clearly determined;

(c) where the interpretation of the provision is so obvious as to leave no scope for any reasonable doubt as to its meaning. This latter instance has to be used with caution given the nature of Community law; for example, the fact that it is expressed in several languages using legal terms which might have different connotations within different jurisdictions. However, it is apparent that, where the meaning is clear, no reference need be made. In undertaking such a task, a purposive and contextual approach is mainly adopted, as against the more restrictive methods of interpretation favoured in relation to UK domestic legislation. The clearest statement of this purposive contextualist approach adopted by the ECJ is contained in its judgment in the *CILFIT* case:

> Every provision of Community law must be placed in its context and interpreted in the light of the provisions of Community law as a whole, regard being had to the objectives thereof and to its state of evolution at the date on which the provision in question is to be applied [*CILFIT Srl v Minister of Health (No 283/81)* (1982)].

Another major difference between the ECJ and the court within the English legal system is that the former is not bound by the doctrine of precedent in the same way as the latter is. It is always open to the ECJ to depart from its previous decisions where it considers it appropriate to do so. Although it will endeavour to maintain consistency, it has, on occasion, ignored its own previous decisions, as in *European Parliament v Council* (1990), where it recognised the right of the Parliament to institute an action against the Council.

The manner in which European law operates to control sex discrimination, through the Equal Treatment Directive, is of significant interest and, in *Marshall v Southampton and West Hampshire AHA* (1993), a number of the points that have been considered above were highlighted. Ms Marshall had originally been required to retire earlier than a man in her situation would have been required to do. She successfully argued before the ECJ that such a practice was discriminatory and contrary to Council Directive 76/207/EEC on the equal treatment of men and women.

The present action related to the level of compensation she was entitled to as a consequence of this breach. UK legislation, the Sex Discrimination Act 1975, had set limits on the level of compensation that could be recovered for acts of sex discrimination. Marshall argued that the imposition of such limits was contrary to the Equal Opportunity Directive and that, in establishing such limits, the UK had failed to comply with the Directive.

The House of Lords referred the case to the ECJ under Art 234 (formerly Art 177) and the latter determined that the rights set out in relation to compensation under Art 6 of the Directive were directly effective, and that, as the purpose of the Directive was to give effect to the principle of equal treatment, that could only be achieved by either reinstatement or the awarding of adequate compensation. The decision of the ECJ, therefore, overruled the financial limitations placed on sex discrimination awards and, effectively, overruled the domestic legislation.

Question 8

> One of the hallmarks of an advanced society is that its laws should not only be just, but also that they be kept up to date and be readily accessible to all who are affected by them [Law Commission, *Proposals for English and Scottish Law Commissions*, Cmnd 2573, 1965].

Consider the mechanisms and procedures for law reform in Britain in the light of the above quotation.

Answer plan

The quotation that forms the basis of this question refers to the Law Commission and, although the question does, indeed, require an examination of the operation of the Law Commission, the temptation must be resisted to launch straight into such a consideration and other means of law reform must also be considered. The following structure avoids this possible error:

- Parliament enacts reforming legislation and this may be in pursuit of party political agendas, or may be the outcome of Private Member's Bills;
- judges may also alter law, especially the common law;

- both of these mechanisms are not unproblematic and the potential problems should be considered;
- reference should be made to Royal Commissions of enquiry, but the major focus of attention should be on the Law Commission;
- the creation, structure and procedure of the Law Commission should be considered in some detail.

Answer

At one level, law reform is either a product of parliamentary or of judicial activity. However, the enactment of new legislation or the statement of a novel *ratio* in a particular case are the end products of a complex process, and to focus on them, and to ignore the various procedures that led up to them, would be to diminish our understanding of the process of law reform.

Legislation is, by definition, the product of Parliament, but, perhaps, of more interest is the actual source or inspiration for any particular piece of reforming legislation. Any consideration of the legislative process must be placed in the context of the political nature of Parliament. Thus, a great deal of law reform can be seen as the implementation of party political policies. Examples of this type of legal reform include the changes in trade union law, education law and the financing of local services introduced by past Conservative administrations, as well as the present Government's introduction of the HRA 1998 and its constitutional reforms in the areas of devolution and the House of Lords.

If Parliament tends to focus on narrow political issues, it, nonetheless, does have access to a wider consideration of law reform through various mechanisms. There is, first of all, the issuing of consultative Green Papers in which the Government sets out its proposals for legislation and invites contributions from interested parties.

More formal advice may be provided through advisory standing committees such as the Law Reform Committee, established in 1952, which is charged with the task – in relation to the civil law – of considering what changes are desirable to such legal doctrines as may be referred to it by the Lord Chancellor. In relation to criminal law, the Criminal Law Revision Committee was established in 1959 to perform similar functions.

A further mechanism for considering the need for law reform in specific areas is the Royal Commission. Examples of such commissions include the Commission on Criminal Procedure (1980), which led to the enactment of the Police and Criminal Evidence Act 1984, and the Royal Commission on Criminal Justice (the Runciman Commission), which examined pre-trial procedure, the conduct of trials, and the provision of redress in the case of alleged miscarriages of justice, reporting in 1993. Also, senior judges may be given the remit of investigating particular aspects of the legal system. The most important recent report of this nature was Lord Woolf's *Access to Justice*, which examined the operation of the procedures of the civil law system. Lord Woolf's recommendations were subsequently given effect by the Civil Procedure Act 1997 and the new Civil Procedure Rules 1998. Lord Justice Sir Robin Auld is currently undertaking a corresponding examination of the criminal law system.

The weakness in this panoply of committees and commissions is that they are all *ad hoc* bodies. Their remit is limited to the particular areas of concern that is put before them and they do not have the power either to widen the ambit of their investigation or to initiate proposals for investigation and reform.

In relation to particular reforms, external pressure groups or interested parties may very often be the original moving force behind them; and, when individual MPs are fortunate enough to find themselves at the top of the ballot for Private Members' Bills, they may well also find themselves the focus of attention from such pressure groups proffering pre-packaged law reform proposals in their own particular areas of interest. The weakness, again, lies in the single issue, *ad hoc* nature of such proposals, at the expense of a general consideration of related issues.

Turning attention to the role of the judiciary, it is a matter of little contemporary controversy to recognise that judges have a potential power to create law. Indeed, it is at least arguable that the whole of the common law is a product of judicial creativity. Given this potential to create law, it would seem equally obvious and uncontroversial to recognise that the judiciary also has a role to play in law reform. An example of this reforming power was evident in the recognition of the possibility of the crime of rape within marriage (see *R* (1991)). Whereas the common law had, previously, denied the possibility of such a crime being committed when the parties were married, both the Court of Appeal and the House of Lords held that a husband is not immune from prosecution for rape in relation to his wife. Another example of this reform of the common law was where a Scottish court extended an old common law offence to cover the sale of solvents to minors.

In both of the above cases, the courts restricted themselves to reforming common law rules and it is in that limited area that some of those who would recognise the power of the judiciary to reform the law would limit its operation. The argument is that, as the judges created the common law, they can be left to reform it. There is an important corollary to this, however, that judges have no place in reforming statutory provisions. They may signal the ineffectiveness of such provisions and call for their repeal or reform, but it would be a usurpation of the legislature's function and power for the courts to engage in such general reform.

A more fundamental attack on the suitability and, indeed, the ability, of judges to initiate reforms in the law has not been without support. In an article on the very question of law reform in the UK, Norman Marsh suggested that judges no longer automatically command the prestige or charismatic authority that they once had and, in an undisguised attack on the reforming activities of Lord Denning, he suggested that the legislative chamber rather than the courtroom is the more appropriate place for the undertaking of such reforms.

If Parliament is overly concerned with particularities of law reform and the judiciary is constitutionally and practically disbarred from reforming the law in other than an opportunistic and piecemeal basis, there still remains the need for some institution to concern itself generally with the question of law reform. That need is, at present, met by the Law Commission.

The Law Commission was established under the Law Commission Act 1965. It was set up under the auspices of Lord Gardiner LC, with the specific aim of improving the previous *ad hoc* consideration of law reform by charging it with the duty of keeping the law *as a whole* under review and making recommendations for its *systematic* reform. Under the Act of 1965, the Law Commission was constituted as an independent body with full time members. It was given duties with regard to the revision and codification of the law, but its prime duty was, and remains, law reform.

The Commission is a purely advisory body and its relationship with Parliament was carefully and cautiously set out by the first chairman of the English Law Commission, Lord Scarman (Sir Leslie, at the time), as follows:

> The Commission has been called into being to advise the Government and Parliament, first, in the planning of law reform; secondly, in the formulation of detailed proposals for the reform of the law. The theory that underlies the Act is that law reform should be the province of the legislature; that the legislature requires specialist advice in the planning and formulation of law reform; and that this advice should be provided by a body independent of the executive and of Parliament ... [*Law Reform: The New Pattern*, 1998].

The scope of the Commission is limited to those areas set out in its programme of law reform, but its ambit is not unduly restricted, as may be seen from the range of matters covered in its seventh programme, set out in 2000. Not surprisingly, the effect of the HRA 1998 is a major aspect of the programme.

It is estimated that, at any one time, there are some 25 law reform projects being actively considered by the Commission and it only ever recommends reform after it has undertaken an extensive process of consultation with informed and/or interested parties. It is this process of general and disinterested consultation, as the basis for the formulation of a genuinely informed recommendation, which distinguishes the procedure of the Commission from the reforms of the judiciary and the partial reforms advocated by interested parties. Reference has already been made to the way in which the judges altered the common law rule relating to rape within marriage, but it is perhaps worthy of mention that the Law Commission already had issued a working paper, entitled *Rape Within Marriage*, in 1990 and its report of the same name was issued in 1992 (Law Com No 205). The Commission continues to consider whether this particular matter, and other important related matters concerning the relationship of married couples, such as the question of compelling of a wife to give evidence against her husband, should be subject to legislative reform. The point to be made is that judges can only change the common law with regard to the problem encapsulated in the case that comes before them: the Commission, on the other hand, is at liberty to consider all matters relating to a specific issue.

Annual reports list all Commission publications and, at the conclusion of a project, a report will be submitted to the Lord Chancellor and Parliament for their consideration and action. The Law Commission claims that, in the period since its establishment in 1965 till the end of 1999, a total of 102 of its law reports have been implemented. For example, the Contracts (Rights of Third Parties) Act 1999 was based on the recommendations of the Commission's Report No 242, *Privity of Contract*, 1996. However, 23 reports containing recommendations for law reform remain to be implemented. According to the current Chairman of the Commission, Robert Carnwath, the most serious failing in implementation is in the criminal law area, where, as yet, none of the Commission's reports have been implemented. Nor has there been any significant move towards the codification of the criminal law as the Commission supports.

The establishment within the Lord Chancellor's Department of a division, one of whose tasks is to promote law reform, may signal an increased recognition of the importance of the process of law reform; alternatively, it may signal a move to marginalise the role of the Law Commission by bringing the law reform process more directly under the control of the Lord Chancellor. It is hoped that the future of the Commission is secure as a disinterested source for the proposal of law reform.

CHAPTER 2

THE COURTS AND THE APPELLATE PROCESS

Introduction

The courts

A sound knowledge of the civil and criminal court structure is essential for a proper understanding of many aspects of the English legal system. You should be aware of the jurisdiction of each court (that is, which types of cases each court is competent to deal with), how its workload compares with other courts, how it is organised and what criticisms have been made of these features. The courts in question are the county courts, magistrates' courts, the Crown Court, the High Court, the Court of Appeal, the House of Lords and the Judicial Committee of the Privy Council.

Very important in this area are the criticisms made of the civil justice system in the Civil Justice Review of 1988, and the Woolf Report of 1997. The proposals are the result of a two year investigation of the system's current weaknesses. Lord Woolf's main aims of are to cut delay, reduce expense and simplify the process of litigation. The system is now being redesigned to fit in more with the interests and conveniences of litigants and less with the financial benefits to lawyers. Lord Woolf had said that costs were the most serious problem to be addressed, because problems arising from costs 'contaminate the whole civil justice system'. Many people have been deterred from proceeding with cases because of the possible costs, and others pressurised into settling their claims for sums lower than they deserve, for fear of costs escalating beyond their means.

The main reform objectives are:

- to encourage parties to explore alternatives to the resolution of a dispute by a court;

- the introduction of a single set of rules governing proceedings in the High Court and the county courts;
- a shorter timetable for cases to reach court, and for the length of trials.

The thrust of the revised system is to give more control to judges in litigation and less influence to lawyers. Most litigants will first be directed to alternative dispute resolution, making court actions a last resort. Community Service funding will become available for such settlements. There will be a three tier system: small claims (up to £5,000, except for personal injury claims for which the £1,000 limit will apply in small claims, and where most will be dealt with on the fast track); a fast track for cases at the lower end of the scale; and a multi-track for the remaining cases. All cases where a defence is received will be examined by a procedural judge who will allocate the case to the appropriate track.

The court structure will remain essentially the same, but heavier and more complex cases will be concentrated at trial centres which have the resources needed, including specialist judges. Judges will be given 'hands on' management of cases, making decisions about the timetabling of the trial and the issues to be resolved. There will be incentives to settle cases early, and penalties for causing unnecessary delay, including the obligation for a litigant to be liable for interest rates of up to 25% on top of costs. A litigant who makes an offer of settlement which is not accepted, but which is matched or exceeded at trial, is entitled to additional interest on his damages. These additions are 25% for damages up to £10,000, 15% for damages between £10,000 and £15,000, and 5% for damages above £50,000. There is a 'fast track' procedure, with a £2,500 limit on costs, for claims of between £3,000 and £10,000 (claims below £3,000 going to small claims courts). These fast track cases will be heard within 30 weeks of being brought and the hearings should not last longer than three hours. For claims over £10,000, and also for claims of less, but where the facts or law are especially complex, or where an issue of public importance is raised, or oral evidence from experts is necessary, the cases will be managed by judges. These cases will have a standard fee for advocacy and use written expert evidence, in contrast to today's norm of using expert testimony. Judges now also have the power to allocate the burden of costs at the end of a case by reference to the conduct of the parties.

The reforms have required funding in order to support new computer systems (for case management in the courts) and to retrain judges, but much of this money will come from savings achieved over time by the future early settlement of cases. The new civil process is designed to be co-ordinated with the development of the Community Legal Service.

Following the publication of a Court Service Consultation Paper in 1999, fees for taking cases to civil courts were updated to reflect more closely the costs involved in a case being tried. The principle idea here is that, where people can afford to pay the costs involved in their bringing a legal action, the taxpayer should not be expected to pay for them. Nonetheless, there is a subsidy for costs associated with some family proceedings. This is to put as few barriers as possible in the way of people using the courts to protect themselves from violence or harassment, or trying to resolve disputes about the care of children.

Should fees be payable by those wishing to use the courts? Some observers point out that payments are not made by members of the public at the point of use in the education and health systems, and that justice can be seen as being just as important as those services. Contrariwise, the Lord Chancellor has pointed out that were the courts to become free at the point of use, the money needed to pay the bill would have to come from closing down large parts of the civil legal aid or shutting schools or hospitals. Thus, legal policy is inextricably bound up with social policy in general.

The appellate process

You should be familiar with:

- what rights of appeal exist and what conditions, if any, apply in relation to all courts (civil and criminal);

- the findings and recommendations of the Runciman Commission on Criminal Justice (1993) about criminal appeals;
- appeals procedure: what powers the appellate courts have;
- the systems for references to be made to the Court of Appeal (Criminal Division) by the Home Secretary and the Attorney General.

You should be familiar with how the Criminal Appeal Act 1995 changes the system of criminal appeals, and changes made from 1998 to the work of the Court of Appeal (Civil Division) as a result of the Bowman Report. The Royal Commission on Criminal Justice, under the chairmanship of Viscount Runciman, reported in July 1993. Many of its 352 recommendations address matters relating to the courts, juries and the appellate process. You should be familiar with these proposals. Wherever appropriate, the relevant proposals have been incorporated into answers here. The Report is also covered in Chapter 7.

Question 9

In what ways are Information and Communications Technology (ICT) being used by the courts and the legal system, and with what justification?

Answer plan

A good answer will:

- recount the historical setting;
- discuss the Consultation Paper, *Modernising the Civil Courts*;
- explain deficiencies of the old system;
- explain the 'virtual court', the proposed uses of email, gateway partnerships, online support and IT (information technology) kiosks;
- consider IT and the judiciary;
- discuss changes in legal practice, for example, conveyancing.

Answer

Changes in technology produce changes in social practice. In the world of law, practice has, from a distant perspective, changed very little over the centuries. The establishment by William Caxton of a printing press at Westminster in 1476 began a series of changes that were drastically to affect the doctrine of precedent, in particular, and, therefore, law in general. Printing enabled judges and lawyers in one part of the country to learn about other judgments with greater speed and accuracy than ever before. The pervasion of the telephone and the photocopier in the 20th century also had significant consequences for law. The effect of ICT on law in the 21st century will undoubtedly run wide and deep.

Making a claim from a computer or digital TV is just one way that people will be able to get access to justice under plans to improve customer service in the civil and family courts, announced in 2001 by David Lock, minister at the Lord Chancellor's Department. The Court Service Consultation Paper, *Modernising the Civil Courts*, outlines how technology and new ways of working can be used to improve the range and quality of services available for people who need to use the civil courts. The proposals, which received a £43 m funding boost in the Spending Review 2000, are the first major reform of the way the civil courts deliver services to the customer. They aim to support the progress made by civil justice reforms launched in April 1999 and create a civil court system fit for the 21st century. The minister said that: 'This is an unparalleled period in the history of the civil justice system. In the space of less than a decade, we have seen significant civil justice reform and the birth of a new era in Human Rights. There have been major changes in the way citizens interact with the State and with each other. Disputes are no longer simply about local problems, and often relate to contracts and agreements made across regional and national boundaries.' Yet, he argued, the structure of the civil courts and the way they work has not kept pace with these changes. Most people using the court are still limited to communicating in writing or by attending in person. While this was entirely appropriate for the time of Dickens, it no longer serves modern day society. Nor does the location of county courts best match service to need. While many of the urban and suburban courts are close to each other with good public transport links, rural courts, where public transport is difficult, are thinly spread.

Developments in technology have given people more direct access to services from their own homes, the library, workplace and even the supermarket. Email has become the communication medium of choice for much of business. People are able to see the benefits of technology in other areas of their lives and, rightly, expect better services and modern facilities from the courts.

The latest proposals show how the civil courts can, with the help of technology and partnerships with other agencies, provide easier and cheaper access to justice.

The proposals include a 'virtual court' – that is, using the internet, email and digital TV to make small claims and other transactions with the court – and 'court on call' – enabling a range of court processes to be available by telephone, for example, to make a request to enter judgment. There would also be 'gateway partnerships', providing improved access to court services through partnerships with advice agencies and links with the Community Legal Service – for example, court staff could act as an outpost of the court office, enabling the customer to have access to procedural advice and court services via laptop an,d similarly, advice agencies could be provided with direct access to court services via the web, so the advisor can counsel the client and assist in transactions with the court at the same time.

The reforms also promise easier access to information and advice, for example, providing 24 hour information about cases and advice about court procedures via the internet and call centres, kiosks in libraries (where people not only get on-screen advice, but can link up to a Citizens' Advice Bureau via video-link), partnerships with advice agencies and links with the Community Legal Service to provide people with web access to court services at the same time as they are getting advice. A restructuring of the civil court network is also envisaged, providing courts according to regional need, population distribution and transport networks rather than historical accident. Improved access to court hearings is expected through partnerships with magistrates' courts, tribunals, use of hired facilities and video-conferencing, in addition to the network of primary court hearing centres.

In addition, improved IT support for the judiciary is planned with the development of electronic case filing, electronic presentation of evidence, digital-audiorecording, video-conferencing and improved electronic communication between the judiciary and court staff and in-court computers to allow access to court files and email. In January 2001, Ian Magee, Chief Executive of the Court Service said: 'These proposals are about extending court services into the heart of the community. Modern technology allows the court into people's living rooms and offices via personal computers and digital TV, making our services available at times and in ways that suit our customers. But so much of our work involves those who have no access to technology, or who are excluded by language or disability. Through partnerships with advice agencies we hope to reach out into society to those who might otherwise be excluded.' He recognised, however, that changes will happen at different speeds. Some ideas are already being tried in the courts and the Report outlines the proposals for more pilot projects. Lord Justice Brooke, who represents the judges on the Board that produced the Consultation Paper, said: 'The Court Service has kept the judges fully informed of these ideas. The judges are keen to see that sensible use is made of modern technology and working methods in the day to day business of the courts.'

The pilot projects include online applications to the court. This pilot, launched on 5 February 2001, will explore the use of email to reduce the need for attendance in court. Parties to cases at Preston County Court will be able to email the judge with their interim applications. Kiosk services will also be given trials. The touch screen kiosk will provide advice, information and court forms from libraries in Telford and, nearby, Madeley in Shropshire. It includes a videolink to the local Citizens Advice Bureau which will enable customers to dial up on-screen advice on, for example, filling in a form or what to do next.

A video-conferencing pilot was launched on 28 July 2000. It seeks to evaluate the effectiveness, uses, benefits and cost savings of video-conferencing. There are currently three suites installed at the Court of Appeal, Leeds and Cardiff Courts, and the network will be extended to more outlying courts in 2001.

Online issue of claims, judgments and warrants are being given trials and will provide the citizen and small businesses with a web-based claims service. Call centres are still at an early stage. This pilot is seeking ways of extending hours of service to obtain court forms, leaflets and simple procedural advice.

The Court Service aims to produce a blueprint for the future of the civil and family courts and a detailed implementation plan by early summer 2001. This will take account of responses to the consultation which ends on 21 April 2001.

The Community Legal Service (CLS) was launched in 2000 and its use of ICT will, if current plans are properly implemented, make legal advice much more accessible for many people than was previously the case. The idea is that the CLS will create local networks of legal services, based on local needs and priorities, and deal with matters that most affect people's everyday lives, such as debt problems, housing or entitlement to benefits.

Local partnerships will identify local needs for legal advice, and set local priorities to ensure funds are directed at the areas of greatest need. There will be a CLS 'Quality Mark' that will identify the legal advisers who provide good quality advice and information. A CLS website will be established to give people direct access to good practical, online information for a range of legal and related issues and to signpost them to organisations which can offer help face to face.

Measures in the Electronic Communications Act 2000 will also have a major effect on the way law works. The time needed to buy a house will probably eventually be cut from months to a matter of weeks, or even days. Under English law, the process of buying and selling houses, flats, buildings and land (called 'real property') is protracted. Computers cannot now be used to facilitate these transactions in the way a non-lawyer (especially, an ICT expert!) might expect. This is because the law requires that contracts for the sale of land and the deed required to convey land must be in writing and signed – a deed must also be witnessed (Law of Property (Miscellaneous Provisions) Act 1989). These requirements date back to 1677 and 1845. Electronic conveyancing is the legal process of the transfer of ownership of land from one person to another. However, the term is often used to describe the whole of the legal work associated with the buying and selling of land from the initial searches (where lawyers check to see if the property has any legal obligations associated with it) and enquiries, through exchange and completion of contracts, to registration of title. In its fullest sense, electronic conveyancing will enable all of that work and registration of title at HM Land Registry to be done without paper and without any manual signatures.

Under the Act, all the conveyancing information needed to sell or buy a property would (via computers) be made available quickly and simultaneously to everybody concerned. This would enable problems to be identified and resolved at the outset of a series of transactions, rather than much later on. The new system will require up to date, widely accessible electronic databases which will provide information to buyers, sellers and their legal representatives. This requires co-operation from local authorities, public utilities and others. Already 15 million properties are registered electronically; and online access is widely available for those who wish to use it. Nonetheless, the creation of a national electronic database of land information sufficient to provide comprehensive online search facilities will take time.

It is clear that, during the next several years, the operation of the courts and the legal system, historically notorious for their prolixity of process and delay, will be dramatically altered by the use of ICT.

Question 10

Describe the work of the coroners' courts and explain what social role this part of the legal system is expected to perform.

Answer plan

You should:

- explain historical setting of coroners' courts;
- note current numbers and duties of coroners;
- consider verdicts and purpose of classifications;
- consider patterns of death;
- discuss the problems posed by the meaning of 'how' in the formula of the purpose of the inquest.

Answer

The coroners' courts are one of the most ancient parts of the English legal system, dating back to at least 1194. They are not, in modern function, part of the criminal courts, although, for historical reasons, they have an association with that branch of the justice system.

Coroners were originally appointed as *custos placitorum coronae*, keepers of the pleas of the Crown. They had responsibility for criminal cases in which the Crown had an interest, particularly a financial interest. By development of their role, however, and, particularly, through the pioneering work of the 19th century coroner Dr Thomas Wakley, the coroner became, in Wakley's phrase, 'the people's judge'. The coroner is the ultimate public safeguard in an area of unmatched importance: the official documenting of how people die. Marilyn Lannigan, an authority on the history of the coroner, has pointed to the fact that it was Wakley who originally campaigned for all suspicious deaths, deaths in police custody or prison, and deaths attributable to neglect, to be brought within the jurisdiction of the coroner. He was an energetic reformer who was also an MP and founder of the medical journal *The Lancet*.

Today, there are 157 coroners' courts, of which 21 sit full time. Coroners are, usually, lawyers (with at least a five year qualification within s 71 of the Courts and Legal Services Act 1990), although about 25% are medical doctors with a legal qualification. The main jurisdiction of the coroner today concerns unnatural and violent deaths, although treasure trove is also something, occasionally, dealt with in these courts. However, the Treasure Act 1996 came into effect in 1997 and introduced new rules relating to the reporting of finds and how they should be dealt with. The number of inquests into treasure trove will, eventually, fall away to zero, although there were still 62 in 1999.

The classifying of types of death is clearly of critical importance, not just to the State, politicians and policy makers, but also to the sort of campaign groups that exist in a constitutional democracy to monitor suicides, drug-related deaths, deaths in police custody and prison, accidental deaths, deaths in hospitals and through industrial diseases. It is important for us to know, for example, that there were 3,750 suicides in England and Wales in 1999, as this should inform public policy related to the health service, community services, custodial policy and the emergency services.

In 1999, there were approximately 600,000 registered deaths in England and Wales (Home Office Statistical Bulletin, *Statistics of Death Reported to Coroners*, 20 April 2000). Deaths must be reported to a coroner, if they seem unnatural or violent; the coroner will order a post mortem and this may reveal a natural cause of death which can be duly registered. If not, or in certain other circumstances, such as where the death occurred in prison or police custody, or if the cause is unknown, then there will be an inquest. There were 201,000 deaths reported to coroners in 1999, resulting in 124,800 post mortem examinations and 24,800 inquests. At the inquests, verdicts showed rises in 1999, for most categories of death like industrial disease (up 200 to 2,300), drug-related deaths (up 80 to 570, a 16% increase) and accidents (up 350 to 9,600). The largest rise was in verdicts of natural causes, up 400 to 3,300, the highest rise for 30 years. Of the industrial disease deaths, 96% of deaths were male.

Most inquests (96%) are held without juries, but the State has been insistent that certain types of case must be heard by a jury in order to promote public faith in government. When, in 1926, legislation, for the first time, permitted inquests to be held without juries, certain types of death were deliberately marked off as still requiring jury scrutiny and these included deaths in police custody, deaths resulting from the actions of a police officer on duty and deaths in prison. This was seen as a very important way of fostering public trust in, potentially, oppressive aspects of the State. In 1971, the Brodrick Committee Report, Cmnd 4810, on the coronial system saw the coroner's jury as having a symbolic significance and thought that it was a useful way to legitimate the decision of the coroner.

The coroners' court is unique in using an inquisitorial process. There are no 'sides' in an inquest. There may be representation for people like the relatives of the deceased, insurance companies, prison officers, car drivers, companies (whose policies are possibly implicated in the death) and train drivers, etc, but all the witnesses are the coroner's witnesses. It is the coroner who decides who shall be summoned as witnesses and in what order they shall be called.

Historically, an inquest jury could decide that a deceased had been unlawfully killed and then commit a suspect for trial at the local assizes. When this power was taken away in 1926, the main bridge over to the criminal justice system was removed. There then followed, in stages, an attempt to prevent inquest verdicts from impinging on the jurisdictions of the ordinary civil and criminal courts. Now, an inquest jury is exclusively concerned with determining who the deceased was and 'how, when and where he came by his death'. The court is forbidden to make any wider comment on the death and must not determine or appear to determine criminal liability 'on the part of a named person'. Nevertheless, the jury may still now properly decide that a death was unlawful (that is, crime). The verdict 'unlawful killing' is on a list of options (including 'suicide', 'accidental death' and 'open verdict') made under legislation and approved by the Home Office.

Some of the legal questions vexing the coronial process are quite significant when one considers the general role of the coroners' system to plot national patterns of death. It is, as noted above, the purpose of an inquest to determine, among other things, how the deceased died, and 'how' in this context means, according to one view, simply by what physical cause of death and in what immediate circumstances. According to another proposition, however, one needs to take a much broader interpretation of the word 'how', in order to give a sufficiently thorough investigation to the issue (in some cases) of whether there was an unlawful killing.

Among the possible scenarios covered by the phrase 'unlawfully killed' is manslaughter through gross negligence committed by a company. The problem here is that, in a case involving a member of the public or an employee who has been killed in an event arising from a company's operations, one often cannot properly tell whether the death has resulted from 'gross negligence' on the company's part, unless and until one has found out the answers to all sorts of questions about how the company ran its business prior to the death. But, to ask such questions can be objected to on the basis that such an explorative exercise involves an excursus into matters beyond the proper scope of the inquest according to the Divisional Court in *R v Sussex Coroner ex p Homberg* (1994).

The meaning of the word 'how' in a coroner's court was addressed in *Homberg*. Simon Brown LJ stated that although the word 'how' is to be widely interpreted, it means 'by what means' the death came about rather than 'in what broad circumstances'. Thus, a coroner or counsel at an inquest can object to any line of inquiry which seeks to find out about 'the broad circumstances of the death'. On the other hand, unless the court knows something about the broad circumstances of a company's operations, it is impossible to determine whether there has been 'gross negligence'. Questions from counsel designed to elicit information from witnesses about the past practices of a company, its record on safety, or who in the company knew what and at what time, could, thus, be objected to on the basis of *Homberg*, while being perfectly defensible on the basis of testing whether the principle of 'gross negligence' manslaughter is applicable.

It is not always possible to identify suspicious deaths, and the recent case of Dr Harold Shipman highlighted the need to have a system which, generally, identifies cases which require further investigation before the cause of death is officially certified and the matter closed. In 2001, it became apparent that Dr Shipman was able, while practising as a GP, to kill over 100 people without the system detecting this homicidal conduct.

Not all of the work of HM Coroners is as riddled with intrigue as a day in the life of the American medical examiner, as portrayed in contemporary fiction and television. Nonetheless, the importance of the system in maintaining an open society and acting as a buttress against sinister conduct is immense.

Question 11

Critically analyse the composition, role and effectiveness of the magistrates' courts in the light of the proposals to allocate more cases to them.

Answer plan

Your answer should deal with the following issues:

- what magistrates' courts are and the powers they exercise – specific mention should be made to summary and either way offences;
- who magistrates are and how they are selected;
- the perceived shortcomings of the system;
- the training that is given to magistrates and the role of the justices' clerk;
- some suggestions for opening up the system to a wider number of people and improving its operation.

Answer

There are approximately 700 magistrates' courts in England and, within these courts, some 30,000 unpaid part time lay magistrates and about 92 full time professional stipendiary magistrates (District Judges (Magistrates' Courts)) are empowered to hear and decide a wide variety of legal matters.

In relation to the criminal law, magistrates are empowered to try summary cases, that is, less serious cases in which the accused has no right to insist on a jury trial. Currently, magistrates may also try 'either way' offences where the accused elects to have their case decided by the magistrates' court. The point is, however, that, for the moment, the decision rests with the accused and they can, if they so choose, insist that that their case is heard before a judge and jury in the Crown Court. The Government has insisted that the power to select the trial forum should be passed from the accused to the magistrates, in relation to these 'either way' offences. Although two previous versions of a Criminal Justice (Mode of Trial) Bill have been defeated in the House of Lords, a third proposal for such a Bill was included in the

Queen's speech to the opening of the new session of Parliament in December 2000. It appears likely, therefore, that the reform will be proceeded with, even if the government has to use the Parliament Acts to force the Bill through the House of Lords. In any event, it is estimated that already 97% of all criminal cases are dealt with by the magistrates' court.

In deciding cases, the magistrates' courts have considerable power; in criminal cases they can sentence guilty parties to prison sentences of up to six months, or 12 months where consecutive sentences are involved, and can impose fines of up to £5,000 under the Criminal Justice Act 1991; and their civil law jurisdiction is equally wide empowering them to hear family law cases, particularly under the Children Act 1989 and the Domestic Proceedings and Magistrates' Courts Act 1978. Yet, to a very great extent, the magistracy is made up of people who have no recognised legal qualifications. (Stipendiary magistrates are legally qualified, being required under the Justices of the Peace Act 1979 to be barristers or solicitors of at least seven years standing.) This apparent anomaly between power and lack of legal qualification is, at one and the same time, the major strength and weakness of the system of magistrates' courts. Magistrates, or justices of the peace, as they are known, are supposed to be ordinary members of the public, chosen to decide cases involving their fellow citizens on the basis of facts presented before them. In this regard, their lack of special legal knowledge is seen as actually legitimising their position as representatives of the general mass of people who are subject to the law.

Of primary concern, however, to those who are critical of the operation of magistrates' courts is the appointment procedure which determines who can act as justices of the peace. Under the Justices of the Peace Act 1979, magistrates are appointed and, indeed, removed from office, by the Lord Chancellor on behalf of the Queen after consultation with local advisory committees. The role of these advisory committees is of considerable importance, but the names of the people who actually serve on them tends to be kept confidential, in order, it is claimed, to prevent their being canvassed on behalf of particular candidates for office.

In the past, proposals for office tended to be generated by local interest groups such as political parties, trade unions, chambers of commerce and like bodies and this limited constituency may have perpetuated the wider perception of the magistracy as representing particular entrenched, not to say conservative, opinions. In an attempt to overcome this perception, however, a significant step towards opening up the whole procedure of appointing magistrates was taken when local committees were granted the power to advertise for people to put themselves forward for selection. And, in August 1998, the Lord Chancellor, Lord Irvine, issued new directions to bring the procedures for appointing lay magistrates, in line with those for the professional judiciary. The new Directions introduced a clear job description for magistrates and set out six defining qualities for appointing someone to the role of magistrate. These characteristics are: good character; understanding and communication; social awareness; maturity and sound temperament; sound judgment; and commitment and reliability. This was followed in March 1999 by a campaign, launched the Lord Chancellor's Department, to attract a wider section of candidates to apply to be magistrates. In announcing the campaign, Lord Irvine stated that:

> Magistrates come from a wide range of backgrounds and occupations. We have magistrates who are dinner ladies and scientists, bus drivers and teachers, plumbers and housewives. They have different faiths and come from different ethnic backgrounds, some have disabilities. All are serving their communities, ensuring that local justice is dispensed by local people. The magistracy should reflect the diversity of the community it serves ... Rest assured appointments are made on their merit, regardless of educational background, social class or ethnic background.

The campaign was supported by adverts in some 36 newspapers and magazines, from broadsheets to tabloids, from TV listings to women's magazines. The campaign was particularly aimed at ethnic minorities, its adverts being carried in such publications as the *Caribbean Times*, the *Asian Times* and *Muslim News*.

It has to be said that the gender balance and ethnic mix of the magistracy does not appear to pose a problem, unfortunately, however, the same cannot be said in terms of its class mix. It remains to be seen, but it is at least to be hoped that this advertising procedure will give the general public more confidence in the representative function of the magistrates' courts as representing general interests, rather than the more usual reliance on the recommendations of political pressure groups.

In a further attempt to encourage wider participation in the magistrates' court, the Employment Protection (Consolidation) Act 1978 provided that employers would be obliged to release their employees for such time as is reasonable, to permit them to serve as magistrates and they are required to sit for at least 25 half-day sessions per year. In the event of an employer refusing to sanction absence from work to perform magistrate's duties, the employee can take the matter before an employment tribunal. Understandably, there is no statutory requirement for the employer to pay their employees in their absence, but magistrates are entitled to claim expenses for loss of earnings in the exercise of their office.

Apart from the actual composition of magistrates' courts, the next most contentious consideration that has to be addressed is the fact that lay magistrates, by their very nature, are not experts in the law. Such a fact, however, does not necessarily invalidate the operation of the magistrates' court, nor should it be assumed that they are completely lacking in any legal understanding. On being accepted onto the bench, magistrates undertake a substantial training/induction course to prepare them for, and in, the proper exercise of the duties of their office. This training course, under the auspices of the Judicial Training Board, is designed to give the new magistrate an understanding of the functions and powers of the bench, generally, and to locate that understanding within the context of national practice, particularly with regard to sentencing. Particular emphasis is placed on Equal Treatment Training. Although particular key legal issues may be considered in the course of the training, it is not the intention to provide the new magistrate with a complete grasp of substantive law and legal practice. Indeed, to expect such would be to misunderstand both the role of the magistrates and the division of responsibility within the magistrates' court. Every bench of magistrates has a legally qualified justices' clerk, whose function it is to advise the bench on questions of law, practice and procedure, leaving matters of fact to magistrates to decide upon. This division of powers raises a further possible area of contention with regard to the operation of magistrates' courts, for, in the case of some particularly acquiescent benches, the justices' clerks appear to run the court and this leads to the suspicion that they actually direct the magistrates as to what decisions they should make. This perception is compounded by the fact that the bench is entitled to invite their clerk to accompany them when they retire to consider their verdicts. A recent *Practice Direction (Justices: Clerks to the Court)* (2000)) set out the role and functions of the Clerk to the Court. Prior to the report of Lord Justice Auld into the operation of the whole criminal justice system, a report entitled *Community Justice*, January 2001, by Professor Andrew Sanders, for the Institute for Public Policy Research called for the replacement of panels of lay justices by panels composed of district judges, former stipendiary magistrates, assisted by two lay magistrates. According to professor Sanders: 'These proposals would increase public confidence, and they would enhance the contribution of ordinary members of the public make to our justice system.' The Magistrates' Association took a rather different view and saw the proposals as an attack on what was already an extremely representative system of justice.

It is often claimed that one of the major strengths of the lay magistracy is the fact that it is composed of local people with local knowledge and commitment to the local community. Indeed, it is a requirement that magistrates live within 15 miles of the place where they perform their judicial function. But, once again, this apparent advantage can be seen as a distinct disadvantage. Local knowledge may lead to a lack of impartiality, but more important perhaps, is the possibility of the emergence of an insularity from general practice. This insularity has particular importance when it leads to the emergence of a distinct divergence across the country with respect to sentencing policy in regard to similar offences. Although a certain variation in sentencing is only to be expected and can, indeed, be justified, the question has to be asked why it should make any great difference where a particular offence is committed. Yet, it has to be recognised that differences in sentencing policy do exist, to the extent that it is 'better' to commit some offences within the jurisdiction of certain benches of magistrates than others. Indeed, the sentence handed down may differ within a particular jurisdiction depending on who is sitting on the bench on any particular day. Such a situation cannot be right and it is continuously addressed, not just in magistrates' training courses, but also the sentencing guidelines produced by the Magistrates' Association, which advise magistrates not just in relation to their powers of sentencing, but also in how to exercise that power.

In conclusion, it is not suggested that the magistrates' courts do not perform a very useful function, but it has to be recognised that there is a perception that the magistracy are not only out of touch with, and unrepresentative of, the views of the public at large, but that they represent entrenched and, specifically, conservative values in society. The suspicion still exists that the magistrates' court is the haven of white, middle aged, middle class, meddlers with time on their hands to pursue their interest in maintaining order as they see it. The various initiatives towards opening up access to membership of the magistracy are to be welcomed, indeed, they are vital for its continued operation, for people can have little respect for institutions which they feel are separate from them and unrepresentative or ignorant of their views and their situations. In a multicultural, multiracial society, it is particularly incumbent upon the basic court in the hierarchy to reflect the composition of the wider society. It is at least arguable that the magistrates' courts, as presently structured, fail to meet this essential requirement.

With specific regard to removing the defendant's right to insist on a jury trial in relation to 'either way' offences, it may well be cheaper to continue with their local amateur service rather than finance a national professional service, but as long as the perception exists, as it certainly does, that the magistrates do not represent 'real' law, as provided by judges in the Crown Court and above, this saving may be made at the expense of the general legitimacy of the legal system.

Question 12

Although there are some problems associated with the current distribution of business between the Crown Court and the magistrates' court, the existing arrangements are generally efficient.

Discuss.

Answer plan

Questions on the division of business between the Crown Court and magistrates' court require discussion of the following:

- the current distribution of work between the two courts;
- the Criminal Justice and Public Order Act 1994;
- the merits and demerits of each courts' procedure;
- the James Committee Report, and the Criminal Law Act 1977;
- the social policy implications of criminal trial categories;
- recommendations of Runciman Commission;
- conclusions.

Answer

Although it has some appellate jurisdiction, the Crown Court is mainly a first instance trial court for serious criminal cases. It is, arguably, suited to its function by the expertise of its judiciary, the fact that it sits with a jury and the formality of its procedures. The magistrates' courts, on the other hand, are much quicker and cheaper (the James Committee, *Distribution of Criminal Business Between the Crown Court and Magistrates' Courts*, Cmnd 6323, 1975) found that dealing with like cases, Crown Court trials cost three times as much as those in magistrates' courts); they act as courts of summary criminal jurisdiction and, by virtue of the Criminal Justice and Public Order Act (CJPOA) 1994 (s 44), as justices in transfers for trial procedures, to ensure that insufficiently strong cases are not sent for trial at the Crown Court.

For those pleading 'not guilty', acquittal rates are higher in the Crown Court jury trials than in magistrates' hearings. In many circumstances, trial by one's peers is thought to be fairer than trial by magistrates. One problem associated with the current distribution of business between the Crown Court and magistrates' court is whether the large and growing proportion of offences triable, only summarily, by the magistrates is unduly harsh on defendants. After all, once it is conceded that as crimes like murder and rape are so serious in their consequences for convicted defendants that only the full precaution of trial by jury will do, then should not the same precaution be available for defendants accused of any crime? The consequences of conviction for *any* crime can be very serious.

In deciding who should be tried where, the State is faced with the conflicting principles of: (a) open access to a full jury trial to anyone who so wishes in the interests of justice in clearing their name; and (b) the relatively cheap, expeditious work of summary hearings. Both options, also, carry disadvantages: the former proceedings are expensive and protracted, the latter are often too 'administrative' and peremptory in the context of criminal hearings.

The relationship between the higher and lower criminal courts was examined by the James Committee which recommended the transfer of considerable categories of case to the lower courts. The Committee considered the criteria which should govern the categorisation of cases. It decided that the most important criterion was the seriousness of the offence in the eyes of the community. Some offences were so serious, they should only be triable on indictment, not just so as to allow for the greater powers of punishment available in the Crown Court but also 'to signify the gravity with which society regards them'. It noted that, at the other end of the scale, were relatively minor offences for which the elaborate procedures and formalities of a jury trial would not be warranted. Between these two categories, was an intermediate class of case.

Following the recommendations of the James Committee in 1975, the Criminal Law Act 1977 provided for three classes of offence regarding modes of trial: (a) offences triable summarily only (for minor offences); (b) offences triable only on indictment in the Crown Court (for serious crimes); and (c) offences triable either way (for crimes which could be serious depending upon the circumstances and facts of their commission, these offences are listed in the Magistrates' Courts Act 1980, or specified as such by individual statutes). Theft, for example, is a crime which covers wrongs as diverse as the unauthorised taking of a single milk bottle to the misappropriation of gold bullion worth many millions of pounds.

This was seen to be the best way to divide the case load between the two courts, balancing the interests of expeditious court process with full, formal trial. Where to draw the line, particularly between offences triable either way and those which are only to be summary offences, is not simply an administrative matter but a critical question of public policy. Moving more categories of crime into the 'summary only' class means, not only will they be dealt with more quickly and cheaply (an advantage for the State), but also that they will be perceived as partially decriminalised. The Government's criminal statistics, often used in political debates and relied upon in the formulation of social policy, do not record summary offences. Therefore, by 'relegating' a type of wrongdoing to the status of a summary offence, the effect can be to make it disappear from serious debate about the extent and developing pattern of crime.

The James Report recommended that the following should become summary only offences: all drink driving offences, using threatening or insulting words or behaviour, homosexual soliciting, theft of value under £20 and criminal damage of value under £100. These proposals were legislated in 1977, although, after considerable opposition to the last two proposals, they were dropped. From 1980, however, cases of criminal damage worth less than £200 became summary offences.

As the throughput of cases in the Crown Courts has increased in recent times (Zander, *The Distribution of Business Between the Crown Court and the Magistrates' Courts*, Home Office, 1986, has demonstrated this by looking at the growth in the number of Crown Court days sat annually: 6,966 in 1957 to 73,507 in 1990), so, the Government has been forced to continue downloading more categories of case into the magistrates' courts. In 1988, criminal damage cases worth less than £2,000, driving while disqualified, taking a motor vehicle without authority and common assault and battery were all downgraded to summary offences.

In 1986, a Home Office Paper again raised for discussion whether low value theft cases should be classified as summary offences. Cases of theft and handling goods worth less than £50 were shown in one survey to have constituted 10% of the Crown Courts workload, 8.8% of its time. As these cases could be dealt with at a third of the cost by magistrates, there is a strong economic argument in favour of such a change, but at what cost to a fair trial? The Home Office Paper suggested that there should be a presumption that these indictable offences should be tried summarily, except where 'special circumstances' aggravating the case made a jury trial preferable. In the face of much opposition, the proposal was dropped, but a similar proposal was submitted to the Royal Commission on Criminal Justice (1991).

The Criminal Law Act 1977 established the procedure for determining the mode of trial in offences triable either way (now, in the Magistrates' Courts Act 1980). The magistrate(s) (a single magistrate may sit) must first decide whether the offence is more suitable for summary trial or trial on indictment. The Bench must consider the nature of the case, whether the circumstances make the offence one of a serious character, whether the magistrates' powers of punishment would be sufficient, any representations made by the prosecution or the accused about the mode of trial and any other circumstances relevant to the mode of trial. Guidelines contained in a Practice Note (see [1990] 3 All ER 979) state that, in general, 'either way' offences should be tried summarily, unless a case has one or more 'aggravating features' *and* the magistrates consider that their sentencing powers would be inadequate in the event of a conviction.

If, after considering all the relevant matters, the court decides that summary trial is the most appropriate mode, it must explain its decision to the accused in ordinary language and ask him if he consents to summary trial, or whether he wishes to elect for jury trial. It must also be explained to the accused that if he is tried summarily and convicted, he may be committed for sentence to the Crown Court, if the magistrates, having heard about his character and antecedents, think that greater punishment should be inflicted than they have power to inflict for the offence. For a summary conviction of a defendant for an 'either way' offence, the maximum sentence is six months' imprisonment and a fine of £5,000 (Criminal Justice Act 1991) or, where the conviction is for two or more offences triable either way, the limit is 12 months' imprisonment in aggregate.

If the defendant does not consent to be tried summarily, then the magistrates proceed to initiate the transfer for trial procedure. If, though, after considering all the relevant matters, the court decides that trial on indictment is more suitable, this decision is final.

A defendant charged with an indictable offence, or someone who on an 'either way' offence has elected for trial at the Crown Court will, first, have his case subjected to committal proceedings.

These proceedings used to take the form of small, preliminary trials (either with witnesses appearing or, more recently, only using paper evidence) to test the strength of the case before allowing it to proceed to a full blown jury trial. Following a recommendation of the Royal Commission on Criminal Justice in 1993, these committal proceedings were abolished by the CJPOA 1994. The new system, however, of 'transfers for trial' which would have expedited the process of deciding whether a defendant should stand trial, encountered great difficulties in being implemented and was never brought into force. The relevant provision of the CJPOA 1994 (s 44) has now been repealed by the Criminal Procedure and Investigations Act 1996, which introduces a new streamlined procedure for committal proceedings. The effect of the new law is to abolish the defendant's right to call witnesses at committal stage. Now, defendants may use only documents and depositions as part of their argument to stop the case from proceeding. Both sides, though, may address the Bench.

Committal proceedings were expensive and the proportion of the more costly old style committals was rising, from 8% in 1981 to 13% in 1986. The methods of committal were of dubious merit as there was, and is, such a high rate of acquittal on the direction of Crown Court judges, indicating that cases are being committed for trial on insufficient evidence. The problem of expensive trials collapsing at the Crown Court could be avoided if magistrates were given better training in rejecting weak prosecutions at what is now the transfer stage.

If implemented, one of the recommendations of the Royal Commission on Criminal Justice (1993) would have a significant impact on the distribution of business between the two courts. Recommendation 114 proposes that, in those cases where the accused can now opt for trial by jury, the right should be removed. It suggests that where the Crown Prosecution Service (CPS) and defendant agree that a case is suited to summary trial, it should proceed to the magistrates' court. It should go to the Crown Court where both sides agree it should be tried on indictment, but, where the defence does not agree with the CPS, the matter should be referred to magistrates to decide. In 1998, the Home Secretary indicated his intention to incorporate this recommendation into forthcoming legislation. This plan has attracted opposition from legal campaign groups, such as Liberty, as it effectively curtails the right to jury trial in relation to some serious criminal offences, such as theft and, according to one viewpoint, everyone should have the right to be tried by his peers when faced with a potentially ruinous conviction. There are no immediate plans to enlarge the magistrates' courts resources, so the thousands of additional cases they would be required to deal with, were the recommendation to be implemented, would be likely to add significant congestion to the courts. This, though, may be cancelled by the abolition of committal proceedings, and the consequential savings in time and resources.

It can be seen that all the issues raised in discussing the distribution of work between the criminal trial courts are issues of economic and political significance, not merely administrative convenience. Crown Court trials might provide a 'Rolls Royce' service, procedurally, in contrast to the magistrates' courts, but they cost too much and take too long to be socially expeditious.

Question 13

What general principles (if any) can be deduced from the existing appeal structure in England and Wales? Is any extension or limitation on existing rights of appeal desirable?

Answer plan

A series of notorious miscarriages of justice were dealt with by the appeal courts in 1991 and 1992. The Government announced the establishment of the Runciman Royal Commission on Criminal Justice, in March 1991, on the day the Birmingham Six were set free. Students should be aware of the Report findings and recommendations of the Commission (Cm 2263, 1993) and incorporate the relevant parts into answers of this sort, as has been done here. A well structured answer should incorporate discussion of the following:

- the principle of finality;
- the principle of orality;
- the principle of controlled accessibility;
- restricted view of 'new evidence';

- changes in criminal appeals, Runciman Commission recommendations;
- changes in civil appeals;
- the new *Practice Direction on Civil Appeals* (2000).

Answer

Several general principles emerge from a study of the current appeal structure, principles which relate to the evolved purposes of the appeal process. These purposes include:

(a) the opportunity for a litigant to have more than one occasion to put his or her case – an idea based upon the premise that people and processes are fallible;

(b) the opportunity to reconsider a problem in the light of new evidence; and

(c) the need for an appellate body to standardise the legal response to particular sorts of problem.

Research undertaken for the Royal Commission on Criminal Justice (1993) revealed that, of 300 appeals in 1990, just over one-third were successful. Almost two-thirds of defendants appealed against conviction on the ground that the trial judge had made a critical mistake and, of these, 43% succeeded in having their convictions quashed. In about 80% of cases where convictions were quashed, there had been an error at the trial, usually by the judge.

In general, the Anglo-Welsh system of appeals avoids 'finality' after just one appeal hearing. There are, for most cases (subject to the approval of the first appeal court or the next intended forum), more than one possible appeal hearing. An appeal from the civil jurisdiction of the magistrates' court, for example, could be taken to the Divisional Court of the Family Division and, thence, to the Court of Appeal Civil Division and, thence, to the House of Lords. Additionally, both the Civil and Criminal Divisions of the Court of Appeal can order retrials where the interests of justice so require.

The appeal structure puts great emphasis on the principle of extempore judicial wisdom. In the USA, the appeal system relies more upon reserved, written judgments and most appellate judges enjoy the services of 'law clerks' (accomplished graduates from law school, paid from public funds), who assist the judges with research work and discussion of complex and contentious points of law. The English system makes much use of unreserved judgments in the Court of Appeal, after listening to oral argument, again in contrast to the American preference for appellate judges considering long, written submissions in respect of the appeals. This principle of orality was reaffirmed by Sir John Donaldson MR (as he then was), in an article in 1982; he said that, 'the conduct of appeals by way of oral hearing lies at the heart of the English tradition' ((1982) 132 NLJ 959).

Another principle clearly governing the operation of the appeal system is that of carefully controlled accessibility. Probably as a deterrent against what might be regarded as overuse of the system by all convicted defendants, there are several obstacles placed in front of anyone contemplating an appeal. Leave must be obtained in all appeals, for example, from the Crown Court to the Court of Appeal Criminal Division unless the matter is concerned only with a point of law. The Court of Appeal, also, has a power to order that time spent appealing will not count toward the sentence. Shortly after this policy was introduced in 1970, the number of applications for leave to appeal in such cases was reduced by about half.

Accessibility to the Courts of Appeal is also restricted by the poor record of trial proceedings in magistrates' and county courts. Additionally, appeals can be based upon fresh evidence but the courts have, sometimes, taken a very narrow view of what is within this term. In criminal cases, the Court of Appeal has discretion whether to admit new evidence if they think it 'necessary or expedient in the interests of justice' (Criminal Appeal Act 1968). The court 'shall' admit the new evidence, that is, it *must*, where it: (a) affords a ground for appeal; (b) looks credible; (c) would have been admissible at the trial; and (d) they are satisfied of a reasonable explanation as to why the evidence was not adduced at the trial.

Similar rules apply in respect of civil appeals. If the new evidence is something that could, with 'reasonable diligence' have been obtained for use in the trial, then it will not be permitted as the foundation of an appeal. In *Linton v Ministry of Defence* (1983), the House of Lords upheld this principle and denied a fresh trial to the appellant in circumstances where it was clear that his case would be very much stronger than in the original trial. This principle also applies to points taken by counsel; if they could have been put at trial, then they cannot form the basis of an appeal. In *Maynard* (1979), Roskill LJ said that if the rule were otherwise, it would enable counsel to keep a point up their sleeve at trial and then, if the case went against them, try to raise them for the first time on appeal, thus, having a second bite at the 'forensic cherry'.

If an appellant has not succeeded in the ordinary appeal process, he or she cannot get around the problem indirectly by taking an action for negligence against his or her lawyers for negligence (*Rondel v Worsley* (1969)). Neither may a convicted person re-open the trial by suing for defamation anyone who says he was rightly convicted (Civil Evidence Act 1968).

Access to the final appellate court, the House of Lords, is very difficult, since it will only hear cases with leave and in criminal appeals there must also be a certificate from the Court of Appeal that the case involves a point of law of general public importance.

Even when access to the appeal process has been granted to the appellant, a constellation of rules is set to prevent technical abuse of the system. Thus, the 'proviso' to s 2 of the Criminal Appeal Act 1968 allows the court to agree with the ground for the appeal, but to keep the conviction if no substantial miscarriage of justice has occurred.

Suggested extensions and limitations

Criminal appeals

It was argued by Lord Devlin that it is wrong whenever judges, rather than juries, try to decide whether a defendant/appellant is guilty. There are still cases, though, where this happens. In cases involving new evidence, Viscount Dilhorne said (*Stafford v DPP* (1974)) that, even if there was a chance that a jury might have come to a different view had it heard the new evidence, the conviction should not be quashed if the appeal court was satisfied that there was no reasonable doubt about the guilt of the accused. An abandonment of this policy would bring appeal practice more in line with the theoretical constitution.

Another important change that the court could make, and might well make under Lord Chief Justice Taylor, is to take a wider view of what constitutes acceptable new evidence. Many recent cases of miscarriage of justice (several exposed originally by the television programme, *Rough Justice*) have demonstrated that, when the Court of Appeal seeks reasons why the new evidence was not adduced at trial, it will not accept explanations involving the negligence of lawyers, questionable practice by the prosecution or problems with legal aid.

In the wake of a string of notorious miscarriages of justice, coming to light in the late 1980s and early 1990s, and its remit to investigate how these occurred and how they could best be avoided, the Runciman Commission (Cm 2263, 1993) made a number of recommendations that are relevant to our discussion here. It suggested that s 2(1) of the Criminal Appeal Act 1968 should be redrafted and the grounds of appeal should be reduced to a single broad ground which would give the court greater flexibility. The law, it states, should be made clear that the court can allow an appeal, even if there is no new evidence and where the jury were properly directed by the trial judge if, after reviewing the case, the court concludes the verdict is or may be unsafe. Recommendation 320 is very important. It says that, in considering whether to receive fresh evidence, the Court of Appeal should take a broad approach to the question whether the fresh evidence was available to the trial court. This, coupled with recommendation 321, could afford a significant change to appellants who have been disadvantaged by poor defence lawyers. The latter recommendation says that, where an appeal is based on an alleged error by trial lawyers, the test to be applied by the Court of Appeal should not be confined to whether there was 'flagrantly incompetent advocacy'. The test to be applied to fresh evidence is (recommendation 322) 'whether it is capable of disbelief'.

The law has now been changed, with the introduction of the Criminal Appeal Act 1995. Sections 1, 2 and 4 of the Act bring particularly significant changes to the criminal appeal system.

Section 1 amends the Criminal Appeal Act 1968, so as to bring an appeal against conviction, an appeal against a verdict of not guilty by reason of insanity and an appeal against a finding of disability, on a question of law alone, in line with other appeals against conviction and sentence (that is, those involving questions of fact, or mixtures of law and fact). Now, all appeals against conviction and sentence must first have leave from the Court of Appeal, or a certificate of fitness for appeal from the trial judge, before the appeal can be taken. Before the new Act came into force, it was possible to appeal without the consent of the trial judge or Court of Appeal on a point of law alone. In Parliament, the reason for this change was given as the need to 'provide a filter mechanism for appeals on a ground of law alone which are wholly without merit' (HC Official Report, SCB (Criminal Appeal Bill), 1995, 21 March, col 6).

Section 2 changes the grounds for allowing an appeal under the 1968 Act. Under the old law, the Court of Appeal was required to allow an appeal where:

(a) the conviction, verdict or finding should have been set aside on the ground that, under all the circumstances, it was unsafe or unsatisfactory; or

(b) the judgment of the court of trial or the order of the court giving effect to the verdict or finding should be set aside on the ground of a wrong decision of law; or

(c) there was a material irregularity in the course of the trial.

In all three situations, the Court of Appeal was allowed to dismiss the appeal if it considered that no miscarriage of justice had actually occurred. The new law requires the Court of Appeal to allow an appeal against conviction under s 1 of the 1968 Act, an appeal against a verdict under s 12 (insanity), or an appeal against a finding (disability), if it thinks that the conviction, verdict or finding is 'unsafe' (as opposed to the old law which used the 'unsafe or unsatisfactory' formula).

During the parliamentary passage of the Act, there was much heated debate about whether the new provisions were designed to narrow the grounds of appeal. That would amount to a tilt in favour of the State, in that it would make it harder for (wrongly) convicted people to appeal. Government ministers insisted that the effect of the new law was simply to restate or consolidate the practice of the Court of Appeal. One Government spokesman said that:

> In dispensing with the word 'unsatisfactory', we agree with the Royal Commission on Criminal Justice that there is no real difference between 'unsafe' and 'unsatisfactory'; the Court of

Appeal does not distinguish between the two. Retaining the word 'unsatisfactory' would imply that we thought there was a real difference and would only lead to confusion.

There were many attempts during the legislation's passage to insert the words 'or may be unsafe' after the word 'unsafe'. The Law Society, the Bar, Liberty and Justice called on the Government to make such a change. Also opposed to the use of the single word 'unsafe' was the eminent criminal law expert, Professor JC Smith. He has argued cogently that there are many cases where a conviction has been seen as 'unsatisfactory', rather than 'unsafe', so that there is a need for both words. Sometimes, the Court of Appeal might be convinced that the defendant is guilty (so the conviction is 'safe'), but still wish to allow the appeal because fair play according to the rules must be seen to be done. Accepting improperly extracted confessions (violating s 76 of the Police and Criminal Evidence Act 1984), simply because it might seem obvious that the confessor is guilty, will promote undesirable interrogation practices, because police officers will think that, even if they break the rules, any resulting confession will, nevertheless, be allowed as evidence.

Professor Smith has given an example (see (1995) 145 NLJ 534) of where there has been a serious breach of the rules of evidence: see *Algar* (1954). In that case, the former wife of the defendant testified against him about matters during the marriage. The Court of Appeal allowed his appeal against conviction, but Lord Goddard said: 'Do not think that we are doing this because we think that you are an innocent man. We do not. We think that you are a scoundrel.' The idea underpinning such remarks is that rules are rules, and the rules of evidence must be obeyed in order to ensure justice. Once you start to accept breaches of the rules as being justified by outcome (ends justifying means), then the whole law of evidence could begin to collapse.

The proposal to include 'or might be unsafe' was rejected for the reason probably best summarised by the former Lord Chief Justice, Lord Taylor, who argued in the Lords that there was no merit in including the words 'or may be unsafe', as the implication of such doubt is already inherent in the word 'unsafe'.

Section 4 provides a unified test for the receipt of fresh evidence in the Court of Appeal. Under the old law, the Court of

Appeal had a discretion, under s 23(1)(c) of the 1968 Act, to receive fresh evidence of any witness, if it was thought necessary or expedient in the interests of justice. Section 23(2) added a duty to receive new evidence which was relevant, credible and admissible, and which could not reasonably have been adduced at the original trial. There was, often, much argument about whether new evidence should be received under the court's discretion or its duty. Gradually, the 'duty' principles came to be merged into the 'discretion' principles. The aim of the latest amendment is to reflect the current practice of the court. The general discretion under s 23(1) has been retained, but the 'duty' principle has been replaced with a set of criteria which the court must consider. These are:

(a) whether the evidence appears to the court to be capable of belief;
(b) whether it appears to the court that the evidence may afford any ground for allowing the appeal;
(c) whether the evidence would have been admissible at the trial on the issue under appeal; and
(d) whether there is a reasonable explanation for the failure to adduce the evidence at trial.

The 1995 Act also legislated for the new Criminal Cases Review Commission (CCRC). The CCRC has taken over the Home Secretary's power to re-investigate already unsuccessfully appealed cases and refer back to Court of Appeal cases of suspected miscarriages of justice. The organisation, Justice, has expressed doubts about the independence of the CCRC, as its members are to be Government appointees. The wide power to re-investigate cases where there appears to be a 'real possibility' (s 13) of miscarriage has been, generally, greeted with approval, but it is a matter of regret in some quarters that those re-investigating cases will not be CCRC investigators but, usually, police officers (s 19). As many allegations of injustice involve accusations against the police, there is a school of thought suggesting that a manifestly impartial, outside body should be responsible for the re-investigation. In order to establish that there is a real possibility of an appeal succeeding regarding a conviction, there has to be:

• an argument or evidence which has not been raised during the trial or at appeal; or

- exceptional circumstances.

In order to establish that there is a real possibility of an appeal succeeding against a sentence, there has to be:

- a legal argument or information about the individual, or the offence, which was not raised in court during the trial or at appeal.

Other than in exceptional circumstances, the Commission can only:

> ... consider cases in which an appeal through the ordinary judicial appeal process has failed, and once a decision is taken to refer a case to the relevant court of appeal, the Commission has no other involvement [Criminal Cases Review Commission, *Annual Report*, 2000].

The Commission cannot overturn a conviction or change a sentence. In those cases where the criteria above are met, the Commission can refer a case to the Court of Appeal (in the case of Crown Court convictions) or the Crown Court (in the case of magistrates' court convictions). Only about 5% of new cases received by the Commission since 1997 have been against summary convictions.

Since its inception, the CCRC has had some notable, high profile 'successes', in the sense that important cases it has referred have resulted in the Court of Appeal allowing appeals.

In 1997, for example, in one of its first referrals, the Commission referred the case of Derek Bentley to the Court of Appeal. Mr Bentley, although hanged for murder in 1953, eventually had his conviction quashed in August 1998 by the Court of Appeal.

Civil appeals

The civil work of the Court of Appeal continues to increase. Figures available in 1995 show that, whereas 1,338 appeals were set down in 1989, this had risen to 1,980 being set down in 1993. The House of Lords, however, has seen a fall in the number of appeals, from 72 to 62, over the same period. There is less clamour for the machinery and rules here to be revised. In part, this follows from the fact that civil appeals are different in nature from criminal appeals. This difference was highlighted by the Court of

Appeal in quashing the convictions of the Birmingham Six (*McIlkenny and Others* (1991)). It said that, in a civil appeal, there is a re-hearing of the whole case and the appeal court is concerned with fact, as well as law, so that it may take a different view of the facts from the court below. In a criminal case, on the other hand, primacy is enjoyed by the jury, so that the appellate court is really just a 'court of review'. It is, thus, easier for the Court of Appeal Civil Division to reverse the decision of a civil trial court than for the criminal courts to do the same.

The Report of the Review of the Court of Appeal (Civil Division), undertaken by Sir Jeffrey Bowman (1997), contains important recommendations for reducing the number of cases coming to the Court of Appeal and for improving practice and procedures in the Civil Appeals Office and in the Court of Appeal itself.

Based on averages, the time between setting down and final disposal of 70% of appeals in 1996 had increased to 14 months. The corollary is that 30% of appeals took over 14 months and, at the end of 1996, some appeals had been outstanding for over five years. The Review's major recommendations include:

(a) that certain appeals which now reach the Court of Appeal (Civil Division) should be heard at a lower level – the largest category of such cases being appeals against decisions in fast track cases;

(b) it should still be possible for appeals which would normally be heard in a lower court to reach the Court of Appeal (Civil Division) in certain circumstances. In particular, an appeal could be considered if it raises an important point of principle or practice, or one which, for some other special reason, should be considered by the Court of Appeal (Civil Division);

(c) the requirement for leave to appeal should be extended to all cases coming to the Court of Appeal (Civil Division), except for adoption cases and child abduction cases; and

(d) an increasing role for appropriate judicial case management;

(e) more focused procedures – cases should be better prepared, at a much earlier stage in the process, and realistic timetables should be set, which must be strictly observed;

(f) the Court of Appeal (Civil Division) should impose appropriate time limits on oral argument – on appeal, the balance of judicial time should lean more towards reading and less towards sitting in court;

(g) the greater use of IT to support the other recommendations of the review;

(h) information for litigants in person about the appeal process and what it can deliver must be available at an early stage. The information must be easily understandable and delivered in a range of different ways.

Some of the Report's more controversial recommendations include the following:

(a) there should be a power to appoint lawyers of outstanding distinction as academics or practitioners to sit as members of the Court of Appeal on occasions; and

(b) there should be a discretion to list cases before a single member of the Court of Appeal; and

(c) that, where specialist knowledge of law, procedure or subject matter is an advantage, the constitution of the Court of Appeal (Civil Division) should usually include one or two members with the appropriate specialist knowledge, but the constitution should not usually consist solely of specialist members.

One problem still remaining, however, with the civil appeal process is whether or not the Court of Appeal should 'correct' the discretionary decision of a trial court which it believes has made an error of judgment. As this matter is unsettled, advice to prospective appellants can be very difficult to give. The traditional rule, expressed by the Court of Appeal in *Culver v Beard* (1937), is that the appeal court should not interfere with a discretionary decision, unless it can be shown to be 'wrong in principle'. A decision can, therefore, be reversed, if it has been based on a mistake of law or of fact or took into account legally irrelevant matters. This approach has been affirmed by the Court of Appeal in *Eagil Trust Co Ltd* (1985), where it was said that lawyers should not use the discretionary decision of a High Court judge as a mere 'conduit pipe' to the Court of Appeal. This is quite clear, but there are other decisions of the Court of Appeal (for example, *D v M* (1982)) which interpret its role as being to arrive at the correct, proper, just decision, even if this means contradicting the discretion of the trial judge – not to do so would be to perpetuate injustice. Legislation, perhaps, should settle this matter. Finally, it is important to note evidence given by Adrian Zuckerman to the Woolf inquiry in 1995. Sometimes, it was pointed out, if a claim or defence is amended, the fate of the amendment may take two appeal hearings to decide. In one case, the issue of whether a writ had been properly served on the opposing side had to be considered by a Master and, on appeal, by a judge, and then by the Court of Appeal. The process is so protracted that the pre-trial dispute can take on a life of its own.

An attempt has recently been made to try to streamline and rationalise the civil appeals system in the wake of the new Civil Procedure Rules. The contents of a Practice Direction from Lord Woolf (*Court of Appeal (Civil Division): Leave to Appeal and Skeleton Arguments*, November 1998) has been now digested in a consolidating Practice Direction about civil appeals (*Practice Direction for the Court of Appeal (Civil Division)* 16 May 2000). The Direction states (2.1.3) that:

> The experience of the Court of Appeal is that many appeals and applications for permission to appeal are made which are quite hopeless. They demonstrate basic misconceptions as to the purpose of the civil appeal system and the different roles played by appellate Courts and courts below. The court below has a crucial role in determining applications for permission to appeal. This guidance indicates how applicants, and courts, should approach the matter.

In answer to the following question 'From which court should permission to appeal be sought?', the Direction articulates the following two key propositions. First (2.2.1), it notes that:

> The court which has just reached a decision is often in the best position to judge whether there should be an appeal. It should not leave the decision to the Court of Appeal. Courts below can help to minimise the delay and expense which an appeal involves. Where the parties are present for delivery of the judgment, it should be routine for the judge below to ask whether either party wants permission to appeal and to deal with the matter then and there. However, if the court below is in doubt whether an appeal would have a realistic prospect of success or involves a point of general principle, the safe course is to refuse permission to appeal. It is always open to the Court of Appeal to grant it.

The Direction then states (2.2.2) that:

> The advantages which flow from permission being considered by the court of first instance are lost if the application cannot be listed before the judge who made the decision which is the subject of the application.

It states that, where it is not possible for the application for permission to be listed before the same judge, or where undue delay would be caused by so listing it, the Court of Appeal will be sympathetic to applicants who claim that it was impracticable for them to make their application to the court below and will not require such an application to be made. The new directions will clearly assist in the introduction of a more nationally uniform response to appeals and to greater expedition in their processing, factors which will, arguably, improve the experience of all those using the system.

Question 14

Explain the role of the Criminal Cases Review Commission (CCRC) in the English legal system, and evaluate how effective it has been in its work.

Answer plan

Your answer should incorporate the following:
- discussion of what led to the establishment of the CCRC;
- description of who is on the CCRC and how it works;
- an explanation of the legal criteria for referring cases;
- some illustration, with an example of a case being processed by the CCRC;
- data to evaluate the CCRC's performance.

Answer

The CCRC is an independent body set up under the Criminal Appeal Act 1995. Its establishment followed a recommendation by the Runciman Royal Commission on Criminal Justice (1993) for an independent body to consider alleged cases of miscarriages of justice. The Runciman Commission itself resulted from the successful appeal of several notorious 'miscarriage of justice' cases in the 1980s and early 1990s, culminating in the release of the 'Birmingham Six' in 1991, after they had spent 16 years in jail for crimes they did not commit.

The CCRC came into being on 1 January 1997. Over 250 cases were transferred from the Home Office around 31 March 1997, when the Commission took over responsibility for casework. It is responsible for investigating suspected miscarriages of criminal justice in England, Wales and Northern Ireland.

There are 14 Commission members from a wide variety of backgrounds, including industrialists, senior lawyers with organisational experience, accountants and academic lawyers. Any decision to refer a case to the relevant court of appeal has to be taken by a committee of at least three members. The CCRC considers whether or not there is a real possibility that the conviction, finding, verdict or sentence would not be upheld were a reference to be made. Under the old system, the Criminal Cases Unit in the Home Office (known as C3) would make a recommendation to the Home Secretary as to whether a case should be referred back to the Court of Appeal. In the CCRC, the decision making role of the Home Office Minister is taken by members of the Commission.

In order to establish that there is a real possibility of an appeal succeeding regarding a conviction, there has to be:

- an argument or evidence which has not been raised during the trial or at appeal; or
- exceptional circumstances.

In order to establish that there is a real possibility of an appeal succeeding against a sentence, there has to be:

- a legal argument or information about the individual, or the offence, which was not raised in court during the trial or at appeal.

Other than in exceptional circumstances, the CCRC can only consider cases in which an appeal through the ordinary judicial appeal process has failed and, once a decision is taken to refer a case to the relevant court of appeal, the CCRC has no other involvement.

The CCRC cannot overturn a conviction or change a sentence. In those cases where the criteria above are met, the Commission can refer a case to the Court of Appeal (in the case of Crown Court convictions) or the Crown Court (in the case of magistrates' court convictions). Only about 5% of new cases received by the CCRC since 1997 have been against summary convictions.

Since its inception, the CCRC has had some notable, high profile 'successes', in the sense that important cases it has referred have resulted in the Court of Appeal allowing appeals.

In 1997, for example, in one of its first referrals, the Commission referred the case of Derek William Bentley to the Court of Appeal. Mr Bentley was convicted of the murder of PC Sidney Miles at the Central Criminal Court on 11 December 1952. Mr Bentley did not actually shoot the officer: the gun was fired by his accomplice during the course of a failed burglary attempt, but Mr Bentley was convicted under the principles of joint enterprise. An appeal against conviction was heard by the Court of Criminal Appeal on 13 January 1953 and was dismissed. Mr Bentley was hanged on 28 January 1953.

Bentley's conviction and sentence were the subject of numerous representations to the Home Office. The trial was seen as unfair in a number of respect. For example, the fact that, although aged 18, Bentley had a mental age of 11 was kept a secret from the jury, and the judge's summing up to the jury was astonishingly biased in favour of the police. In July 1993, on the recommendation of the Home Secretary, Her Majesty The Queen, in the exercise of the Royal Prerogative of Mercy, granted to Mr Bentley a posthumous pardon limited to sentence.

Following submissions from the applicants' solicitors and the completion of its own enquiries, the CCRC concluded that Mr Bentley's conviction should be reconsidered by the Court of Appeal. In August 1998, on a momentous day in legal history, the Court of Appeal cleared Bentley of the murder for which he was hanged 46 years earlier. In giving judgment, the Lord Chief

Justice, Lord Bingham, said: 'The summing up in this case was such as to deny the appellant that fair trial which is the birthright of every British citizen.'

Assessing the success of the CCRC, more generally, is difficult. The volume of documents it has to deal with (albeit electronically) is formidable, averaging around 2,000 pages per case. This is a considerable workload, as the CCRC is currently dealing with about 1,500 cases per year.

In a report to the House of Commons Home Affairs Committee, at the end of 1997, the Chairman of the CCRC, Sir Frederick Crawford, stated that, at that time, it had received 892 applications for review of cases. Of that total, 738 had had CCRC files opened on them, with 251 being actively worked on. One hundred and thirty one had been closed for reasons of ineligibility (for example, they were, at that time, still being appealed in the court system, or no appeal had been made through the court system).

By the Autumn of 1998, only five cases had successfully come through the system, in the sense that convictions were regarded by the Court of Appeal as unsafe. Set against the number of applications, this might seem a low number, but then, it would be wrong to gauge the efficiency of the CCRC on the basis of 'successful' appeals. The important thing is that all those cases requiring attention beyond the ordinary trial and appeal process are dealt with promptly, fairly and thoroughly, and the evidence suggests that these objectives are being achieved. This is, perhaps, particularly positive, since, to begin with, the CCRC inherited an enormous caseload from both the old Home Office system and all the existing prisoners (from the entire prison population of 60,000), who were waiting to apply to the new body. During 1997, the Chairman received 112 letters from 80 MPs and replied to them in an average of less than six working days.

As the members of the Commission establish their working practices and routines, and accustom themselves to their new roles, their efficiency is likely to improve. Even during the first 12 months of its operations, the CCRC saw a rapidly decreasing case completion time for its members.

The third Annual Report of the Commission (ccrc.gov.uk ISBN 1 84082 480, 15 June 2000) was published in the summer. In a letter to the Home Secretary published at the outset of the Report, the Chairman, Sir Frederick Crawford, says that, although the number of case review manager positions has been increased from 28 to 40 during 1999–2000, there was still a backlog of about 900 cases to be reviewed. This meant that 'if the legitimate expectations of Parliament and the Commission's other stakeholders are to be satisfied, the gap between resources and casework must be closed'. The backlog of cases will probably rise now since the coming into force (October 2000) of the Human Rights Act 1998.

Since 1997, the Commission has received 3,193 applications to review convictions and sentences. It has referred 80 cases to courts of appeal, 27 of which have resulted in convictions being quashed or sentences modified. The Report notes (2.4) that a long term objective of the Commission is 'to analyse the causes of miscarriages of justice, and to suggest ways in which the criminal justice system might be improved to minimise their occurrence'. It notes that, considering its experience to date, the leading reasons for its 80 referrals are:

(a) prosecution failings (27 cases of breaches of identification and interview procedure, or use of questionable witnesses);

(b) scientific evidence (26 cases, for example, DNA, medical and psychiatric, fingerprint);

(c) non-disclosure (23 cases, for example, of police information, interviews or statements).

It is likely that the number and range of applications made to the CCRC will multiply prodigiously as a result of the coming into force of the Human Rights Act 1998. Citizens facing a criminal charge will have a new domestic right, as provided for by Art 6 of the European Convention on Human Rights, to 'a fair and public hearing' and Art 6(3)(d) 'to examine or have examined witnesses against him and to obtain the attendance and examination of witnesses on his behalf'.

Ultimately, though, the test of success for the CCRC will be the same one as that which was apparently failed by its predecessor – carrying the confidence of the general public and of politicians – that it represents a safe, quick and impartial method of dealing with cases not given justice in the ordinary courts.

CHAPTER 3

JUDICIAL REASONING

Introduction

This chapter examines the way in which judges reach decisions in particular cases and, central to the common law, is the doctrine of judicial precedent. This means that, depending on the level of the court in the hierarchy, previous 'decisions' of one court are supposed to be binding on later courts. The implication of the traditional approach to precedent is that it is a strictly applied, highly rational and almost scientific, process. However, as will be demonstrated, the mechanisms deployed by judges in deciding cases allows them a large degree of discretion in reaching decisions. This introduction of the possibility of discretion necessarily opens the question of the accountability of the judges, which will be addressed directly in the following chapter.

Whilst the common law is, by definition, judge made, the extent to which judges can influence the operation of statute law, through interpreting it in particular ways, should not be underestimated.

It is obvious, but no less important for that, that the outcome of cases to a large extent depends upon what evidence the parties to the action can put before the court. That, in turn, is dependent upon the rules of evidence which apply in the courts.

Checklist

You should be familiar with:
- the nature of legal reasoning, as opposed to reasoning in general;
- the hierarchy of the courts;
- the doctrine of binding precedent;
- how judges avoid the strict operation of precedent;
- the rules of, and presumptions relating to, statutory interpretation;
- the rules of evidence.

Question 15

Consider how the doctrine of binding precedent operates in the English courts, having particular regard to its advantages and disadvantages.

Answer plan

This is a very straightforward, traditional question. It requires a consideration of the following points:

- define what binding precedent is in such a way as to explain how it is supposed to operate, with appropriate reference to *ratio decidendi* and *obiter dictum/dicta*;
- it is important to emphasise the authoritative hierarchy of the court structure in the UK legal system, although mention should be made of the European Court of Justice (ECJ) and the European Court of Human Rights;
- the relationship between the various courts within the hierarchy must be considered and, also, the extent to which they are governed by their own previous decisions;
- the difference between the criminal and civil law should be considered at the level of the Court of Appeal;
- reference should be made to the process of distinguishing cases on the basis of their facts;
- advantages and disadvantages should be considered – it is essential to note that some of the supposed advantages are, in fact, problematic, not to say, contradictory.

Answer

The doctrine of binding precedent, or *stare decisis*, lies at the heart of the English legal system. In essence, the doctrine refers to the fact that, within the hierarchical structure of the English courts, a decision of a higher court will be binding on a court below.

The House of Lords stands at the summit of the English court structure and its decisions are binding on all courts below it in the hierarchy. It always has to be borne in mind, as regards European Community (EC) law, that the ECJ is superior to the House of Lords, and its decisions are binding on all UK courts. Also, as a consequence of the Human Rights Act (HRA) 1998, the decisions of the ECJ are now part of the jurisprudence of the UK courts. This latter factor, means that it is possible that the superior courts will find it necessary to alter previous precedents where they have been generated without reference to the European Convention on Human Rights (ECHR). Those issues apart, as regards its own previous decisions, up until 1966, the House of Lords regarded itself as bound by its previous decisions. In the *Practice Statement (Judicial Precedent)* of that year, however, Lord Gardiner indicated that the House of Lords would, in future, regard itself free to depart from its previous decisions where it appeared right so to do. It should be noted that, given the, potentially, destabilising effect on existing legal practice based on previous decisions of the House of Lords, this is not a discretion that the House of Lords exercises lightly, although there have been a number of cases in which it has elected to exercise it (for example, *Miliangos v George Frank (Textiles) Ltd* (1976), in which it decided that damages in English court cases did not have to be awarded in sterling).

The next court in the hierarchical structure is the Court of Appeal, but, in order to consider its place within the doctrine of binding precedent, it is necessary to consider its civil and criminal jurisdiction separately.

In a civil case, the situation is that, as an inferior court, the Court of Appeal is, generally, bound by previous decisions of the House of Lords. Although the Court of Appeal, notably under the aegis of Lord Denning, attempted, on a number of occasions, to escape from what it saw as the constraints of *stare decisis*, the House of Lords repeatedly reasserted the binding nature of its decisions on the Court of Appeal in such cases as *Broome v Cassell* (1972) and *Miliangos v George Frank (Textiles) Ltd* (1976).

The Court of Appeal is, generally, also bound by its own previous decisions. As explained, however, by Lord Greene MR in *Young v Bristol Aeroplane Co Ltd* (1944), there are a limited number of exceptions to this general rule. These exceptions arise where:

(a) there is a conflict between two previous decisions of the Court of Appeal, in which circumstances the later court must decide which decision to follow and, as a corollary, which to overrule

(b) a previous decision of the Court of Appeal has been overruled, either expressly or impliedly, by the House of Lords, in which case, the Court of Appeal is required to follow the decision of the House of Lords

(c) one of its previous decisions has been given *per incuriam* or, in other words, that previous decision was taken in ignorance of some authority that would have led to a different conclusion, in which case, the later court can ignore the previous decision in question.

In addition to the above, there is also the possibility that, as a consequence of s 3 of the European Communities Act 1972, the Court of Appeal can ignore a previous decision of its own which is inconsistent with EC law or with a later decision of the ECJ.

Once again, there was an attempt by the Court of Appeal, under Lord Denning to widen these exceptions in *Gallie v Lee* (1971), but again, the House of Lords reaffirmed the limited nature of these exceptions and reasserted the strict operation of the doctrine of *stare decisis*.

Although, on the basis of *Spencer* (1987), it would appear that there is no difference in principle between the operation of the doctrine of *stare decisis* between the criminal and civil divisions of the Court of Appeal, it is generally accepted that, in practice, precedent is not followed as strictly in the former as it is in the latter. Courts in the criminal division are not bound to follow their own previous decisions which they subsequently consider to have been based on either a misunderstanding or a misapplication of the law. The reason for this increased measure of apparent laxity is the fact that the criminal courts deal with matters involving individual liberty and, therefore, require a wider ambit of discretion to prevent injustice.

Further down the hierarchy, the Divisional Court is bound by the doctrine of *stare decisis* in the normal way and must follow decisions of the House of Lords and of the Court of Appeal. It is, also, normally bound by its own previous decisions, although, in civil cases, it may avail itself of the exceptions open to the Court of Appeal, in *Young v Bristol Aeroplane Co Ltd*, and in criminal appeal cases the Queen's Bench Divisional Court may refuse to follow its own earlier decisions where it feels the earlier decision to have been wrongly made.

As regards the High Court, decisions by individual High Court judges are binding on courts inferior in the hierarchy. Such decisions are not binding on other High Court judges, although they are of strong persuasive authority and tend to be followed in practice.

Although subject to binding precedent from superior courts, Crown Courts cannot create precedent and their decisions can never amount to more than persuasive authority.

The decisions of county courts and magistrates' courts are never binding.

The operation of the doctrine of binding precedent is, of course, dependent on the existence of an extensive reporting service to provide access to judicial decisions. But, it should not be thought that the doctrine is as hard and fast as it originally appears. The technique of 'distinguishing' cases on their facts provides judges with scope for declining to follow precedents by which they would otherwise be bound. The legal decision in any case is an abstraction from the immediate facts of the case. If a judge decides, for some reason, that the facts in the case before him are so different from those of a case setting a precedent, he is at liberty to ignore the precedent and treat the case in question as not being covered by it. He can then decide the case as he thinks fit, without being bound by the, otherwise binding, precedent.

Scope for further uncertainty is introduced by the necessary distinction between *ratio decidendi* and *obiter dicta*. The only part that is binding in any judgment previously decided is the *ratio* of the case; the actual legal reason for the decision. Anything else in the judgment is by the way, or *obiter*. Difficulty arises from the fact that judges do not label their judgments in this way. They do not, actually, nominate the *ratio* of the case. Additionally, their judgments may be of great length, or there may be as many as five judges delivering individual judgments on the case and there is no requirement that all the judgments should agree on the principle of law governing the decision in the case. In any event, it is later judges who, in effect, determine what the particular *ratio* of any case was. The problem in relation to binding precedent is that it is open to later judges to avoid precedents by declaring them to be no more than *obiter* statements.

There are numerous *advantages* to the doctrine of *stare decisis*. Amongst these are:

(a) the fact that it saves the time of the judiciary, lawyers and their clients, for the reason that cases do not have to be re-argued – this also has the benefit of saving the money of potential litigants;

(b) it provides a measure of certainty to law – thus, lawyers and their clients are able to predict what the outcome of a particular legal question is likely to be in the light of previous judicial decisions;

(c) it provides for a measure of formal justice, to the extent that like cases are decided on a like basis;

(d) it provides an opportunity for judges to develop the common law in particular areas without waiting for Parliament to enact legislation.

There are, however, corresponding *disadvantages* in the doctrine. Amongst these are:

(a) the fact that the degree of certainty provided by the doctrine is undermined by the absolute number of cases that have been reported and can, therefore, be cited as authorities – this uncertainty is compounded by the ability of the judiciary to select which authority to follow through use of the mechanism of distinguishing cases on their facts;

(b) law may become ossified on the basis of an unjust precedent with the consequence that previous injustices are perpetuated – an example of this is the long delay in the recognition of the possibility of rape within marriage, which has only recently been recognised;

(c) in developing law, it might be claimed that the judiciary is, in fact, overstepping its constitutional role by making law rather than simply deciding its application.

Question 16

How can the common law progress if judges are bound by precedent?

Answer plan

A question of this type requires the following approach:

- consider what is meant by the common law;
- explain what is involved in the declaratory view of the role of the judiciary;
- analyse the operation of the system of *stare decisis* as it is supposed to operate;
- highlight some of the loopholes in the traditional version of *stare decisis*, for example, *Curry v DPP* (1994);
- provide some examples where the judges have continued to create new law;
- consider the constitutional role of the judiciary in the UK and whether they should or should not be allowed to go on making new law.

Answer

This question requires a consideration of the scope of judges to avoid the consequences of *stare decisis* in order to reach their own subjective decisions and the dangers inherent in so doing. In answering the question, it is necessary to consider the place and function of the judiciary within the Constitution of the UK and to consider their role in the creation and development of the common law.

Within the constitutional division of powers in the UK, it is the function of the legislature to make law and it is merely the function of the courts to apply that law. The declaratory view of the function of the English judiciary accepts this constitutional division of power and portrays them as not making law, but merely deciding cases in accordance with existing legal rules. The doctrine of binding precedent operates in such a way that judges in deciding particular cases are not merely referred to earlier decisions for guidance, but are actually bound to apply the rules of law contained in those decisions. The operation of this principle depends on the established hierarchy of the court structure: all courts standing in a definite relationship of superiority/inferiority to every other court. Usually, a court is bound by decisions of a court of equal standing, or of higher authority than itself in the court structure. Allowing for the fact that the doctrine of *stare decisis* is supposed to have binding force within this hierarchical framework, two questions still arise.

Firstly, it is axiomatic that legal rules cannot be subject to infinite regression; every rule of the common law must have had an origin. If one rejects as untenable the proposition of natural law – that it is possible for law to exist as an entity outside of, and distinct from social practice – then it follows that, if a particular law was not created by statute, it must have been created by a judge; even if this creative activity is no more than recognising the legitimacy, or otherwise, of the practice in question. As a matter of course, it follows that, where there is no established precedent, the doctrine of *stare decisis* breaks down and the courts are faced with the alternatives of either refusing to decide a case, or stating what the law should be. Even in modern times, courts are still required on occasions to consider situations for the very first time without access to precedent. These cases, described as cases of first impression, inevitably involve judges in the establishment of new law.

Secondly, the question arises as to how the law is to develop and change to cater for changed circumstances, if cases are always to be decided according to ageless precedent. In practice, flexibility is achieved through the possibility of previous decisions being either overruled, or distinguished, or the possibility of a later court extending or modifying the effective ambit of a precedent. At this stage, it must be emphasised that, strictly speaking, it is wrong to speak of a decision being binding, just as it is, technically, incorrect to refer to a decision being overruled. It is not the actual decision in a case that sets the precedent, but the rule of law on which that decision is founded. This rule, which is an abstraction from the facts of the case, is known as the *ratio decidendi* of the case. Thus, the *ratio decidendi* of a case may be understood as the statement of the law applied in deciding the legal problem raised by the concrete facts of the case. Moreover, not every statement of law in a judgment is binding; only those which are based on the particular facts of the case, as found and upon which the decision was based, are binding. Any other statement of law is, strictly speaking, superfluous and any such statement is termed *obiter dictum*, that is, said by the way. It is significant that, although *obiter dicta* do not form part of the binding precedent of the case in which they occur, and, therefore, do not have to be followed by judges deciding later similar cases, they do amount to persuasive authority and can be taken into consideration in later cases, if the judge in the later case considers it appropriate to do so. This, apparently small measure of discretion, in relationship to whether later judges are minded to accept the validity of *obiter* statements in precedent cases, opens up the possibility that judges, in later cases, have a much wider degree of discretion than is originally apparent in the traditional view of *stare decisis* when it is realised that it is the judges in the later cases who actually determine the *ratio decidendi* of previous cases. In delivering judgments in cases, judges do not separate and highlight the *ratio decidendi* from the rest of their judgment and this can lead to a lack of certainty in determining the *ratio decidendi*. This uncertainty is compounded by the fact that reports of decisions in cases may run to considerable length and where there are a number of separate judgments, although the judges involved may agree on the decision of a case, they may not agree on the legal basis of the decision reached. This difficulty is further compounded where there are a number of dissenting judgments. In the final analysis, it is for the judge deciding the case in which a precedent has been cited to determine the *ratio* of the authority and, thus, to determine whether he is bound by the precedent or not. This factor provides the courts with a considerable degree of discretion in electing whether to be bound or not by a particular authority.

It is somewhat anomalous that, within the system of *stare decisis*, precedents gain increased authority with the passage of time. As a consequence, courts tend to be reluctant to overrule long standing authorities, even though they may no longer accurately reflect contemporary practices or morals. Allied to the wish to maintain a high degree of certainty in the law, the main reason for judicial reluctance to overrule old decisions would appear to be the fact that overruling operates retrospectively. Overruling a precedent might, therefore, have the consequence of disturbing important financial arrangements previously settled in line with what were thought to be settled rules of law. It might also, in certain circumstances, lead to the imposition of criminal liability on previously lawful behaviour. It has to be emphasised, however, that the courts will not shrink from overruling authorities where they see them as no longer representing an appropriate statement of law. The legal recognition of the possibility of rape within marriage is simply one example of this process (see *R* (1991)).

In comparison to the mechanism of overruling, which is rarely used, the main device for avoiding binding precedents is that of distinguishing. As has been previously stated, the *ratio decidendi* of any case is an abstraction from, and is based upon, the material facts of the case. This opens up the possibility that a court may regard the facts of the case before it as significantly different from the facts of a cited precedent and, thus, not binding. The cases have been distinguished on their facts and the court is at liberty to ignore the precedent in the prior case.

Judges use the device of distinguishing where, for some reason, they are unwilling to follow a particular precedent. The law reports provide many examples of strained distinctions, where a court has, quite evidently, not wanted to follow an authority that it would otherwise have been bound by. A recent example is *Curry v DPP* (1994), in which the Court of Appeal attempted to remove the previous presumption that children between the ages of 10 and 14 charged with a criminal offence do not know that there actions are seriously wrong and requirement that the prosecution provide evidence to rebut the presumption. Mann LJ justified reversing the presumption by stating that, although it had often been assumed to be the law, it had never actually been specifically considered by earlier courts. On such reasoning, he felt justified in departing from previous decisions of the Court of Appeal which, otherwise, would have bound him. The House of Lords subsequently restored the original presumption. Although their Lordships recognised the problem, they thought it was a matter more for parliamentary action than judicial intervention.

A further way in which judges have a creative impact on the law is in the way in which they adapt and extend precedent in instant cases. Judicial reasoning tends to be carried out on the basis of analogy and judges have a large degree of discretion in selecting what are to be considered as analogous cases. They also have a tendency continuously to extend existing precedents to fit new situations, as the historical evolution of the tort of negligence will show.

The foregoing has demonstrated how the doctrine of *stare decisis* can be obverted by the judiciary and it is now, probably, a common place of legal theory that judges do make law. Perhaps, the more interesting question is not whether judges make law, but why they deny that they do so. In spite of the protestations of the judiciary, law and judicial decision making is a political process to the extent that decisions have to be made about which values are to be given priority within society. Through their choice of values, the judiciary sanction or prohibit particular forms of behaviour. To the extent that the judiciary can maintain the general belief in the fact that they do not take part in a political process, but simply declare what existing law is, they provide their inevitably partial decisions with the aura of objectivity, neutrality and fairness, whilst at the same time apparently respecting their limited role in regard to the separation of powers. For judges to do other than that, and to blatantly decide cases on the basis of their personal views as to 'rightness', would be not simply to undermine the hierarchy of binding precedent as the question suggests, but, more fundamentally and more dangerously, to undermine the whole judicial process and the constitutional role of the judiciary.

Question 17

Consider critically the rules of interpretation which guide judges in the interpretation of statutes and the presumptions they apply in this process.

Answer plan

This is quite a common type of question, although it can, sometimes, take the form of a problem question. Students must know the rules of statutory interpretation and the presumptions, but they must also show that they are fully aware that the various rules and presumptions are not as certain as a straightforward exposition of them might suggest. They are not all compatible, nor do they form a clear hierarchy. Judges, therefore, have a measure of freedom to select which ones they wish to follow. Answers should:

- address the point that interpretation is creative by its very nature;
- note that statutes may partake of the general uncertainty inherent in language;
- set out the three rules of statutory interpretation and highlight the use of each with reference to cases;
- consider the presumptions that will be applied in the consideration of statutes;
- consider the relationship of the rules and presumptions;
- refer to the HRA 1998;
- conclude with observations about the discretion that judges possess in deciding which rule/presumption to apply.

Answer

According to the traditional theory of the division of powers, the role of the judiciary is simply to apply the law that Parliament has created. This view is, however, simplistic to the extent that it denies, or at least ignores, the extent to which the judiciary has a measure of discretion and creative power in the manner in which it interprets the legislation that comes before it.

Contrary to common sense views, communication is not a passive receptive process. Language, necessarily, involves the listener in a process of active interpretation in order to determine the content and meaning of what is actually being communicated to him. Legislation can be seen as a form of communication. It represents and passes on to the judiciary and society at large what Parliament has determined should be the law governing a particular situation. To that extent, legislation shares the general problem of uncertainty inherent in any mode of communication. The conflicting aims of legislation, however, give rise to particular problems of interpretation; these conflicting aims are the need to be clear whilst at the same time being general. Clarity and precision tend to be achieved only in inverse proportion to generality, but legislation must, by and large, endeavour to be of general applicability. There is, therefore, in all legislation, a penumbra of uncertainty that can only be illuminated, and made certain, by judicial interpretation. That interpretation is a creative process and, inevitably, involves the judiciary in the process of creating law.

The question arises, therefore, as to how judges actually interpret legislation that comes before them and, the usual answer is that, in determining the actual meaning of legislation, they make use of the three primary rules of statutory interpretation and a variety of other secondary aids to construction.

The three rules of statutory interpretation are: (a) the literal rule; (b) the golden rule; and (c) the mischief rule. Before any detailed consideration of these rules of interpretation is undertaken, however, it must be emphasised that they are not really rules, but, as will be shown, they may best be considered as *post hoc* justifications for decisions taken in line with judicial preference.

The literal rule

Under this rule, the judge is required to consider what the legislation *actually* says, rather than considering what it *might mean*. In order to achieve this end, the judge should give words in legislation their literal meaning; that is, their plain, ordinary, every day meaning, even if the effect of this is to produce what might be considered as an, otherwise, unjust or undesirable outcome. A classic example of this approach from the area of contract law is *Fisher v Bell* (1961). In this case, a shopkeeper, who had put a flick-knife in his shop window, together with a price tag, was charged under a particular statute with 'offering the knife for sale'. The charge was dismissed on the basis that, in line with the general contract law principles, the placing of an article in a window did not amount to an offer, but was merely an invitation to treat and, therefore, the charge was inaccurate. There is no doubt that the flick-knife was an offensive weapon and that the legislation was aimed at controlling the sale of such weapons, nor was there any doubt that the shopkeeper would have sold the knife, but the court stood by the literal interpretation of the Act in question and refused to extend the usual legal interpretation of the word 'offer'.

The golden rule

This rule is used when it appears that the application of the literal rule will result in, what appears to the court to be, an obviously absurd result. An example of application of the golden rule is *Adler v George* (1964). Under the Official Secrets Act in operation at the time, it was an offence to obstruct HM Forces *in the vicinity of* a prohibited place. George had, in fact, been arrested whilst obstructing such forces *within* such a prohibited place. The court found no difficulty in applying the golden rule to extend the literal wording of the statute to cover the action committed by the defendant.

The mischief rule

This rule is of venerable age, being clearly established in *Heydon's Case* (1584). It gives the court a justification for going behind the actual wording of a statute in order to consider the problem that the particular statute was aimed at remedying. At one level, the mischief rule is, clearly, the most flexible rule of interpretation, but it is limited by being restricted to using previous common law to determine the particular mischief the statute in question was designed to remedy. In *Heydon's Case*, it was stated that in making use of the mischief rule the court should consider the following four things:

(a) what was the common law before the passing of the statute?;

(b) what was the mischief in the law with which the common law did not adequately deal?;

(c) what remedy for that mischief had Parliament intended to provide?;

(d) what was the reason for Parliament adopting that remedy?

An example of the use of the mischief rule is clearly found in *Corkery v Carpenter* (1951), where a person was arrested for being drunk in charge of a bicycle. He was subsequently charged under the Licensing Act with being drunk in charge of a carriage, as the legislation made no actual reference to cycles. It is certainly arguable that a cycle is not a carriage, but, in any case, the court elected to use the mischief rule to decide the matter. The purpose of the Act was to prevent people from using any form of transport on the public highways whilst in a state of intoxication. The cycle was clearly a form of transport and, therefore, its user was correctly charged.

It is usually suggested that the above three rules are ranked in a hierarchical order, the first being the preferred rule only giving way to the second in certain circumstances, and the third rule only being brought into use in a perceived failure of the other two to deliver an appropriate result. On consideration, however, it becomes obvious that there is no such hierarchy. The literal rule is to be used, unless it leads to a manifest absurdity, in which case it will give way to the golden rule; but what determines whether any particular result is an absurdity, other than the view of the judge deciding the case? The rules are contradictory, at least to a degree, and there is no way in which the outsider can determine in advance which of them the courts will mobilise to decide the meaning of a particular statute. In reality, it may be seen, therefore, that the three rules are simply different rules which are no more than devices by means of which the judges justify their particular decisions.

In addition to using the usual rules of interpretation, judges are now required by the HRA 1998 to construe statutes in such a way as, so far as possible, to give effect to the rights provided under the ECHR. This new requirement might well have the effect of invalidating previous interpretations of statutes which had to be decided without reference to the Convention. No doubt, the future will see many strained interpretations of statutes in an endeavour to keep them within the parameters of the Convention.

Apart from the supposed rules of interpretation considered above, the courts may also make use of certain presumptions. As with all presumptions, these are open to rebuttal. They can be listed as follows:

(a) since Parliament is sovereign, it can, of course, alter the common law by express enactment, but, otherwise, a statute is presumed not to make any fundamental change to the common law in the face of an alternative interpretation which maintains the existing common law position;

(b) a statute does not impose criminal liability without proof of *mens rea* – thus, in *Sweet v Parsley* (1970), the owner of property was acquitted of being concerned with the management of premises which had been used for the smoking of cannabis.

The House of Lords decided that, as she did not know her property was being used for that purpose, she could not be guilty of the offence with which she was charged. As stated previously, this presumption can be rebutted either expressly by the wording of the legislation, as in many strict liability offences, or by implication, on the basis of the judge's interpretation of the statute;

(c) a statute is presumed not to operate retrospectively. It is, however, always open to Parliament to enact such legislation, as it did with the War Damage Act 1965 in order to prevent the Burmah Oil Company from collecting damages which the courts had decided were owed to it from the State;

(d) a statute is presumed not to intend to deprive individuals of their property or interfere with their rights without compensation;

(e) a statute is presumed not to apply to the Crown unless there is a clear statement that it is to be so bound;

(f) a statute is presumed not to run counter to international law and, where possible, it should be interpreted in such a way as to give effect to existing international legal obligations.

As with the 'rules' of interpretation, simply being able to list the various presumptions does not, in fact, mean a great deal in the face of judicial discretion in deciding which particular ones to follow.

The various contradictions and weaknesses evident in the manner in which judges interpret legislation mentioned above were encapsulated in the Law Commission's Report entitled *The Interpretation of Statutes*, Law Com No 21, 1969. There has been no action on this Report to date.

Question 18

Consider the implications of *Pepper v Hart* (1993) within the context of the material available to courts in the construction of legislation.

Answer plan

This contemporary question may well prove popular in future exams, for the reason that it alters a long standing rule. Students must, of course, have a close knowledge of the case and, in particular, do the following:

- refer to the rules of interpretation and the secondary aids to construction;
- distinguish between intrinsic and extrinsic aids to construction, providing explanatory examples of each;
- consider the previous use of parliamentary debates in court cases;
- consider the decision in *Pepper v Hart* in some detail and offer a view as to its likely effect.

Answer

The primary mechanisms by means of which judges construe legislation are the three rules of interpretation: the literal, the golden and the mischief rules; together with the various presumptions upon which they are expected to base their decisions. In addition to these, are a number of secondary aids to construction, which can themselves be further categorised as either intrinsic or extrinsic.

Assistance is said to be *intrinsic* when it is derived from the statute which is immediately under consideration. For example, there are a number of ways in which the judge can use the full statute to understand the meaning of a particular part of that statute.

One possible source of such illumination might be the title of the Act under consideration. Titles, however, whether long or short, tend not to be used by the courts in determining the purpose of legislation and, in any case, any general intention derived from the title must give way in the face of clear statements to the contrary in the actual body of the Act. There are, however, some circumstances in which the courts will refer to the long title of an Act in making their decision as to its particular effect and operation; an example of this is *Royal College of Nursing v DHSS* (1981).

A second possible intrinsic source of guidance, although this one tends only to be found in older Acts, is the preamble, a statement preceding the actual provisions of the Act which sets out it purposes, sometimes in full and fulsome detail. Again, such assistance is only of limited value, in that it has to give way in the face of specific provisions to the contrary within the body of the legislation.

A third source of assistance for courts can be found in the schedules to Acts which appear as additions at the end of the main body of the legislation. These form part of the Act and may be used to shed light on any obscurity in the main text.

Of less certain help to judges in deciding the meaning of sections are the headings which may precede particular sections of an Act or the marginal notes which accompany them. The legitimate use of either is doubtful, although authority for the use of the former is provided in *DPP v Schildkamp* (1971).

Finally, in regard to intrinsic aids to interpretation, it is now recognised that punctuation has an effect on the meaning of words and can be taken into account in determining the meaning of legislation.

It is only with regard to external aids to construction that controversy really enters the picture. The question is, and always has been: 'What sources are judges entitled to look to in order to determine either the meaning or the intent of legislation?' It is in answering this particular question that *Pepper v Hart*, at least arguably, has had a major impact, for it may be seen as overturning the previous, fundamentally restrictive, approach of the courts to what they can legitimately look at in order to determine the meaning or purpose of a statute.

Some external sources are without problems. For example, it has always been open to judges to use dictionaries to determine the meaning of non-legal words and they have been able to consider textbooks for elucidation with respect to particular points of law. They have also been able to refer to other earlier statutes to determine the mischief, at which the particular statute they are endeavouring to construe, is aimed.

Problems arise with respect to what other works courts can refer to. There are many stages in the preparation of legislation; reports, commissions, working papers (generally, known as *travaux preparatoires*) and, indeed, the debates in Parliament during the passage of the Act in question. Each of these is a potential source for finding out the real purpose of the final Act or the real meaning of any provision within it. The question is which of these sources is open to the courts? Historically, English courts have adopted a restrictive approach to what they are entitled to take into consideration; although some judges, such as Lord Denning, have been notorious for trying to avoid those restrictive rules. The restrictive approach has been gradually relaxed to the extent that judges can use extrinsic sources to, at least, determine the mischief at which particular legislation was aimed at and, in pursuit of this end, they were entitled to look at Law Commission reports, the reports of royal commissions and the reports of other official commissions.

However, until now, access to the debates of Parliament, as reported in *Hansard*, has remained, at least in theory, if not in practice, a closed book to the courts.

In *Pepper v Hart*, the House of Lords decided to overturn the previously prevailing rule that judges were not at liberty to consult the reports of Parliamentary debates in *Hansard* in order to assist them in their construction of legislation. In a majority decision, it was held that, where the precise meaning of legislation was uncertain or ambiguous, or where the literal meaning of an Act would lead to a manifest absurdity, the courts could refer to *Hansard*'s reports of parliamentary debates and proceedings as an aid to construing the meaning of the legislation.

As Lord Browne-Wilkinson stated in his judgment, there were good reasons for making a limited modification to the existing rules, the most obvious of which was the fact that such reports might actually provide a clear indication of what Parliament had actually intended in using particular words.

In permitting this extension, however, the House of Lords did not grant absolute freedom to future courts. For one thing, any such reference to *Hansard* should be made only to reveal the legislative intention of the statute, rather than find the precise meaning of statutory language. In other words, the extension still only applies to the determination of the mischief at which the particular legislation is aimed, rather than the determination of the precise explanation of the remedy provided. In addition to this restriction, it was made clear that consideration should only be made, subject to strict safeguards. For example, it is evident that, even now that the possibility of examining *Hansard* has been opened up to provide a means of determining the purpose behind a statute, it is likely that only statements made by a Government minister, or some other sponsor, responsible for the provisions and passage of the legislation will be considered as authoritative in determining the mischief at which a particular statute was aimed.

Until its removal in 1980, there had been a parliamentary rule preventing counsel in any court case from citing any debates in the House of Commons without the prior approval of the House and a further constitutional question was considered in *Pepper v Hart*. This question was whether the use of *Hansard* in courts would question the freedom of parliamentary debate and, thus, constitute a breach of the 1689 Bill of Rights. But, as the House of Lords pointed out, the relaxation of the old rule would actually lead to the courts giving effect to the wishes of Parliament and, thus, could not in any way be seen as an infringement on parliamentary privilege or sovereignty.

The operation of the principle in *Pepper v Hart* was extended in *Three Rivers DC v Bank of England (No 2)* (1996), to cover situations where legislation under question was not itself ambiguous, but might be ineffective in its intention to give effect to some particular EC directive. However, in *Melluish v BMI (No 3) Ltd* (1995), the court refused to extend the rule to situations where ministers had made statements as to the meaning of statutes, at some time, other than at the passing of the particular piece of legislation.

Question 19

> Evidence must be sufficiently relevant to be admissible, but sufficiently relevant evidence is only admissible in so far as it is not excluded by any rule of the law of evidence. The consequence … is that some relevant evidence is excluded [Keane, A, *The Law of Evidence*, 4th edn, 1996].

Explain the exclusionary rules of evidence and assess how far they are successful in promoting a fair trial.

Answer plan

A good approach to this discussion and assessment would be to:

- introduce the different types of excluded evidence;
- consider evidence unduly prejudicial to the defendant – Criminal Evidence Act 1898, *Selvey v DPP* (1968), *Boardman v DPP* (1974), *P* (1991);
- include discussion of inherently unreliable evidence – children's evidence, hearsay evidence (with exceptions, discuss *Rogers* (1994));
- evidence against the public interest should be dealt with – legal professional privilege, confessions obtained by oppression;
- conclude with some discussion of the need to balance the interests in question.

Answer

The exclusionary rules of evidence are a characteristic of the common law tradition and are not favoured by continental jurisdictions. There are three main types of evidence which can be excluded from a trial even though containing information relevant to the case: (a) evidence which might be unduly prejudicial to the defendant; (b) evidence which is inherently unreliable; and (c) evidence which it would be against the public interest to admit into the hearing.

It is, generally, unduly prejudicial to the defendant for the court to learn, during the trial, of his previous convictions. He must be judged according to the evidence relating to the crime in question (*Coombes* (1960)). This exclusionary rule, however, does not apply if the defendant asserts his own good character. Here, the prosecution can rebut the assertion with the defendant's criminal record. A defendant's past misconduct can also be disclosed if he attacks a co-accused, even a co-accused not charged with the same offence. The defendant who is attacked may cross-examine the attacker about his criminal record.

There are two further exceptions to the 'unduly prejudicial' exclusion rule. The defendant's record can be admitted if he attacks a prosecution witness, or where there is a marked similarity of facts between the crimes under consideration and earlier ones for which the defendant has been convicted. Both these exceptions have proved problematic in practice.

Section 1 of the Criminal Evidence Act 1898 states that a defendant's record can be admitted where the 'nature or conduct of the defence is such as to involve imputations on the character of the prosecutor or the witnesses for the prosecution'. The rationale of the rule is that, in circumstances of a simple quarrel on evidence between the sides, where the defence explains the prosecution's story by alleging that the prosecution witness is lying, it is proper for the court to know of any evidence that the defendant is a liar, so as best to judge which side is telling the truth. The problem here is for an innocent defendant who does have a criminal record and against whom there is being put some dishonest evidence. He cannot attack the prosecution's improper case without exposing his criminal record and, thus, probably, damaging his defence. Additionally, as Zander has argued, if it is regarded as generally correct to withhold evidence of past misconduct from the court because it is unduly prejudicial, it does not become any the less prejudicial simply because the accused has impugned a prosecution witness.

In *Selvey v DPP* (1968), the House of Lords ruled that, where previous convictions of a defendant are admitted, they are to be treated by the court only as evidence of the defendant's creditworthiness, not of his propensity to commit the offence in question. This, however, is a rather pious hope. Once jury members learn of the defendant's convictions, they are likely to draw unfavourable conclusions about the person and probably do just what the House of Lords have declared should not be done.

As to the 'similar fact' exception, it was held in *Straffen* (1952), that previous convictions can be admitted where the facts in a case are so strikingly similar to the facts in previous cases for which the defendant has been convicted as virtually to rule out co-incidence. The test for when the exception can be used was relaxed by the House of Lords in *Boardman v DPP* (1974), where it was suggested that the similarity did not need to be 'striking'. In *P* (1991), the House of Lords held that the real test was whether the 'probative force' of the evidence to be admitted was great enough to justify the prejudice given to the accused. Thus, in a charge of rape and incest against P, it was acceptable for the evidence of one of two victimised daughters to be used in the same hearing as her sister's evidence. Both girls had testified about prolonged misconduct and the probative value of each girl's evidence outweighed the prejudice to the father in using one allegation to fortify another.

Another category of evidence which English law excludes from the trial is that which is inherently unreliable. Thus, a judge can exclude the evidence of a proposed witness who does not have the mental capacity to testify. Two more problematic types of evidence in this class are children's evidence and hearsay evidence.

Traditionally, there was an assumption that young children were not reliable witnesses. Children could give sworn testimony if the judge believed that they appreciated the solemnity of the occasion and understood the importance of the oath. There was a more relaxed rule in criminal cases, where unsworn evidence could be taken from a child who was sufficiently intelligent. Evidence has been heard from children as young as six (Z (1990)). Psychological research (for example, Davies, Tarrant and Flin, 'Close encounters of the witness kind' (1989) British Journal of Psychology) has now shown, however, that children are more reliable witnesses than was earlier thought. Now, s 52 of the Criminal Justice Act 1991 requires that all witnesses under 14 years of age are to give unsworn evidence ,unless a judge rules that such a person is incompetent. Another reform was made by s 34 of the Act, which abolished the requirement for the unsworn evidence of children to be corroborated and provided that the unsworn evidence of children could corroborate any other witness' testimony. The law, prior to these reforms, had made it extremely difficult to get convictions in serious cases of sexual abuse.

Hearsay evidence – that of someone not actually present in court – is regarded as inherently unreliable because the person who actually saw or heard something relevant cannot be tested by cross-examination in court. A document is hearsay, unless its author is also present to testify. In *Sparks v R* (1964), a white man was convicted for sexual assault on a three year old girl. When asked just after the event, by her mother, who had assaulted her, the girl allegedly said, 'It was a coloured boy', but the Privy Council ruled that the mother could not give this as part of her evidence, as it would be hearsay. There are now so many exceptions to this exclusionary rule that it has been described by Zander as being in 'an advanced state of disintegration' (*Cases and Materials on the English Legal System*, 7th edn, 1996).

The hearsay rule only applies if the statement is to be introduced in order to establish the truth of its contents. It is not counted as hearsay, if it is to be introduced as 'direct evidence'. The law on this is somewhat erratic, for example, it was held in *Taylor v Chief Constable of Cheshire* (1987), that a video recording was not hearsay, but direct evidence, whereas, in *Townsend* (1987), a robbery victim had scribbled down the registration number of the defendant's car. The pen was defective and made only indentations which the police had managed to boost, but they lost the original note. The technical evidence was ruled to be hearsay. Hearsay evidence is admissible where the original statement was made as a dying declaration, or as part of the *res gestae* (a statement made so close to the incident in question that it can be regarded as part of the event).

An interesting recent decision is *Rogers* (1994). The appellant had been convicted of possession of heroin with intent to supply. He had sought to have admitted as evidence a statement made by the wife of an old associate of his who had died before the trial. The wife's statement was a report of what she said her husband, L, had told her before he died. The statement began: 'L said there were a number of guys after him for the money for the heroin that the police had found.' It continued to the effect that L had been supplying the appellant with heroin for his personal use only and that the appellant knew nothing of the larger stock (which the prosecution alleged he did control). The appellant submitted that Mrs L's evidence fell within an exception to the hearsay rule – that statements made by a deceased were admissible if they were against his pecuniary interest (the rationale being that no one would acknowledge an obligation against his pecuniary interests, unless it was true) – in that, the first sentence was such a statement as the deceased was acknowledging that he owed money and the remainder of the statement was admissible as collateral evidence. The appeal was dismissed. It was held that, on the facts, the first sentence was not against the deceased's pecuniary interests, since he was not saying that he actually owed anyone any money and, so, was not acknowledging any obligation. Furthermore, even if that sentence was admissible, the rest of the statement, which was the part on which the defence wished to rely, was not admissible as collateral evidence as, it would only be so admissible, if further information was needed to explain the nature of the transaction in question, which was not the case.

Documentary hearsay evidence has been admissible in civil cases since 1938 and, in 1968, the rule was widened to include oral evidence with the consent of the other side. In 1991, the Law Commission recommended that the hearsay rule should be abolished in civil proceedings to bring the rules of evidence in line with the recent changes facilitating pre-trial exchange of witness statements. Many erosions of the hearsay rule in criminal cases have also been made, for example, statements of the dead, people who have (since they made the statement) become unfit, the untraceable, business documents and expert evidence are all admissible under the Criminal Justice Act 1988. Zuckerman has argued that these examples of 'non-hearsay' are just convenient ways of avoiding the rule, where it is thought that a certain type of statement will be reliable.

The third category of relevant evidence excluded from trial is that which it would be against the public interest to admit. There are several types of evidence which fall under this heading. Legal professional privilege means that any communications between a client and his legal adviser (arising from an existing, or contemplated case, or to enable advice to be given), generally, cannot be adduced in evidence by the lawyer without the permission of the client. The privilege is afforded to promote openness between the client and the lawyer. The privilege is not absolute, however, where the material sought to be produced in court would help to establish someone's innocence. This has arisen in cases with several co-accused and the judge must decide whether the legitimate interest of the defendant, who wants to keep the privilege, outweighs that of the client, who wants to breach it.

Since *Marks v Beyfus* (1890), it has been accepted by the courts that it is in the public interest that the identity of police informers should be kept secret. Nonetheless, this principle can be superseded by the principle that the defendant should not be unfairly impeded from establishing his innocence. In *Brown* (1988), convictions were quashed where the trial judge had refused to allow police officers to be questioned about their surveillance operation.

Section 76 of the Police and Criminal Evidence Act (PACE) 1984 allows for the exclusion of evidence of a confession which has, or might have been, obtained by 'oppression' or in consequence of anything said or done which was likely to render it unreliable. 'Oppression' is defined as including torture, inhuman or degrading treatment and the use or threat of violence. There have been very few successful appeals using this section and the courts appear to have taken the contentious view that, whether police questioning is oppressive or not, depends upon the intention of the interrogating officers, rather than the actual effect the questions have on the defendant. This reasoning was adopted in *Miller* (1986).

Much more effectively used has been s 78 of PACE 1984. Under this, the court can refuse to admit evidence if it appears to the court that, in all the circumstances, the evidence would have such an adverse effect on the fairness of proceedings that the court ought not to admit it. The majority of cases where the section has been successfully used have concerned breaches of PACE 1984 or its Codes of Practice with facts involving wrongful refusal to provide legal advice or the failure to record interviews (see, for example, *Samuel* (1988), defendant denied access to solicitor; *Doolan* (1988), defendant not cautioned; *Weekes* (1993), defendant not provided with appropriate adult).

In *AG's Reference (No 3 of 1999)* (2000) *The Independent*, 20 December, the House of Lords gave a ruling which shows how subtle in their reasoning the courts should be when balancing: (a) the interests of the accused not to have prejudicial evidence used against him; and (b) the interests of the public in convicting offenders. In this case, a man was accused of burglary and rape. He was alleged to have broken into the house of a 66 year old woman and raped her anally. He was arrested and prosecuted after a DNA sample taken from the victim was found to match his

DNA taken from a sample he had provided in the investigation of an earlier unconnected burglary. According to s 64(1) of the PACE 1984, the sample he gave at the time of the first burglary should have been destroyed because he was tried for, but acquitted of that crime. If that sample had been destroyed, then the police would not have had it, so, when the DNA sample was taken from the woman in the later burglary it would not have matched any sample in the police records. In the second case, the police had, once they apprehended the defendant, taken a new sample from him to match with that found on the victim. But, they would not have been doing that, had they not identified him as a suspect in the first place, which they only did because of the first, improperly held, sample. The Lords held that, in future cases, where there were exceptional circumstances, the courts could, by analogy with s 78(1), admit evidence apparently rendered inadmissible by s 64(3B).

In conclusion, it can be noted that the real difficulty in this area is the familiar legal problem of balancing the interests of two sides. English law has taken the view that the judge should be the gatekeeper of much evidence brought to court by lawyers, deciding whether the jury can hear it and make up their own minds. The judge is given guidance by the law on how to decide these matters but, ultimately, many of his decisions are matters of personal opinion, for example, whether a child is fit to give evidence, or whether the defendant is imputing the character of a prosecution witness or simply asserting his or her own innocence.

CHAPTER 4

JUDGES AND JURIES

Introduction

Judges obviously occupy a central role in the legal system with regard to both civil and criminal law and, for that reason, questions about the judiciary are found in most examination papers on English legal system courses. It is frequently claimed that judges represent the views of a highly limited section of society, being mainly white middle aged men. The point to consider, however, is whether this social placement has a deleterious effect on the decisions that the judges make. If judges are simply the mouthpieces of the law and their decisions represent no more than the automatic outcome of a strictly logical process of reasoning, then the actual social situation and background of the judge is immaterial, for the decisions are contained in the law itself. If, on the other hand, legal reasoning is not as prescriptive as outsiders generally consider it to be and judges actually have a substantial measure of discretion in the way in which they reach their decisions, then the social placement of the judiciary does become a matter to be critically analysed with regard to the decisions that they reach. Law becomes, not the expression of some imminent authority, but the expression of individual and, perhaps more importantly, group prejudice.

For the above reasons, it is important to avoid reliance on superficial and anecdotal assertions as to the lack of awareness of judges, in favour of a reasoned and well supported critique of the nature of legal reasoning, before attention is focused on the social background of the judiciary. The answers offered in this chapter locate weaknesses in the process of legal reasoning as of central importance and, indeed, as prior to any critical understanding of how judges operate.

Juries

The role of the jury in the English legal system is the subject of contentious debate. You should be familiar with recent research on this theme and some particular questions which have been addressed by researchers; for instance, how often do juries return 'perverse' verdicts and are such practices desirable? Are juries capable of properly following the details of complex trials? Be careful to observe how much the question you are answering requires a factual account or explanation of procedure, as opposed to evaluative, argumentative material. In any event, you will need a good knowledge of the legal and historical aspects of the jury in order to be able to rehearse the controversial parts of this topic.

Checklist

You should be familiar with:
- the way in which judges are appointed and the role of the Lord Chancellor in their appointment;
- how judges can avoid the strict operation of precedent and their powers in relation to the interpretation of statutes;
- the difference between individual and corporate prejudice;
- the social background of the judiciary;
- possible ways of diminishing perceptions of judicial bias;
- the historical justification for trial by jury;
- the rules concerning eligibility (including disqualification and excusal);
- the powers of the prosecution and defence to alter the composition of the jury;
- the practice of jury vetting and issues of selection procedure and impartiality;
- the arguments for and against retaining the jury for criminal trials.

Question 20

Critically examine the way in which judges are appointed to office and consider alternative methods of appointment.

Answer plan

This question raises issues relating to the way in which judges are appointed to office. The obvious part of the question involves a brief consideration of the qualifications required to hold judicial office, but the more important part relates to the way in which judges are actually selected for office. The latter issue requires an examination of the office of the Lord Chancellor and the role he plays in the selection process. Mention should be made of the – at least alleged – shortcomings in the present system and alternative means of selecting judges. Some reference should be made to the current social, ethnic and gender make-up of the judiciary. Equally, attention should be focused on why the issue is one of contemporary importance and, in addition, reference should be made to the role of the judges in judicial review and in relation to the Human Rights Act (HRA) 1998. A possible structure is as follows:

- qualifications for judicial office;
- selection process and the role of the Lord Chancellor;
- criticisms of current procedure;
- current ethnic/gender mix of judiciary;
- why the criticisms are important;
- proposals for improving the system – proposed;
- proposals for improving the system – possible.

Answer

The Courts and Legal Services Act (CLSA) 1990 introduced major changes into the qualifications required for filling the positions of judges. Judicial appointment is still, essentially, dependent upon the rights of audience in the higher courts, but, at the same time as the Act of 1990 effectively demolished the monopoly of the Bar to rights of audience in such courts, it opened up the possibility of achieving judicial office to legal practitioners, other than barristers. The necessary qualifications are, as follows.

Lord of Appeal in Ordinary (House of Lords):
- the holding of high judicial office for two years;
- possession of a 15 year Supreme Court qualification under the CLSA 1990.

Lord Justice of Appeal (Court of Appeal):
- the holding of a post as a High Court judge;
- possession of a 10 year High Court qualification under the CLSA 1990.

High Court judge:
- the holding of a post as a circuit judge for two years;
- possession of a 10 year High Court Qualification under the CLSA 1990.

Deputy judge:
- must be qualified in the same way as permanent High Court judges.

Circuit judge:
- the holding of a post as a recorder;
- possession of either a 10 year Crown Court qualification, or a 10 year county court qualification under the CLSA 1990;
- the holding of certain offices, such as district judge, social security commissioner, chairman of an industrial tribunal, stipendiary magistrate, for three years.

Recorder:
- candidates must possess 10 year Crown Court or county court qualification under the CLSA 1990.

District judge:
- requires a seven year general qualification under the CLSA 1990.

Selection of judges

The foregoing has concentrated on the specific requirements for those wishing to fulfil the role of judge; but, it remains to consider the more general question, relating to the general process whereby people are deemed suitable and selected for such office. All judicial appointments remain, theoretically, at the hands of the Crown. The Crown, however, is guided, if not actually dictated to, with regard to appointments, by the Government of the day. The Lord Chancellor, himself, is of course a direct political appointment with a seat in the cabinet. The Prime Minister also advises the Crown on the appointment of other senior judicial office holders, the Law Lords and Court of Appeal judges. Judges at the level of High Court judges and Circuit Bench are appointed by the Crown on the advice on the Lord Chancellor and the Lord Chancellor, personally, appoints district judges, lay magistrates and the members of some tribunals.

This system has not gone without challenge; the question being raised as to how the Chancellor actually reaches his decision to recommend or appoint individuals to judicial offices. It is accepted that the Lord Chancellor's recommendations are made on the basis of the opinions of the existing judiciary as to the suitability of the potential candidates. Although the Lord Chancellor's Department publishes a guidance booklet entitled 'Judicial appointments', the problem with the system – at least, as perceived by both the Bar and the Law Society – is reflected in the widespread belief that it is oversecretive and leads to a highly conservative appointment policy; with judges, perhaps not unnaturally, favouring those candidates who have not been 'troublesome' in their previous cases and who have shown themselves to share the views and approaches of the existing office holders.

In his 1993 Hamlyn Lecture, the former Lord Chancellor, Lord Mackay stated that the arrangements in the UK for the collection of data about candidates for the judiciary are comparatively well developed and provide those who have to take the decisions (essentially, the Lord Chancellor himself) with fuller information than would otherwise be available to them. The reasoning behind this claim would appear to be that, because the procedure is secret and limited, people commenting on the suitability of candidates are willing to be more frank and open than would otherwise be the case were the references open to wider inspection. This complacency is continued by the present Lord Chancellor, Lord Irvine, who was recently quoted as saying:

> The press and, I am sorry to say, many in the profession, refer to these consultations as 'secret soundings'. This makes them sound sinister. They are not ... [they] are confidential. But it is no secret that they happen. And they are not soundings, they are an information gathering exercise.

The meetings aren't secret; only what takes place in them is secret – so that's all right then.

However, no doubt as a consequence of the sustained criticism of the closed nature of the appointment process, Lord Chancellor Mackay announced that advertisements would be used to recruit likely candidates from the professions for the positions of assistant recorder, deputy district judge and circuit judge. Lord Irvine has carried this further by advertising for High Court judges. These advertisements stated:

> The Lord Chancellor will recommend for appointment the candidates who appear to him to be best qualified, regardless of ethnic origin, gender, marital status, sexual orientation, political affiliation, religion or (subject to the physical requirements of the office) disability.

And, in a speech to the Association of Women Barristers in 1998, Lord Irvine showed a desire to encourage an increase in female members of the judiciary. In the course of the speech, he stated:

> In December 1994, 7.6% of the main tiers of the judiciary – by which I mean the Lords Justices of Appeal, High Court, circuit judges ... – were women. It is now a little over 9%. Not a meteoric rise, true, but a steady one.

Lord Irvine is clearly a master of understatement: an increase of 1.4% in four years and from such a low base level, is certainly not meteoric. In fact, there are no women amongst the 12 judges in the House of Lords, only one amongst the 35 in the Court of Appeal and seven amongst the 97 High Court judges.

He showed an equal desire to encourage judicial appointments from ethnic minorities in a 1997 speech to the Minority Lawyers Conference. With regard to ethnicity, there are no black, full time judges at any level and only four from other ethnic minorities amongst the 558 circuit judges.

Their statements clearly indicate the willingness of the Lord Chancellors to consider changes, but some have questioned their effectiveness in opening up the judicial appointment process. This distrust and suspicion in relation to the way judges are selected has been heightened as judges increasingly take on overtly political roles in relation to judicial review and the HRA 1998. Criticism came to a head with the announcement of the appointment of two new Lords of Appeal in July 1998. The news that both Sir John Hobhouse and Sir Peter Millet were to be elevated from the Court of Appeal to the House of Lords infuriated a number of commentators. It was pointed out that the commercial law background of both men did nothing to convince that they were suitable candidates for such a high office which would, increasingly, be called upon to deal with human rights cases, as the HRA 1998 came into effect. The view was expressed that, as the House of Lords assumed a role within the UK more akin to the United States Supreme Court, so the judges in that court should be open to the same degree of public scrutiny that members of the Supreme Court are subject to.

Some called for the setting up of a judicial appointments committee to oversee the selection of appropriate people to judicial office. Interestingly, it was Labour Party policy, before the 1997 election, to have just such a commission. The then Labour Party spokesman on legal affairs and former chairman of the Bar Council, Lord Williams of Mostyn, attacked the reforms introduced by Lord Mackay, calling them 'cosmetic tinkering to no lasting or sensible purpose ... offer[ing] nothing which is likely to improve either judicial performance or public confidence in the judiciary'.

Lord Williams' call for an independent judicial commission had been supported not only by the law reform group Justice, but also by the Bar and the Law Society. It was, also, advocated by Derry Irvine QC, as he was then, in a Society of Labour Lawyers publication entitled 'Law reform for all'. Since his accession to the office of Lord Chancellor, Lord Irvine, as he now is, would seem to have changed his opinion, but such a proposal, combined with an opening up of access to judicial posts from the existing, very narrow, constituency would go some way to increasing public confidence in the judiciary, which still seems remote, isolated and insular, to the majority of people.

However, it has to be recognised that some, if relatively faltering, steps have been taken in this regard. In 1999, Sir Leonard Peach conducted an independent review of the systems for appointing both judges and Queen's Counsel. The report, delivered in December of that year, was broadly supportive of the existing system. It, nonetheless, advocated the establishment of a Commission for Judicial Appointments, the task of which would be to provide an ombudsman facility for unsuccessful candidates and to carry out an ongoing audit into the procedures of appointment. The Commission would have authority in relation to all judicial positions, except the Lord Chief Justice and the Lords of Appeal in Ordinary (the House of Lords) and, of course, the Lord Chancellor. The recommendation was accepted by the Lord Chancellor and the job of Commissioner has already been filled by Sir Colin Campbell, Vice Chancellor of Nottingham University.

Question 21

Why does the social composition of the judiciary matter?

Answer plan

This question appears to be of the type that asks candidates to consider whether the particular class/race/gender background of the judges leads to a bias in their decisions. It has assumed a contemporary importance, however, given the continued increase in judicial review and the incorporation of the European Convention on Human Rights (ECHR) into UK law in the form of the HRA 1998. This question still requires a reference to Professor Griffith's views on *The Politics of the Judiciary* (5th edn, 1997). A good answer might take the following form:

- examine the actual constitution of the judiciary referring to any available statistics;
- consider why the composition of the judiciary matters, paying particular regard to judicial review and the HRA 1998;

- refer to Professor Griffith's claim as to the biased nature of the judiciary;
- adduce argument to the contrary;
- offer some proposals as to how the perceived problems might be remedied.

Answer

Central to the general idea of the rule of law is the specific proposition that it involves the rule of *law* rather than the rule of *people*. From this perspective, judges are seen as subservient to, and merely the instruments of, the law; and the outcome of the judicial process is understood as being determined through the straightforward application of legal rules, both statute and precedent, to particular factual situations. In applying those rules, the judge is expected to act in a completely impartial manner, without allowing his personal preferences to affect his decision in any way. A further assumption is that, in reaching a decision, the judge is only concerned with matters of law and refuses to permit politics, economics or other non-legal matters to influence his decision. The law is assumed to be distinct from, and superior to, those non-legal issues and the assumption is that the judge operates, in the words of Professor JAG Griffith, as a 'political, economic and social eunuch'. In reality, however, judges have a large measure of discretion in determining which laws to apply, what those laws actually mean and how to apply them. Equally, judges are, by necessity, involved in political issues when they are called upon to provide judicial review of the actions of the State and its functionaries. Although some judges have denied the political nature of such decisions, others have actually welcomed and justified the growth in judicial review, on the grounds that it permits the judiciary to protect individuals from the abuse of the power by, what they perceive, as an overmighty State and an otherwise uncontrolled executive. This overtly political role, which sets the courts up against the State, cannot but be increased by the enactment of the HRA 1998. This Act, which incorporates the ECHR into UK law, places the courts in the position of acting as the protectors of individual rights from incursions by the State. Although the Act expressly declines to challenge the supremacy of Parliament, by denying the courts the power to strike down particular legislation as being unconstitutional, it does permit them to make declarations to the effect that such legislation is incompatible with the human rights protected under the Act. Such declarations, and there are bound to be some, if not many, will, inevitably, place the judiciary in a political, not to say confrontational, relationship with Parliament.

In the light of this potential creative power, it is essential to ensure that the judiciary satisfactorily represents society at large, in relation to which it has so much power, and to ensure, further, that it does not merely represent the views and attitudes of a self-perpetuating elite. This desideratum could be reformulated in the form of a stark question: are judges biased and do they use their judicial positions in such a way as to give expression to that bias?

Bias can operate at two levels. The first is personal bias and occurs where individual judges permit their own prejudices to influence their understanding and implementation of the law. Such bias is a serious matter and reprehensible, but the very fact that it is individual makes it more open to control and, in the long run, less serious than the accusation of corporate bias that some observers, such as Professor Griffith, level against the judiciary. Corporate prejudice involves the assertion that the judiciary, as a body, do not decide certain types of cases in a fair and unbiased way; rather, that, as a consequence of their shared educational experience, shared training and practical experience at the Bar, along with shared social status, they have developed a common ideology comprising a homogeneous collection of values, attitudes and beliefs as to how the law should operate and be administered. The claim is that because, as individuals, they share the same prejudices, this leads to the emergence of an in-built group prejudice which precludes the possibility of some cases being decided in a neutral way.

The essence of Griffith's argument is that judges in the UK are in the position of being required to make political choices in the many cases that come before them which require a determination of public interest. This situation will, necessarily, become more frequent as the judges are required, under the HRA 1998, to weigh individual rights against public interest. His further point is that, in determining what constitutes the public interest, the judges give expression to their own values which are in turn a product of their position in society as part of the Establishment, the group in society which is the location of established authority. The argument runs that, as the judiciary are part of the machinery of authority within the State, they cannot exercise their functions in a truly neutral way, but must, whether consciously or not – and Griffith himself suggests that it is unconscious – further the interests of that State. The consequence of this is that they decide cases in a, fundamentally, conservative manner, operating in such a way as to maintain the status quo and resist challenges to the established authority.

It is claimed that the most obvious examples of the judiciary's overzealous solicitude for the State's interests occur when those interests come into conflict with individual interests or the right to public information. Griffith claims that in such cases the courts will tend to give undue preference to the State and cites various examples – such as the unilateral withdrawal of rights of trade union representation at the GCHQ – the total ban on publication of extracts from the *Spycatcher* book being simply the most recent of a number of notorious cases demonstrating the courts' readiness to promote the interests of the State and the Government above those of the individual.

With regard to the maintenance of law and order generally, but with particular reference to direct challenges to the State, Griffith cites the way in which the courts have reacted to alleged terrorists. It cannot but be admitted that the history of the trials and appeals of the Guildford Four, the Maguire Seven, the Birmingham Six and the solitary Judith Ward have resounded to the extreme discredit of the British courts, the British appeal system and British justice in general. The question has to be asked, however, do these cases reflect an inherently and inescapably conservative judiciary or are they simply unfortunate instances of errors which can occur within any system? Indeed, it could be argued that, as the accuseds were all ultimately released, these cases actually demonstrate the neutrality and long term validity of the British legal system. But, at the culmination of his attack on the judiciary, Griffith accuses them of actually promoting Conservative Party political views in their attitudes towards race relations, immigration and trade unions.

It is hardly surprising to find that Professor Griffith's attack on the judiciary has met with opposition. One notable response (and presumed rebuttal) was provided by Lord Devlin in a review article on Griffith's book, *The Politics of the Judiciary*. Lord Devlin pointed out that, in most cases, and on most issues, there tended to be plurality rather than unanimity of opinion and decision amongst judges. He also explained any apparent Conservative bias on the part of judges as a product of age rather than class; and that, in any case, even if the judiciary were biased, its bias was well known and allowances could be made for it. It has to be stated that Lord Devlin's response is extremely complacent and, in the light of the alleged terrorist cases mentioned previously, it is worryingly so.

It is apparent that senior judges are still being appointed from the same limited social and educational elite as they always have been and that this gives rise to the accusation, if not necessarily the reality, that the decisions made by this elite merely represent the interest of a limited and privileged segment of society, rather than society as a whole. It is arguable that, even if the accusations of those commentators such as Professor Griffith are inaccurate, it remains appropriate and, indeed, essential that, in order to remove even the possibility of those accusations, the present structure of the judiciary be examined and altered. At present, the Lord Chancellor appoints High Court judges; with appeal court judges and Law Lords being appointed by the Prime Minister, upon consultation with the Lord Chancellor. It is an open secret, however, that such appointments are made on the basis of the Lord Chancellor's and the senior judiciary's perception of the suitability of prospective candidates for such preferment. It is suspicion of precisely how this elite cabal makes its decisions that lends weight to the charges of those such as Professor Griffith. The repeated, almost strident, denials by Lord Irvine of the existence of any 'secret soundings' does little to undermine those of a suspicious mind. It has to be recognised, however, that the appointment system was investigated by Sir Leonard Peach, whose broadly supportive report was delivered in December 1999. The main proposal suggested by Sir Leonard, the establishment of a Commission for Judicial Appointments, was accepted by the Lord Chancellor in what might be seen as an attempt at legitimising the whole appointments procedure. Nonetheless, it would surely be better if the whole procedure of appointing judges, and not just those in senior positions, were opened up to public scrutiny, as it is in the USA. For example, judges in the Supreme Court have real and obvious power, as has been seen, all too obviously for their comfort, in relation to the 2000 presidential election, but, in order to exercise such power, they must have their positions ratified by the elected representatives of the people. There is no such proposal in relation to judicial appointments in this country, where our judges have real and increasing, but disguised power.

Question 22

Critically examine the law governing the circumstances in which a judge should excuse him or herself from presiding in a case because of a possible partiality.

Answer plan

This question involves a consideration of the circumstances under which judges should decline to sit in a particular case. It is one of the rules of natural justice that a person should not be the judge in an action in which they have a personal interest, and the Latin expression of this rule, *nemo judex in causa sua*, goes back a long way. Answers should be able to provide an explanation of the historical context in which the question is set but the question really demands an examination of the contemporary situation, starting with the various actions relating to the application to extradite the former Chilean dictator Augusto Pinochet and going on to consider the *Locabail* action. A good answer might adopt the following structure:

- an explanation of the *nemo judex* rule citing cases that show how it has been applied in the past;
- an explanation of how the law understands bias as it affects the judiciary considering *R v Gough*;

127

- a fairly detailed explanation of the facts and law in the *Pinochet* case;
- a consideration of the post-*Pinochet* applications and the Court of Appeal's ruling in the *Locabail* case.

Answer

The law in this area was, until recently, quite meagre. Judges related to parties before them, or judges with a pecuniary interest in one side of a case were clearly required to stand down. Beyond that, however, in the areas of social interest, things were much less clear. In 1999, in *Re Pinochet*, the House of Lords set aside one of its earlier decisions on the grounds that one of the Lords who delivered an opinion in the first case had a connection with Amnesty International – a body which had issued an opinion on the case.

The English legal system has a rule that no one may be a judge in their own cause, that is, they cannot judge a case in which they have an interest. This is sometimes known by the phrase *nemo judex in causa sua*. Thus, a judge who is a shareholder in a company appearing before him or her as a litigant must decline to hear the case: *Dimes v Grand Junction Canal* (1852). Even if a judge is unaffected by his or her interest in coming to a decision, it would still be wrong to preside in such a case because it might look as if the judge was improperly swayed, even if, in fact, there was no such sway. Thus, in the famous *dictum* of Lord Hewart, it is of fundamental importance that: 'Justice must not only be done but should manifestly and undoubtedly be seen to be done.' (*R v Sussex JJ ex p McCarthy* (1924), p 259.)

This rule was given another dimension in *Re Pinochet Ugarte*. General Pinochet, a former ruler of Chile, was over in England on a visit when he was arrested for crimes of torture and mass killing allegedly orchestrated by him in Chile during the 1970s. His extradition had been requested by Spain. The legal question for the English courts was whether General Pinochet enjoyed a diplomatic immunity.

His case was eventually rejected by the House of Lords (by a 3:2 majority) in November 1998. Pinochet's lawyers then alleged that the Lords' decision was invalid as one of the majority Law Lords, Lord Hoffmann, could not be seen to be impartial as he had a connection with the organisation Amnesty International which had been granted leave to intervene in the proceedings, and had made representations to the Lords through counsel. Lord Hoffmann, at this time, was an unpaid director of the Amnesty International Charitable Trust. Amnesty International was in favour of General Pinochet being brought to trial. In January 1999, on an appeal brought by Senator Pinochet, another panel of Law Lords set aside the decision of the earlier hearing on the basis that no one should be a judge in his own cause.

Whereas, previously, only pecuniary or proprietary interests had led to automatic disqualification, the House of Lords held that if the absolute impartiality of the judiciary was to be maintained, there had to be a rule which automatically disqualified a judge who was involved, whether personally or as a director of a company, in promoting the same causes in the same organisation as was a party to the suit.

It was important not to overstate what was being decided. It was suggested by counsel in the case, in argument, that a decision which stated that Lord Hoffmann's action was wrong would lead to a position where judges would be unable to sit on cases involving charities in whose work they were interested. That was not correct. The facts of the present case were exceptional. The critical elements were: (i) that Amnesty was a party to the appeal; (ii) that Amnesty was joined as a party in order to argue for a particular result; (iii) that the judge was a director of a charity closely allied to Amnesty and sharing, in that respect, Amnesty's objects. Only in cases where a judge was taking an active role as trustee or director of a charity, which was closely allied to and acting with the party to the litigation, should that judge, normally, be concerned either to recuse himself (that is, refuse to offer himself as a judge), or disclose the position to the parties. However, there might well be other exceptional cases in which the judge would be well advised to disclose a possible interest.

Whatever one's views about the merits, sagacity or neutrality of the current judiciary, there is considerable evidence to support the proposition that, historically, judges have often been biased towards certain causes and social classes. Griffith's book, *Politics of the Judiciary*, for example, is brimming with concrete examples of judges who have shown a noted leaning towards one side of debate in cases involving workers, trade unions, civil liberties, Northern Ireland, police powers, religion and other matters. Lord Hoffmann was wrong because he was a director of an organisation which was represented in the case before him. Nonetheless, it is ironic that, while for centuries judges have been permitted to preside in cases where their highly contentious political views have quite evidently affected their decisions (sexist, racist, anti-union, etc), the first senior judge actually to be acted against successfully for bias is someone whose agenda was nothing more than being against torture and governmental killings. It will be very interesting, now, to see what other 'associations' are declared by presiding judges in the wake of the Lords' decision.

Following a number of other cases in which lawyers sought to challenge a judgment on the grounds that, through a social interest or remote financial connection, the judge was potentially biased, the Court of Appeal has now given authoritative guidance on this area. The extraordinary judgment was delivered by Lord Bingham of Cornhill, Lord Chief Justice, Lord Woolf, Master of the Rolls and Sir Richard Scott, Vice Chancellor (*Locabail (UK) Ltd v Bayfield Properties Ltd and Another* (1999)). In respect of five decisions in which the judge's impartiality was questioned, the Court of Appeal ruled on general principles as follows:

(a) a judge who allowed his judicial decision to be influenced by partiality or prejudice deprived a litigant of the right to a fair trial by an impartial tribunal and violated a most fundamental principle on which the administration of justice rested;

(b) the most effective protection of his right was, in practice, afforded by disqualification and setting aside a decision where real danger of bias was established;

(c) every such case depended on its particular facts, real doubt being resolved in favour of disqualification. It would, however, be as wrong for a judge to accede to a tenuous objection as it would be for him to ignore one of substance;

(d) in determination of their rights and liabilities, civil or criminal, everyone was entitled to a fair hearing by an impartial tribunal. That right, guaranteed by the European Convention for the Protection of Human Rights and Fundamental Freedoms (1953, Cmd 8969), was properly described as fundamental.

The Court of Appeal ruled that all legal arbiters were bound to apply the law, as they understood it, to the facts of individual cases, as they found them, without fear or favour, affection or ill will: that is, without partiality or prejudice. Any judge, that term embracing every judicial decision maker whether judge, lay justice or juror, who allowed any judicial decision to be influenced by partiality or prejudice deprived the litigant of his important right and violated one of the most fundamental principles underlying the administration of justice.

There was one situation where, on proof of the requisite facts, the existence of bias was effectively presumed and, in such cases, it gave rise to automatic disqualification: namely, where the judge was shown to have an interest in the outcome of the case which he was to decide or had decided: see *Dimes v Proprietors of the Grand Junction Canal* (1852); *R v Rand* (1866); and *R v Camborne Justices ex p Pearce* (1955).

In any case where the judge's interest was said to derive from the interest of a spouse, partner, or other family member, the link had to be so close and direct as to render the interest of that other person, for all practical purposes, indistinguishable from an interest of the judge.

The automatic disqualification rule until recently, had widely, if wrongly, been thought to apply only in cases of a judge's pecuniary or proprietary interest in the outcome of the litigation. However, *R v Bow Street Metropolitan Stipendiary Magistrate ex p Pinochet Ugarte (No 2)* (1999) made it plain that the rule extended to a limited class of non-financial interests, such as an interest in the subject matter in issue arising from the judge's promotion of some particular cause.

The law was settled in England and Wales by the House of Lords in *R v Gough* (1993) and, in consequence, the relevant test was whether there was, in relation to any given judge, a real danger or possibility of bias. When applying the real danger test, it would often be appropriate to inquire whether the judge knew of the matter relied on as appearing to undermine his impartiality. If it were shown that he did not, the danger of its having influenced his judgment was eliminated and the appearance of possible bias dispelled. It was for the reviewing court, not the judge concerned, to assess the risk that some illegitimate extraneous consideration might have influenced his decision.

The position of solicitors was somewhat different, for a solicitor who was a partner in a firm of solicitors was legally responsible for the professional acts of his partners and did, as a partner, owe a duty to clients of the firm for whom he, personally, might never had acted and of whose affairs he, personally, might know nothing. While it was vital to safeguard the integrity of court proceedings, it was also important to ensure that the rules were not applied in such a way as to inhibit the, increasingly valuable, contribution which solicitors were making to the discharge of judicial functions. Problems were more likely to arise where a solicitor was sitting in a part time capacity, and in civil rather than criminal proceedings. But, such problems could usually be overcome if, before embarking on the trial of any assigned civil case, the solicitor conducted a careful 'conflict search' within his firm, even though such a search, however careful, was unlikely to be omission-proof.

While it would be dangerous and futile to attempt to define or list factors which might, or might not, give rise to a real danger of bias, since everything would depend on the particular facts, the court could not conceive of circumstances in which an objection could be soundly based on the religion, ethnic or national origin, gender, age, class, means or sexual orientation of the judge. Nor, at any rate ordinarily, could an objection be soundly based on his social or educational or service or employment background or history, nor that of any member of his family; nor previous political associations, membership of social, sporting or charitable bodies; nor Masonic associations; nor previous judicial decisions; nor extra-curricular utterances, whether in textbooks, lectures, speeches, articles, interviews, reports, responses to consultation papers; nor previous receipt of instructions to act for, or against, any party, solicitor or advocate engaged in a case before him; nor membership of the same Inn, circuit, local Law Society or chambers.

By contrast, a real danger of bias might well be thought to arise if there were personal friendship or animosity between the judge and any member of the public involved in the case; or if the judge were closely acquainted with any such member of the public, particularly, if that individual's credibility could be significant in the decision of the case; or if, in a case where the credibility of any individual were an issue to be decided by the judge, he had, in a previous case, rejected that person's evidence in such outspoken terms as to throw doubt on his ability to approach such a person's evidence with an open mind on any later occasion.

In one way, the Court of Appeal was bound to come to this conclusion. Had it ruled that membership of certain societies, or a particular social background, or the previous political associations of a trial judge *were* grounds for appeal, two consequences would follow. First there would be a rapid expansion of the use by law firms of special units that monitor and keep files on all aspects of judges' lives. Second, there would be a proliferation of appeals in all departments of the court structure at the very time when there is such a concerted effort to reduce the backlog of appeals. What this decision leaves us with is a question of profound jurisprudential importance: how far can judges judge in an entirely neutral and socially detached manner? Under the new Court of Appeal guidelines, a judge who was a keen hunter and member of the pro-hunting Countryside Alliance would not be required to stand down from presiding in a case involving anti-hunt protesters. It is difficult, however, to see a practicable alternative way to operate a judiciary.

Question 23

According to Lord Denning:

> Our philosophy is that the jury should be selected at random from a panel of persons who are nominated at random. We believe that 12 persons selected at random are likely to be a cross-section of the people and, thus, represent the views of the common man [R v Crown Court at Sheffield ex p Brownlow (1980)].

What assumptions underlie this statement and to what degree are they accurate or, indeed, justifiable?

Answer plan

This particular question on the jury asks for attention to be focused on the composition of the jury, rather than the jury system generally, and seeks to elicit information about how the composition is determined and how it can be interfered with. The following procedure would address those issues:

- detail the process whereby a jury is actually selected, distinguishing between 'panels of jurors' and juries;
- consider how random this process is, in practice;
- is randomness always fair? Consider the need for racially mixed juries;
- consider rights of the defence and prosecution to challenge potential jurors;
- explain the process of jury vetting and consider its general legitimacy;
- offer a conclusion as to whether randomness is, fundamentally, necessary or, indeed, valuable *per se*.

Answer

The procedure of deciding cases on the basis of the deliberations of a jury is an ancient one and one that has attracted much praise within the British legal system. The implicit assumption underlying this quotation is that the presence of 12 ordinary lay persons, randomly introduced into the trial procedure to be the arbiters of the facts of the case, strengthens the legitimacy of the legal system. It, supposedly, achieves this end by introducing a democratic humanising element into the abstract impersonal trial process, thereby reducing the exclusive power of the legal professionals who would otherwise command the legal stage and control the legal procedure without reference to the opinion of the lay majority. A corresponding assumption is that jury service is a public duty that citizens should readily undertake, although it is made compulsory and failure to perform one's civic responsibility is subject to the sanction of a £1,000 fine. According to the Lord

Chancellor's Department, around 250,000 people serve as jurors in any one year.

The procedure for determining the actual composition of a the jury to hear any particular case is as follows. An officer of the court summonses a randomly selected number of qualified individuals and, from that group, draws up panels of potential jurors for various cases. The actual jurors are then randomly selected, by means of a ballot in open court.

The Juries Act 1974, as amended by the Criminal Justice Act 1988 and the Criminal Justice and Public Order Act (CJPOA) 1994, sets out the law relating to juries. It provides that any person between the ages of 18 and 70, who is on the electoral register and who has lived in the UK for at least five years, is qualified to serve as juror. The dependency on electoral roles to determine and locate jurors, however, raises a very real shortfall from the ideal assumptions made in relation to the jury system. The problem arises from the fact that electoral registers tend to be inaccurate. Generally, they have misreported the number of young people who are in an area, due to the fact that such people tend to have a greater degree of mobility than older people and, as a result, tend not to appear on the electoral role of the place they currently live in. Electoral registers have also underreported the true number of members of ethnic minorities who have simply declined to notify the authorities of their existence. The difficulty arising from the inaccuracy of electoral roles has been compounded by the disappearance of a great many people from electoral registers in order to try to avoid payment of the former Poll Tax. It is a matter of some doubt whether such people have registered, even with the passing of that particular tax. The Runciman Commission on Criminal Justice (Cm 2263, 1993) recognised the above problems and urged electoral registration officers to ensure that registers included all those who were liable for jury service: whether this will be achieved is, at least, a moot point.

In any case, the general qualification for serving as a juror is subject to a number of exceptions. For example, a number of people, such as members of the clergy or the legal profession or, as a consequence of s 168(2) of the CJPOA 1994, custody officers, are deemed to be ineligible on the basis of their employment; and others, such as those who have served particularly lengthy or recent prison sentences, are disqualified in order to maintain the unquestioned probity of the procedure. Following the recommendation of the Runciman Commission, s 40 of the CJPOA 1994 introduced a provision that a person on bail in criminal proceedings cannot serve as a juror in the Crown Court, although it follows that such individuals are not disqualified from serving as jurors in civil proceedings. It should also be noted that any disqualification automatically comes to an end at the end of the bail period.

Others, such as members of the medical professions, MPs and members of the armed forces, may be excused jury service as matter of right on the basis of their employment. Practising members of religious sects which object to jury service may also be excluded from service as a result of s 42 of the CJPOA 1994. There is, additionally, a discretionary power given to the court to release a person from jury service or, alternatively, to defer their service to some time in the future, if they show grounds for such treatment. Grounds for such excusal or deferral are usually made on the basis of special hardship, but, as Professor Zander points out:

> The operation of the discretion exercised by summoning officers and judges varies widely ... It is common in ... immensely long cases for the judge to ask jurors whether they can manage such a case and to excuse any who say they cannot. The jury is in a sense, therefore, self-selected [*Cases and Materials on the English Legal System*, 7th edn, 1996].

The fact that juries can, even to this limited extent, be 'self-selecting' provides grounds for concern as to the random nature of the jury, but the traditional view of the jury is further undermined when the extent to which others, both prosecution and defence, seek to influence its constitution.

The traditional procedure for determining the actual composition of the jury to hear any particular case is as follows. An officer of the court summonses a randomly selected number of qualified individuals and, from that group, draws up panels of potential jurors for various cases. The actual jurors are then randomly selected by means of a ballot in open court. This, somewhat antiquated, procedure, with its accompanying disparity of treatment, is in the process of being modernised by the introduction of a central summoning bureau based at Blackfriars Crown Court Centre in London. Progressively, from

October 2000, the new bureau will use a computer system to select jurors at random from the electoral registers and issue the summonses, as well as dealing with jurors' questions and requests. It is intended to link the jury summoning system to the national police records system to allow checks to be made against potentially disqualified individuals.

The aim of the new procedure is to ensure that all jurors are treated equally and fairly and that the rules are enforced consistently, especially in regard to requests to be excused from service and, thus, to reduce at least some of the potential difficulties mentioned above. Under s 12(6) of the Juries Act 1974, both prosecution and defence have a right to challenge the array, where the summoning officer has acted improperly in bringing the whole panel together. Such challenges are rare, although an unsuccessful action was raised in the *Danvers* case (1982).

As regards individuals, the defence until fairly recently had the right to issue peremptory challenges, that is, challenges without reason, to potential jury members, up to a maximum of three. In spite of arguments for its retention on a civil liberties basis, the right was abolished in the Criminal Justice Act 1988. The defence, however, still has the power to challenge any number of potential jurors for cause, that is, with reason; although following the attempt of the defence to exclude numerous classes of people from the jury in the *Angry Brigade* trial in 1972, the Lord Chief Justice issued a Practice Direction in which it was laid down that potential jurors were not to be excluded on account of race, religion, politics or occupation.

In *Danvers*, the defence had sought to challenge the array on the basis that a black defendant could not have complete confidence in the impartiality of an all white jury. And, the question of the racial mix of a jury has exercised the courts on a number of occasions. In *Ford* (1989), the trial judge's refusal to accept the defendant's application for a racially mixed jury was supported by the Court of Appeal on the grounds that 'fairness is achieved by the principle of random selection', as regards the make-up of a jury, and that, to insist on a racially balanced jury, would be contrary to that principle and would be to imply that particular jurors were incapable of impartiality.

It has been argued that the desire of civil libertarians to retain the right of the defence to select a jury that might be more sympathetic to its case is contradictory, because although, in theory, they usually rely on the random nature of the jury to ensure the appearance of justice, in practice, they seek to influence its composition. When, however, the shortcomings in the establishment of panels for juries is recalled, it might be countered that the defence is attempting to do no more than counter the in-built bias that ensues from the use of unbalanced electoral registers. To deny people of colour the right to have their cases heard by representatives of their own race on the basis of a refusal to recognise the existence of racially discriminatory attitudes, cannot but give the appearance of a society where such racist attitudes are institutionalised. Without suggesting that juries, as presently constituted, are biased, it remains arguable that if, in order to achieve the undoubted appearance of fairness, jury selection has to be manipulated to ensure a racial mix, then it should at least be considered. This was, apparently, the view of the Runciman Commission, which suggested that, in exceptional circumstances, it should be possible for either the prosecution or the defence to apply to the judge before the commencement of a trial to ensure that the jury should contain up to three people from ethnic minority communities, with at least one from the same ethnic minority as the defendant or victim.

Of, perhaps, even more concern than challenges by the defence, is the extent to which the prosecution can challenge potential jurors. For, in addition to the right to challenge for cause, the prosecution also has the option of excluding particular individuals, simply by asking them to 'stand by' until a jury has been empanelled. The manifest unreasonableness of this procedure, in view of the limited power of the defence, led to the Attorney General issuing a *Practice Note* ([1988] 3 All ER 1086) to the effect that the Crown should only exercise its power to stand down potential jurors in the following two circumstances:

(a) to prevent the empanelment of a 'manifestly unsuitable' juror;

(b) where the Attorney General has approved the vetting of the potential jury members and that process has revealed that a particular juror might be a security risk and the Attorney General has approved the use of the 'stand by' procedure.

This latter point leads, naturally, to another contentious subject, that of jury 'vetting'; the process in which the Crown checks the background of potential jurors. The practice of vetting potential jurors developed after the *Angry Brigade* (1972), but did not become public until the Official Secrets Act case, known as the *ABC Trial*, in 1978. Subsequently, the Attorney General published the guidelines for vetting panels. The most recent guidelines were published in 1988 and, interestingly, they support the general propositions that jury members should normally be selected randomly from the panel and should be disqualified only on the grounds set out in the Juries Act 1974. The guidelines do, however, make reference to exceptional cases of public importance where potential jury members might properly be vetted. Such cases are broadly identified as those involving national security, where part of the evidence may be heard in camera, and terrorist cases. Vetting is a twofold process. An initial check in police criminal records and police Special Branch records should be sufficient to reveal whether a further investigation by the security services in required. This further investigation cannot take place without the prior approval of the Attorney General. The purpose of the vetting is to ensure that jury members will not be likely to divulge any secrets made open to them in the course of a trial, or to ensure that jurors with extreme political views do not get the opportunity to permit those views to influence the outcome of a case.

In conclusion, therefore, it can be seen that juries are, by and large random, subject to some particular and important shortcomings. However, as has been suggested above, randomness is not necessarily a virtue in itself, especially if it leads to ethnically unrepresentative juries.

Question 24

To what extent is the jury system under attack and is such an attack justifiable?

Answer plan

This question differs from the previous one in that it looks for attention to be focused, not on the composition of the jury, but on the use of the jury. There is an implicit suggestion in the question that the use of the jury is in decline. A candidate must offer an evaluation of this process. A suggested plan for dealing with the topic is:

- consider the use of juries in civil procedures and the effect to which the use of juries has declined;
- carry out a similar procedure in relation to criminal law paying particular attention to the various Criminal Justice (Mode of Trial) Bills;
- in both of the above cases, where possible, reference should be made to Judicial Statistics to substantiate any claims made;
- reference should be made to the Roskill Committee (*Report on Fraud Trials*, 1986);
- mention should be made of the juryless 'Diplock courts' in Northern Ireland;
- the ideological power of the jury trial should not be ignored.

Answer

There can be no doubt as to the antiquity of the institution of trial by jury, nor can there be much doubt as to its supposed democratising effect on the operation of the legal system. Neither, unfortunately, can there be any grounds for denying the diminishment that has occurred in the fairly recent past in the role of the jury as the means of determining the outcome of trials, nor can the continued existence of the jury, as it is presently constituted, be taken for granted.

In respect of civil law, the use of juries has diminished considerably and automatic recourse to trial by jury is restricted to a small number of areas and, even in those areas, the continued use of the jury is threatened. Prior to 1854, all cases that came before the common law courts were decided by a judge and jury. The Common Law Procedure Act of the same year provided that cases could be settled without a jury where the parties agreed and, since then, the role of the jury has been gradually curtailed until, at present, under s 69 of the Supreme Court Act 1981, the right to a jury trial is limited to only four specific areas; fraud, defamation, malicious prosecution and false imprisonment. (Similar provisions are contained in the County Courts Act 1984.) Even in those four areas, however, the right is not absolute and can be denied by a judge under s 69(1), where the case involves 'any prolonged examination of documents or accounts or any scientific or local investigation which cannot be conveniently be made with a jury'.

In *Beta Construction Ltd v Channel Four TV Co Ltd* (1990), the Court of Appeal held that, whether or not a libel action could be decided without a jury under s 69(1) depended upon a number of considerations, such as whether the involvement of a jury would lengthen the trial, make it more expensive, lead to practical problems in regard to the hearing of the case, or whether the documents or accounts would prove too complicated for a jury to understand.

The question of whether or not juries should be used in libel cases has gained wider consideration in the case involving McDonalds, the fast food empire, and two environmentalists, Dave Morris and Helen Steel (*McDonalds v Steel and Morris* (1997)). McDonalds claimed that their reputation was damaged by an allegedly libellous leaflet issued by members of an organisation called London Greenpeace, including Morris and Steel, which linked McDonalds' products to heart disease and cancer, as well as the despoliation of the environment and the exploitation of the Third World. In a preliminary hearing, later confirmed by the Court of Appeal, it was decided that the evidence to be presented would be of such scientific complexity that it would be beyond the understanding of a jury.

In all other civil cases, there is a presumption against trial by jury although, under s 69(3) of the Supreme Court Act 1981, the judge has the discretion to order a trial by jury. How judges should exercise a similar discretion under previous legislation was considered by the Court of Appeal, in *Ward v James* (1966), and the conclusion reached was that, in civil cases, a jury should only be used in 'exceptional circumstances', although no exhaustive list as to what amounted to exceptional circumstances was provided. One of the major reasons given for excluding juries was the uncertainty and unpredictability of the level of damages awarded by juries in personal injury cases.

Even the right to jury trial in defamation cases has not gone without direct attack and the Faulks Committee on the Law of Defamation (Cmnd 5909, 1975) recommended that the availability of jury trial should be subject to the same judicial discretion as all other civil cases. It is of interest to note that the Faulks Report shared the Court of Appeal's view in *Ward v James* as to the unsuitability of juries in determining damages and prefigured the attacks that have been made on juries in view of recent notorious defamation cases, such as *Sutcliffe v Pressdram Ltd*, in which the wife of a convicted serial killer was awarded damages of £600,000 (reduced, on appeal, to £60,000) and *Aldington v Watts and Tolstoy* in which damages of £1.5 m were awarded.

Section 8 of the CLSA 1990 gave the Court of Appeal the power to alter damages awarded by juries to a level they considered to be 'proper', but the most recent example of interference in jury decisions in defamation cases arose in January 2001 in the case involving the ex-footballer Bruce Grobbelaar. Although Grobbelaar had been accused of accepting payments for fixing football games, he had been found not guilty in a criminal charge and had won damages in a civil action against the Sun newspaper, which originally had accused him of the match fixing. On appeal, however, the Court of Appeal took the extraordinary step of overturning the decision of the jury, citing its decision as perverse and 'a miscarriage of justice'. The Defamation Act 1996 also increased the courts' powers to hear defamation cases without a jury. In situations where the judge decides that, either there is no realistic prospect of success, or, alternatively, that there is no realistic defence to the claim, the judge may award summary relief.

In relation to criminal law, the use of the jury has also been subject to significant attack. Before considering this, however, it is necessary consider the precise role of the jury in this area. It has to be borne in mind that the criminal jury trial is essentially restricted to the Crown Court. The magistrates' courts know no juries, but deal with 97% of criminal cases and, in practice, juries determine the outcome of less that 1% of the total of criminal cases. The reason for this being that, of the all the cases decided in the Crown Court, 72% of defendants plead guilty on all counts and, therefore, have no need for jury trial and a further 2% plead guilty to some counts.

It can be seen, therefore, that, in absolute and proportional terms, the jury does not play a significant part in the determination of criminal cases. The statistics furnish another fact that tends to undermine the case for the jury as the protector of the individual's liberties. Criminal offences can be divided into three categories;

(a) summary offences, dealt with in the magistrates' courts without a jury;

(b) indictable offences, heard in the Crown Court before a jury; and

(c) offences 'triable either way'.

In this latter category, the defendant can opt for either trial in the magistrates' court or the Crown Court, unless the magistrates insist that the case goes to the Crown Court. The significant point, in relation to the role of the jury, is that, in cases involving allegations of offences 'triable either way', the great majority of those accused, amounting to about 80%, actually give up the right to jury trial and opt to have their cases dealt with in the magistrates' court. Nonetheless, proposals have been made to remove the right of defendants to elect for jury trial in relation to 'either way' offences.

Just such a proposal was recommended by the Runciman Commission on Criminal Justice in 1993 (Cm 2263) and in July 1998 a Home Office Consultation Paper canvassed the issue of reducing the role of juries in minor criminal cases. Following the consultation paper, the Labour Home Secretary, Jack Straw, introduced a Criminal Justice (Mode of Trial) Bill in 1999, which proposed giving magistrates the power to decide whether particular cases should be decided before juries. That Bill was generally criticised as an illiberal measure by civil liberties organisations and the legal professions, but was particularly attacked for the manner in which it sought to protect the rights of individuals with reputations to protect. Such solicitude for those with reputations to protect, apparently as opposed to the common majority of people, was seen as inherently unjust and dangerously class based. The Bill was defeated in the House of Lords. However, undeterred by this defeat the Home Secretary introduced the Criminal Justice (Mode of Trial) (No 2) Bill in

February 2000. As a measure of appeasement, the reference to individuals' reputations was removed and magistrates were directed to decide the location for trials on the basis of the circumstances of the offence rather than the circumstances of the accused. Even that measure of conciliation was not sufficient to protect the Bill from, once again, being defeated by the House of Lords. The Government reaffirmed its commitment to the Bill by including it in its proposals for legislation in 2001 and indicating its willingness to use the Parliament Acts to force the Bill through, against any continued opposition from the House of Lords.

If trial by jury is (generally) statistically insignificant, it cannot be denied that it is still of major significance in the determination of the most serious cases. Even this role has not gone without scrutiny, however, and the Roskill Committee on Fraud Trials (1986) critically examined its role in complex criminal fraud cases and, in its report, recommended the abolition of trial by jury in such cases. It is interesting to note, once again, the same alleged weaknesses in jurors that were mentioned in the Faulks Committee Report and the *Beta Construction* case, namely, the difficulties that jurors had in understanding complex cases: 'The most complex of fraud cases will exceed the limits of comprehension of members of a jury.' (Roskill Committee, *Report on Fraud Trials*, 1986, para 8.34.)

The Roskill Committee did not go so far as to recommend that all fraud cases should be taken away from juries, only the most complex, of which it was estimated that there were about two dozen, or so, every year. It was suggested that these cases would be better decided by a judge assisted by two lay persons drawn from a panel with specialist expertise in the arcane world of complex business transactions. The Government declined to implement the recommendations of the Roskill Committee and, instead, introduced procedures designed to make it easier to follow the proceedings in complex fraud cases.

It might be claimed that the hugely complex cases concerning the various participants in the Guinness affair relating to the takeover of Distillers plc and those involved in the *Blue Arrow* share issue case have given retrospective validation to the Roskill findings. The blame for those fiascos, however, lies not so much with the juries in each of the cases, but with the procedural shortcomings of the Serious Fraud Office.

It has been, repeatedly, suggested by those in favour of abolishing (or at least severely curtailing) the role of the jury that the general public views the operation of the system of trial by jury in an over-romanticised and unrealistic way. Thus, the Roskill Committee expressed the view that: 'Society appears to have an attachment to jury trial which is emotional or sentimental, rather than logical.' (*Report on Fraud Trials*, 1986, para 8.21.)

A similar point had been made, previously, by the Faulks Committee, but that report also recognised the source of the public's opinion and was careful not to dismiss it as unimportant:

> ... much of the support for jury trials is emotional and derives from the undoubted value of juries in serious criminal cases where they stand between the prosecuting authority and the citizen [Faulks Committee, *Report on Defamation*, 1975, para 496].

One should not underestimate the ideological power of the existence of the jury system, which represents not only the ordinary person's input into the legal system, but also provides the whole legal system with an sense of legitimacy. In this regard, mention can be made of the cases where juries have introduced what some have called 'jurors' equity' and others termed 'perversity', into the, otherwise, abstract formal rationality of the legal process. Examples of this include repeated cases where juries have refused to bring in guilty verdicts against invalids using cannabis for medicinal purposes. And, in the political arena, juries have declined to convict peace campaigners for damaging military aircraft and environmentalists for damaging genetically modified crops. It is, at least, arguable that these apparently irrational and perverse decisions go a long way to maintain the general legitimacy of the legal system by introducing a sympathetic element. It is not unlikely that it was concern as to the possibility of the exercise of jurors' equity that led McDonalds to oppose the empanelling of a jury to decide the libel case against Morris and Steel.

Nor should the effect of the removal of the right to jury trial in Northern Ireland since 1973 be ignored. In response to the problem of the intimidation of jury members, the *Report of the*

145

Commission to Consider Legal Procedures to Deal with Terrorist Activities in Northern Ireland (1972) recommended that the best way to deal with the problem was to do away with juries in particular cases. Lord Diplock headed the Commission and to him went the honour of giving his name to the new juryless courts. The so called Diplock courts operate in relation to certain 'scheduled offences' particularly, but by no means exclusively, associated with terrorism. It would be an understatement of the grossest kind to state that the Diplock courts have been the subject of controversy in the Northern Irish community; for, it is argued by some civil libertarians that, to the extent that they appear as no more than the unrestricted mechanism of the State, they bring the whole of the legal system into disrepute. It remains to be seen whether, as part of the normalisation of the situation in Northern Ireland, the Diplock courts will be replaced by jury trials.

CHAPTER 5

THE CRIMINAL PROCESS

Introduction

In 2000, the Lord Chancellor appointed Lord Justice Auld, a senior judge of the Court of Appeal, to report on the working of the criminal courts. The report is expected in 2001. His terms of reference are:

> A review into the practices and procedures of, and the rules of evidence applied by, the criminal courts at every level, with a view to ensuring that they deliver justice fairly, by streamlining all their processes, increasing their efficiency and strengthening the effectiveness of their relationships with others across the whole of the criminal justice system, and having regard to the interests of all parties including victims and witnesses, thereby promoting public confidence in the rule of law.

This latest move to systematise the operation of criminal justice can be seen within a particular setting. This has been, for many years, an accepted descriptive term used by social scientists, journalists and, occasionally, lawyers. Officially, however, there is no such thing as the 'criminal justice system'. Governmental responsibilities, for example, overlap in this area. The Home Secretary is responsible for the Metropolitan Police, criminal statistics, the probation service and the Crown Prosecution Service (CPS) (and, more broadly, for 'law and order'), while the Lord Chancellor is responsible for all the criminal law courts, the appointment of magistrates and the judges. Nonetheless, in recent times, there has been increasing governmental recognition of something called the 'criminal justice system'. On 30 December 1998, for example, a single official statement entitled 'Joint Press Release on the Criminal Justice System Public Service Agreement' was issued on behalf of the Home Office, the Lord Chancellor's Department and the Attorney General's Office. It stated:

> The overarching aims, objectives and performance measures for the criminal justice system have been published for the first time in a cross-departmental Public Service Agreement. The three

> Departments, and their respective services, will be working more closely than ever before to ensure that *the criminal justice system* protects the public and delivers justice. Inter-agency co-operation will be promoted at regional, local, as well as at the national level. Ministers believe that these arrangements are a good example of 'joined-up government' in practice [emphasis added] [www. nds.coi.gov.uk/coi/coipress.ns].

The significance of such a pronouncement is that it reveals an attempt to make co-ordinated policy in respect of each of these branches of operation. In fact, the statement goes on to become quite explicit. It said that the three ministers had set two overarching aims to provide a strategic direction for the system as a whole. They had made clear that every part of the criminal justice system (including the police, courts, CPS, prison and probation services) should work together so as to best serve and protect the public.

The two overarching aims are:

- to reduce crime and the fear of crime and their social and economic costs; and
- to dispense justice fairly and efficiently and to promote confidence in the rule of law.

It will be a major achievement if the government can, by reforms, establish a long term reversal in the high annual crime figures and re-invigorate public confidence in the criminal justice system. According to the latest *Recorded Crime Statistics for England and Wales* (Government Statistical Service, Issue 1/00, 18 January, 2000), there were 5.2 m notifiable offences (that is, the more serious offences) recorded by police in the period October 1998–September 1999. This shows a 2.2% increase on the figure for the previous 12 months. The majority of crimes were property offences (84% of all recorded crime).

Checklist

In particular, you should be familiar with the following recommendations and changes in the law:

Appeals

The recommendation of an independent authority, the Criminal Cases Review Authority, to investigate alleged miscarriages of justice, and its creation by the Criminal Appeal Act 1995; recommended new powers for the Court of Appeal; the recommendation of a single new broad ground of appeal should be instituted to enhance flexibility of the process; the Court of Appeal decision in *Secretary of State for the Home Department ex p Hickey and Others* (1995).

Trial by jury

Recommendation of abolition of the defendant's right to elect for jury trial in cases triable 'either way' and the Mode of Trial (No 2) Bill 2001.

Right to silence

Sections 34–37 of the Criminal Justice and Public Order Act (CJPOA) 1994 which explain what inferences may now be drawn in what circumstances from the silence of the accused.

Confessions

Sections 32–33 of the CJPOA 1994 which abolish the rules requiring the court to give the jury a warning about convicting the accused on uncorroborated evidence of a person who is an accomplice or, in sexual cases, the victim.

Standards

Runciman recommended that judges should be urged to penalise poor defence lawyers and call additional witnesses if necessary; independent supervision of police rejected.

Plea bargaining

Limited introduction was recommended by Runciman – reduced sentences for guilty pleas.

Juries

Judge should be able to order that a jury include up to three ethnic minority members, Contempt of Court Act 1981 should be amended to allow for research into juries' reasons for decisions. The CJPOA 1994 changes the rules relating to disqualifications, persons excusable as of right, physical disability and jury service, and separation of the jury.

In general, you will need to know the major provisions of the Police and Criminal Evidence Act (PACE) 1984 and other provisions relating to criminal procedure:

- the general powers of arrest – s 24 of PACE 1984;
- the general arrest conditions – s 25 of PACE 1984;
- the common law powers of arrest;
- procedure on arrest;
- information on arrest;
- stop and search – ss 1 and 2 (and revised Code A) of PACE 1984;
- search of arrested person – s 32 of PACE 1984;
- search on detention – s 54 of the PACE 1984;
- search of premises – ss 17, 18, 32 of PACE 1984;
- search warrants – ss 8, 15, 16 of PACE 1984;
- interrogation, confession and admissibility of evidence – PACE 1984;
- bail – the CJPOA 1994 changes;
- plea bargaining.

Question 25

How far is it correct to say that the right to silence has been abolished in the English legal system? Discuss the arguments for and against the changes that have been made to this area of law by the CJPOA 1994.

Answer plan

A good response to this type of question will incorporate the following:

- an explanation of the 'right to silence';
- a brief explanation that the right has not been 'abolished';
- consideration of pre-Act law in relation to silence when questioned by police, and silence in court;
- examination of the background to the 1994 reform;
- discussion of the consequences of ss 34–37 of the Act;
- some description of the alleged advantages of the changes;
- some description of the alleged disadvantages of the changes;
- conclusions.

Answer

Several meanings have been credited to the phrase 'the right to silence'. Six such meanings were identified by Lord Mustill in *Director of Serious Fraud Office ex p Smith* (1993). These ranged from the right to refuse to co-operate with a police inquiry, to the principle against self-incrimination. The changes made by the CJPOA 1994 are concerned with the legal effect of a suspect or accused failing to respond to questions by police officers, or failing to give evidence in his defence in court.

Notwithstanding the new Act, any person may refuse to answer questions put to him or her out of court. There are only a few exceptions to this (as with s 2 of the Criminal Justice Act 1987, which concerns the investigation of serious fraud and requires certain questions to be answered under pain of punishment for refusal) and they existed before the new Act. The CJPOA 1994 does not alter the position of the accused person as a witness – he remains a competent but not compellable witness in his own defence (s 35) – although now the prosecution, as well as the judge, may comment upon such a failure to give evidence (s 168). Thus, the Act does not really 'abolish the right to silence'; a person can quite legally remain silent when questioned, although adverse comment may be made about such silence in some circumstances.

Except in so far as the new law makes changes, the old law still applies and we need briefly to consider this first in order properly to explain how far the CJPOA changes the legal framework.

Answering police questions and the right to silence

The police are free to ask anyone any questions. The only restriction is that all questioning is supposed to cease once a suspect has been charged.

There is no obligation on a citizen to answer police questions. A person cannot be charged, for example, with obstructing the police in the execution of their duty simply by failing to answer questions, nor, before the CJPOA 1994 could the judge or prosecutor suggest to the jury that such silence was evidence of guilt. This was confirmed in *Rice v Connolly* (1966), where Lord Parker CJ said:

> It seems to me quite clear that, though every citizen has a moral duty or, if you like, a social duty to assist the police, there is no legal duty to that effect, and, indeed, the whole basis of the common law is the right of the individual to refuse to answer questions put to him by persons in authority, and to refuse to accompany those in authority to any particular place; short, of course, of arrest.

There was an established common law rule that neither the prosecution nor the judge could make adverse comment on the defendant's silence in the face of questions from police officers at the time of arrest. The dividing line, however, between proper and improper judicial comment was a matter of great debate. There are many reasons why a suspect might remain silent when questioned (for example, fear, confusion, reluctance to incriminate another person) and the 'right of silence' has been a long established general principle in English law. Thus, in *Davis* (1959), a judge was ruled on appeal to have misdirected the jury when he told them that:

> ... a man is not obliged to say anything, but you are entitled to use your common sense ... can you imagine an innocent man who had behaved like that not saying anything to the police? ... He said nothing.

Silence in court

Before the Act, the law relating to a defendant who did not give evidence in court was neatly summed up by the Lord Chief Justice, Lord Taylor, in *Martinez-Tobon* (1993). Where a defendant did not testify at his trial, the trial judge should have given the jury a direction that the defendant was under no obligation to testify and the jury should not assume that he is guilty because he had not given evidence. The judge could, however, comment on the defendant's failure to give evidence, where the defence case involved alleged facts which were at variance with prosecution evidence, provided that the judge did not equate silence with guilt. In this case, involving charges of importing cocaine, the judge, commenting on the defence argument, had said that, if the appellant 'thought it was emeralds and not drugs, one might have thought he would be very anxious to say so' (defence *counsel* had made this suggestion but this cannot be evidence). The judge's observations were held by the Court of Appeal to be quite proper, as he had also given a standard direction to the jury explaining that silence does not necessarily imply guilt.

Reform

The right to silence was considered by the Runciman Royal Commission on Criminal Justice. It had to decide whether to adopt a practice like the Northern Ireland system and the similar one recommended by the Home Office in 1989, or whether to retain the right to silence as the Philips Royal Commission on Criminal Procedure had recommended in 1981 (Cm 8092). In evidence to the Runciman Royal Commission, the proposal to retain the right to silence was supported by the Law Society, the Bar Council and the Magistrates' Association. It was opposed by the police, the CPS, HM Council of circuit judges and senior judges.

In a study commissioned by the Lord Chancellor's Department, only 2% of 527 suspects exercised their right to silence. The Runciman Royal Commission eventually decided to recommend retaining the right to silence. Its report (1993) states:

> The majority of us believe that adverse inferences should not be drawn from silence at the police station and recommend retaining the present caution and trial direction [para 82].

The Commission did, however (para 84), recommend the retention of the current law regarding silence in investigations of serious and complex fraud under which adverse consequences can follow from silence. The report notes that a large proportion of those who use the right to silence later plead guilty. The majority of the Commission felt that the possibility of an increase in convicting the guilty by abolishing the right would be outweighed by the considerable extra pressure on innocent suspects in police stations. The Commission did, however, meet the police and CPS concern about 'ambush defences' where a defence is entered late in at a trial, thus, leaving the prosecution no time to check and rebut the defence. The Commission recommends that, if the defence introduces a late change or departs from the strategy it has disclosed in advance to the prosecution, then it should face adverse comment (para 136). Professor Zander, however, issued a note of dissent that the principle must remain that the burden of proof always lies with the prosecution. He stated that:

> The fundamental issue at stake is that the burden of proof throughout lies with the prosecution. Defence disclosure is designed to be helpful to the prosecution and, more generally, to the system. But, it is not the job of the defendant to be helpful either to the prosecution or the system.

The Government ignored the recommendation of the Royal Commission. The general purpose of the Act was to assist in the fight against crime. The Government took the view that the balance in the criminal justice system had become tilted too much in favour of the criminal and against the public, in general, and victims, in particular. The alleged advantage of the change in law is that it helps convict criminals who, under the old law, used to be acquitted because they took advantage of the right to keep quiet when questioned without the court or prosecution being able to comment adversely upon that silence. Introducing the legislation, the Home Secretary said that the change in the law was desirable because 'it is professional criminals, hardened criminals and terrorists who disproportionately take advantage of and abuse the present system'.

The new law is contained in ss 34–37 of the Act. Section 34 states that, where anyone is questioned under caution by a police officer, or charged with an offence, then a failure to mention a fact at that time which he later relies on in his defence will allow a court to draw such inferences as appear proper about that failure. Inferences may only be drawn if, in the circumstances, a suspect could reasonably have been expected to mention the fact when he was questioned. The inferences which can be drawn can be used in determining whether the accused is guilty as charged. The section, however, permits adverse inferences to be drawn from silence in situations that do not amount to 'interviews', as defined by Code C of PACE 1984 and, thus, which are not subject to the safeguards of access to legal advice and of contemporaneous recording which exist where a suspect is interviewed at the police station. The amended caution to be administered by police officers reads as follows (with appropriate variants for ss 36 and 37):

> You do not have to say anything. But it may harm your defence if you do not mention when questioned something which you later rely on in court.

As Card and Ward have warned, a temptation may arise for police officers to give this caution at the earliest possible stage in any situation in which they are talking to someone in connection with a crime, given that the caution may be understood (incorrectly) by some suspects as creating an obligation to speak:

> The Act does not affect earlier law on alibi defences. Under s 11 of the Criminal Justice Act 1967, the defence at trial on indictment cannot adduce evidence in support of an alibi defence (that is, where the accused claims to have been away from the crime at the time of its occurrence) unless notice of the details of that defence have been served on the prosecution within seven days of the transfer for trial. Nevertheless, this rule does not prevent an adverse inference being drawn by a court from a failure to have disclosed that alibi at an earlier stage (when, for instance, the accused was arrested) [*The Criminal Justice and Public Order Act 1994*, 1994].

Section 35 allows a court or jury to infer what appears proper from the refusal of an accused person, aged 14 or over, to testify in his own defence, or from a refusal without good cause to answer any question at trial. Section 36 permits inferences to be drawn from the failure or refusal of a person under arrest to account for any object, substances or mark in his possession, on his person, in or on his clothing or footwear, or in any place at which he is at the time of arrest. Section 37 permits inferences to be drawn from the failure of an arrested person to account for his presence at a particular place where he is found.

Thus, as Lord Taylor, the late Lord Chief Justice has observed, the legal changes do not, strictly speaking, abolish the right to silence:

> If a defendant maintains his silence from first till last, and does not rely on any particular fact by way of defence, but simply puts the prosecution to proof, then [ss 34–37] would not bite at all.

This is, of course, correct, but it ignores the change in the general structure of proofs. Article 6 of the European Convention on Human Rights aims to protect the rights of a suspect to a fair trial. It states that:

> Everyone charged with a criminal offence shall be presumed innocent until proved guilty in accordance with law.

The European Commission on Human Rights has already ruled as admissible a complaint that provisions in the law of Northern Ireland equivalent to those in ss 34–37 infringe Art 6 and the point can now be taken as applicable in the UK, since the Human Rights Act 1998 came into force in October 2000.

Since the abolition of the court of Star Chamber in 1641, no English court has had the power to use torture or force to exact confessions from suspects. The so called 'right to silence' really meant that a suspect could remain silent when questioned by police or in court without prosecution counsel or the judge being allowed to make adverse comment to the jury about such a silence. Traditionally, silence could not be used in court as evidence of guilt.

In support of the old rule, it could be said, that:

(a) people are innocent until proven guilty of a crime by the State; and

(b) people should never be under force to condemn themselves; and

(c) there are several reasons other than genuine guilt why someone may wish to remain silent in the face of serious accusations – he might be terrified, confused, retarded, wish to protect someone else or fear that the truth would get them in some other type of trouble. The 11th Report of the Criminal Law Revision Committee (1972) gives several examples. The accused might be so shocked at an accusation that he forgets a vital fact which would acquit him of blame; his excuse might be embarrassing like being in the company of a prostitute; or he may fear reprisals from another party.

The 'right' is widely protected in other aspects of society: the police, for example, when facing internal disciplinary charges are not bound to answer questions or allegations put to them.

Limitation of the right to silence has been widely and strongly opposed by lawyers, judges and legal campaign groups. Liberty, for example, has said that drawing adverse inferences from silence would undermine the presumption of innocence. Silence is an important safeguard against oppressive questioning by the police, particularly for the weak and vulnerable.

Michael Mansfield, the leading QC, opposing the planned undermining of the right, pointed out that the Government was ignoring the recommendations of no fewer than three Royal Commissions (1929, 1981 and 1993), all of which had resolved in favour of keeping the right intact. He stated that:

> The presumption of innocence should be across the board – I do not think anyone should have to prove their innocence or we will be going towards an inquisitorial system [(1994) *The Guardian*].

John Alderson, former chief constable of Devon and Cornwall (1973–82) and a respected writer on constitutional aspects of policing, has written of the impending danger when police are able to 'exert legal and psychological pressure on individuals held in the loneliness of their cells'. He states that:

> History tells us that when an individual has to stand up against the entire apparatus of the modern State, he or she is very vulnerable. That is why, in criminal cases, the burden of proof has always rested on the State rather than on the accused. The

Founding Fathers of America amended their constitution to that effect in 1791 [(1994) *The Independent*].

Another opponent of the change is James Richardson, the leading criminal law barrister and editor of the authoritative practitioners' text *Archbold on Criminal Evidence, Pleading and Practice*. He has described the Act as 'an ill thought out package of expedients'.

Undermining the right to silence may constitute a significant constitutional change in the relationship between the individual and the State. It may be doubted whether the majority of suspects should be put under greater intimidation by the system because of the conduct of a few 'hardened criminals' – the justification for the legislation given by the Home Secretary when he introduced the legislation.

In conclusion, however, two points should be noted to put the debate in its proper historical context. First, it should not be forgotten that there were, prior to the Act, several instances in English law where there was already a legal obligation for a suspect to answer questions. These included the obligation to speak under s 2 of the Criminal Justice Act 1987 (above); the obligations under ss 431–41 of the Companies Act 1985 (concerning investigations in respect of company officers and agents whose companies are being investigated by the Department of Trade and Industry); the obligations under ss 22 and 131 of the Insolvency Act 1986 (concerning inquiries upon the winding up of companies); s 18 of the Prevention of Terrorism (Temporary Provisions) Act 1989 (concerning information relating to terrorism); and the law under s 11 (as amended) of the Official Secrets Act 1911.

Secondly, in the few cases where the right to silence was used under the pre-Act law, we need to ask how far juries were genuinely sympathetic to the judge's directions that they could not assume guilt from silence. Juries convicted in half of such cases, so there is evidence that jurors were suspicious and sceptical about people who exercised the right, just as they may be today when someone exercises the right (that is, remains silent from arrest until the jury retires, without relying on any fact he could have mentioned earlier).

Question 26

After a shop has been set on fire late one night, Detective Constables Whistle and Cuff, in a nearby road, hear about the incident on their car radio. They then see two youths, Gas and Spark, running down the road away from the area of the shop. The officers stop the youths who smell of petrol and ask them some questions. Gas and Spark are then arrested for arson and taken to the police station.

Before questioning, the officers untruthfully told Gas that his fingerprints had been discovered on a discarded bottle of petrol found in the burnt out shop. The solicitor, unaware of the deceit, advised Gas to disclose any involvement he had had in the incident and Gas admitted having taken part.

Spark declined to accept any legal advice after the proper notices about its availability had been given to him. Spark was a drug addict and after a session of relentless questions being fired at him for over two hours he asked whether the police would agree to bail if he admitted to being involved in the incident. The officer in the room agreed and Spark made a statement in which he said he was at the shop at the time the fire was just becoming serious and had gone in to see if any property could be salvaged, but he had not started the fire.

Advise Gas and Spark on the admissibility of their statements.

Answer plan

Advice to Gas

In your advice to Gas, you should:

- explain the significance of s 82(1) of PACE 1984;
- explain the relevance of ss 76 and 78 of PACE 1984;
- explain and apply *Sang* (1980);
- explain and apply *Mason* (1988).

Advice to Spark

When advising Spark, include discussion of:

- the rule in *Zavekas* (1970);
- s 76 of PACE 1984, Code C and *Sharp* (1988);
- *Goldenberg* (1988) and the drug issue;
- three possible arguments on appeal, ss 76, 78 and 82 of PACE 1984;
- precedent on 'oppressive', for example, *Miller* (1986).

Answer

Advice to Gas

A confession is defined in s 82(1) of PACE 1984 as a statement 'wholly or partly adverse to the party who made it'. Gas, within these terms, appears to have made a confession. The admissibility of a confession is governed by several sections of PACE 1984. Section 76(2) states that in relation to confessions which have allegedly resulted from 'oppression', or in consequence of anything said or done which was likely, in the circumstances existing at the time, to render unreliable any confession made, the court shall not admit the evidence unless the prosecution proves that the confession was not obtained in such a manner.

Section 78 allows a court to refuse to admit evidence if it appears, having regard to all the circumstances including the circumstances in which the evidence was obtained, that admission of the evidence would have such an adverse effect on the fairness of the proceedings that the court ought not to admit it. It was held by the Court of Appeal, in *Mason* (1988), that, regardless of whether the admissibility of a confession falls to be considered under s 76(2), a judge has the discretion to deal with it under s 78.

Section 82 states that 'nothing in this part of the Act [Pt VIII, dealing with evidence] shall prejudice any power of a court to exclude evidence'. The general view is that s 82 preserved the whole of the common law existing prior to PACE 1984, so that a confession could also be excluded under decisions like that of the House of Lords in *Sang* (1980). That case permitted exclusion of evidence where its prejudicial effect outweighs its probative value. Lord Diplock thought that a discretion only existed at common law with regard to admissions and confessions and 'generally with regard to evidence obtained from the accused after commission of the offence'. One observation of Lord Diplock's which is especially helpful to Gas (although *obiter dicta*) is that the purpose of such judicial discretion is to ensure that an accused was not induced to incriminate himself by deception.

It would be possible for Gas to argue for the exclusion of his admission on all three of the above sections (ss 76, 78 and 82).

In *Mason* (1988), on facts similar to those in question, the defendant was tricked into making an admission of instigating an arson attack on the car of an enemy after a police officer had told both him and his solicitor that the defendant's fingerprints had been found on a bottle of inflammable liquid used in the attack. Following the solicitor's advice to give an explanation, the defendant then admitted his role in the arson. The Court of Appeal quashed the defendant's conviction as having such an adverse effect on the fairness of the proceedings (s 78) that the court should have excluded it. It is not certain, however, that this case would assist Gas. In *Mason*, the trial judge had admitted the evidence of the defendant's admission, but, in saying the trial judge wrongly exercised his discretion, the Court of Appeal said he had omitted one 'vital factor' from his considerations: that of the deceit practised on the defendant's solicitor. Evidently, a deceit practised only upon the defendant – as in our case – would not in itself warrant discretionary exclusion of the admission.

Advice to Spark

Zavekas (1970) was a case decided using the old Judges' Rules which held that admissions, to be admissible, had to be voluntary in the sense of being obtained without 'fear of prejudice or hope of advantage, exercised or held out by a person in authority'. The Court of Appeal quashed a conviction because the trial judge had admitted a confession made after the defendant asked the police whether he could have bail if he made a statement and, receiving an affirmative reply, proceeded to confess. Such law has, however, been effectively overruled by s 76(2)(b) of PACE 1984 and Code C which give a much narrower compass to the notion of unreliability in respect of confessions. Spark's admission is 'mixed', in that it contains parts which are incriminating (he was at the scene of the crime and he did go into the shop) and parts which are self-serving, self-exculpatory (he did not start the fire). The combination of the provisions of PACE 1984 and the decisions of the House of Lords in *Sharp* (1988) and *Aziz* (1996), appear to have put the law on this subject beyond doubt. Their Lordships in both *Sharp* and *Aziz* specifically approved the judgment of Lord Lane in *Duncan* (1981), which held that the simplest and, therefore, the method most likely to produce a just result, is for the jury to consider the whole statement, both the incriminating parts and the excuses and explanations, in deciding where the truth lies. Section 82(1) of PACE 1984 defines 'confession' as including 'any statement wholly or partly adverse to the person who made it'. Accordingly, statements of 'mixed' content count as confessions and are admissible in evidence subject to s 76 of PACE 1984 being satisfied.

The Code says that, if a suspect asks an officer a 'direct question' as to what action will be taken in the event of his answering questions, making a statement or refusing to do either, 'the officer may inform him what action he proposes to take in that event provided that the action itself is proper and warranted' (Code C, para 11.3).

Provided that the police officer, in agreeing that the police would agree to bail in consequence of an admission, was answering a direct question from Spark, then the police conduct is lawful and the evidence not rendered inadmissible or vulnerable to exclusion.

The fact that Spark was a drug addict and might have been sufficiently desperate for more drugs to have admitted to anything in order to get bail would not, on current case law, appear to affect the matter. Provided, of course, that his confession was not prompted by any other factor of police conduct in breach of the Act or the Codes. In *Goldenberg* (1988), the defendant, a heroin addict, requested an interview five days after his arrest and, during this interview, he allegedly gave information about someone whom he claimed had supplied him with heroin. At trial, counsel for the defendant argued that the evidence of the interview might be unreliable under s 76, because:

(a) the admissions were made in an attempt to get bail; and
(b) because of his addiction, it might be expected that the defendant would do or say anything – however false – to get

bail and, thus, to be able to feed his addiction. This argument was rejected both at trial and on appeal. There was no argument that the interviewing officer had said or done anything improper, and the words 'in consequence of anything said or done' in s 76(2)(b) meant said or done by someone other than the suspect.

If it can be shown that the police interview with Spark was 'oppressive', then the argument for the exclusion of the confession could be run in any or all of three ways: (a) that it should be excluded by virtue of s 76(2)(a), as the police conduct was oppressive *simpliciter* or that, in conjunction with the fact of Spark's addiction and in view of the *ratio* of *Goldenberg* (where the appeal was dismissed because of no evidence of police misconduct), it was a confession gained by oppression; or (b) that it should be excluded by virtue of s 78 (see advice to Gas, above); or (c) that it should be excluded by virtue of s 82, as its prejudicial effect greatly outweighs its probative value and it is within Lord Diplock's formula from *Sang* (1980), of protecting a suspect's right not to incriminate himself.

It will be difficult to show that the police interview was 'oppressive', as the courts have been very reluctant to make such findings. In *Fulling* (1987), the Court of Appeal gave 'oppression' its dictionary meaning, which involves 'the exercise of power or authority in a burdensome, harsh or wrongful manner'. *Fulling* was applied in *Emmerson* (1991). Questioning that was 'rude and discourteous', with a raised voice and some bad language and which gave the impression of 'impatience and irritation', was not considered oppressive. *Paris* (1993) produced a different result. The police were held to have behaved oppressively after shouting at a suspect what they wanted him to say over 300 times, after he had denied involvement in the offence charged. However, in *L* (1994), tactics similar to those employed in *Paris* appear to have been regarded as acceptable. The length of the interviews and the nature of the questioning are, of course, the important considerations.

Rules in Code C govern how interviews should be conducted. It is provided (Code C, para 12.7) that breaks from interviewing shall be made at recognised meal times and that 'short breaks for refreshment shall also be provided at intervals of approximately two hours'. An officer has the discretion to delay a break, but only where there are reasonable grounds for believing that it would involve: (a) a risk of harm to persons or serious loss or damage to property; or (b) unnecessarily delay the suspect's release from custody; or (c) otherwise prejudice the outcome of the investigation. It, thus, seems unlikely that Spark's interview, which lasted 'for over two hours' (but, presumably, nearer to two than three hours), was oppressive, unless he can show that it was deliberately aimed at producing a state of confusion, or that it transgressed the fairly wide Code rules.

One final consideration is that Spark is described as a 'youth'. Code C, para 1.5 says that if anyone appears to be under the age of 17, then he shall be treated as a juvenile. Code C, para 11.14 states that a juvenile, whether suspected or not, must not be interviewed or asked to provide or sign a written statement in the absence of an appropriate adult (unless para 11.1 or Annex C applies).

Question 27

After a series of burglaries in Grimtown, Pat and Billy were arrested by police and taken to the local police station. Pat and Billy were taken to separate rooms for interrogation.

Pat asked to see a solicitor. A police officer wrote something down, went out of the room and came back saying that there would need to be a little delay as: 'We would not want word to get out to the wrong people that you're in here.' The officer then said: 'You know the ropes, Pat, we would just like to ask you a few simple questions.' Pat then made some confessions which were admitted in court and he was convicted for offences of burglary.

In the other room, Billy also asked about a lawyer. 'We can arrange for one or you can have your own,' he was told. Billy thought for a moment and then replied that it would probably be too expensive so he would not opt for legal advice. Billy asked the police to inform the president of the Civil Freedom League of his arrest. A senior officer told Billy that would not be possible. Billy has now also confessed to certain burglaries and has been tried and convicted.

Advise Pat and Billy on the possibility of appealing against their convictions.

Answer plan

Advice to Pat

In your advice to Pat, you should:

- give the meaning of s 58 of PACE 1984;
- explain the significance of s 116, 'serious arrestable offence';
- state whether burglary falls within this category – see s 24(1)(b);
- explain and apply *McIvor* (1987);
- explain and apply *Smith (Eric)* (1987), *Samuel* (1988) and *Parris* (1989);
- explain and apply Code C, Annex B, Note B4.

Advice to Billy

In your advice to Billy, you should examine:

- his entitlement to free advice: revised Code C, para 3.1;
- provide some examination of s 56 – meaning of 'friend or relative' (s 56(6));
- the application of *Beycan* (1990);
- the relevance of s 76(2)(b).

Answer

Advice to Pat

PACE 1984 came into effect in 1986 and, since that time, the access a suspect in a police station has to a lawyer has been governed by the Act. Section 58(1) of PACE 1984 states that a person arrested and held in custody in a police station shall be entitled, if he so requests, to consult a solicitor at any time. The request must be recorded in the custody record and the request must be granted 'as soon as is practicable', except to the extent that delay is permitted by the section. Delay in compliance with Pat's request is only permitted by the section if he is being held in connection with a 'serious arrestable offence' and an officer of at least the rank of superintendent authorises it. 'Serious arrestable offences' are defined in s 116 and Sched 5. The term includes named offences such as murder and rape and, also, any arrestable offence which has, *inter alia*, led to 'substantial financial gain to any person' (s 116(6)(e)) or 'serious financial loss to any person' (s 116(6)(f)).

Burglary is an 'arrestable offence', by virtue of s 24(1)(b) of PACE 1984 as someone over 21 (without previous conviction) could, upon conviction for it, be sentenced to a term imprisonment of five years. It is arguable whether Pat has been arrested in connection with a 'serious arrestable offence'. It would depend on the value of the stolen goods and on the respective financial positions of: (a) those who were burgled; and (b) Pat. It was held in *McIvor* (1987) that the theft of 28 beagles worth £880 from a hunt was not a serious arrestable offence. The theft of the dogs, which were owned collectively by the hunt, did not cause 'serious financial loss'. In *Smith (Eric)* (1987), a robbery from Woolworths involving two video recorders (valued at £800) plus cash of £116 was regarded by the trial judge as probably not a serious arrestable offence: the loss to such a large national store would be small and the gain to the robbers would not necessarily be substantial.

Under Code C, Annex B, Note C1, an officer of at least the rank of superintendent may only delay Pat's access to a solicitor on the grounds stated in s 58 of PACE 1984. He must have 'reasonable grounds' for believing that such access *will*: (a) lead to interference with, or harm to, evidence connected with a serious arrestable offence, or interference with, or physical injury to, other persons; or (b) the alerting of other persons involved in the offence but not yet arrested; or (c) that such access would hinder the recovery of any property obtained as a result of the offence.

The words used by the officer to Pat, 'We would not want word to get out to the wrong people that you're in here,' are consistent with any of the statutory reasons in (a) to (c) above. The Act says, however, that, if the delay is authorised, then the suspect must be told the reason for the delay and the reasons must be recorded on the custody sheet. The officer's words here are quite vague, so neither of the requirements (the explanation to Pat and the recording of the reason) appear to have been complied with.

Moreover, it was held in *Samuel* (1988) that it was insufficient for an officer simply to believe that giving a suspect access to a solicitor *might* lead to the alerting of accomplices: the defendant was being questioned about offences of burglary and robbery. His request to see a solicitor was refused on the grounds that the offences were serious and that there was a risk of accomplices being inadvertently alerted. The defendant subsequently made confessions which were admitted at trial. The Court of Appeal quashed his conviction stating that access to a solicitor was a 'fundamental right' of a citizen and that a police officer who sought to refuse access had to justify the refusal by reference to the specific circumstances of the case. The court noted that 'solicitors are intelligent professional people' whereas most suspects were 'not very clever', so the likelihood of the latter being able to hoodwink the former into inadvertently passing on a coded message to fellow criminals was very low. This would probably only be a sustainable point in very few cases.

In *Parris* (1989), it was held that, where the lawyer called was the duty solicitor, there would usually be no grounds for the police fearing that he would alert other parties to the crime. Here, the court quashed a conviction for armed robbery because of breaches of s 58. In *Davidson* (1988), it was held by the Court of Appeal that the police had to be 'nearly certain' that a solicitor granted access to the suspect would warn another criminal or get rid of the proceeds of the crime. The power to delay access to a solicitor could not be exercised until the suspect had nominated an actual solicitor. This was not the case here; the court excluded the confessions given by the suspect without legal advice and, as a result, the prosecution's case collapsed.

The revised Code of Practice (Code C, Annex B, Note B4) clarifies the position further. This says that the officer may only authorise a delay if he has reasonable grounds to believe that the specific solicitor in question will, inadvertently or otherwise, pass on a message from the detained person which will lead to the alerting of accomplices, or interference with evidence. It is uncertain from the question whether Pat is asking to see a specific solicitor. Unless this is the case and the officer has reasonable grounds for the relevant suspicions, then he will be in breach of the Code and s 58. Such a breach, though, does not entail automatic exclusion by the court of any resulting statement made by the suspect. The court will evaluate all the circumstances.

In *Dunford* (1990), the defendant had a record and was aware of his right not to answer any questions put by the police. Before reaching the police station, he had refused to answer questions and had, thereafter, answered several questions with the phrase 'no comment'. In such circumstances, the Court of Appeal ruled that the judge had been entitled to allow the confession made in the police station. Moreover, the Court of Appeal ruled in *Walsh* (1990), that an 'adverse effect of the fairness of proceedings' within the meaning of s 78 would no doubt follow from a 'significant and substantial breach' of s 58, but that did not necessarily mean that the evidence thus obtained had to be excluded. The court had to decide, not simply whether there had been an adverse effect on the fairness of proceedings, but whether it had been such an adverse effect that justice required the evidence to be excluded.

In sum, Pat's appeal could succeed if he could persuade the Court of Appeal that s 78 should have been used to exclude evidence of his confessions because of significant breaches of s 58 and Code C, which had such an adverse effect on the fairness of proceedings that justice requires they be excluded. Pat's access to a lawyer is delayed, but was s 58 of PACE 1984 complied with? The officer 'wrote something down' but was this the required entry on the custody sheet? He went out the room, but was it to get the required permission of the superintendent? Was the vague reason given to Pat for the delay sufficient to exclude Pat's 'fundamental right'? There are also significant doubts about whether the offence was a 'serious arrestable offence' and whether, if so, the police had reasonable grounds to believe that any of the criteria in s 58(8) were applicable. Overall, this gives a strong case to Pat, only slightly counterposed by virtue of Pat's possible criminal record (that is, '... you know the ropes Pat ...') by the decisions in *Dunford* and *Walsh* (see above).

Advice to Billy

The duty solicitor schemes at police stations, set up under PACE 1984, are run by the Legal Aid Board. The provision of legal advice to suspects at police stations is not means tested. It is paid for by the State. Research has shown that many suspects who previously did not take up the opportunity for legal advice abstained because they were unaware that it was free. The revised Code of Practice (April 1995) dealt with this problem by requiring the police to inform the suspect that the advice is free (Code C, para 3.1(ii)). The Code also requires (para 6.3) that a poster advertising the right to have legal advice must be prominently displayed in the charging area of every police station.

We are not told whether there is a poster for Billy to see, but in not informing Billy that advice is free, the officer is in breach of the Code.

Under s 56 of PACE 1984, an arrested person held in custody, like Billy, has the right to have someone informed of his arrest. The person to be informed must be a 'friend or relative or other person who is known to him or who is likely to take an interest in his welfare'. Whether the president of the Civil Freedom League is within this category is a moot point. He would be if he was a friend or associate of Billy's and even, possibly, in his capacity as someone publicly concerned with civil liberties but, if the only link was the latter one, it is uncertain whether this would be sufficient. A circular issued to police to assist them with the operation of s 56's forerunner (s 62 of the Criminal Law Act 1977) excluded public figures, like pop stars and football players, from the sorts of person who could be notified. Those groups, however, are of course not related to civil liberties.

The only other reasons given in the Act to justify a delay in notifying a specified person are when, in a case of a serious arrestable offence (see under advice to Pat), an officer of at least the rank of superintendent authorises it for any of the reasons in s 56(5), which are the same as those dealt with above in Pat's case under s 58(8). Section 56(6) states that the suspect must be told of the reason for the delay and it must be recorded on the custody sheet, neither of which appear to have been done in this case.

It seems more likely that there has been a breach of Code C (in respect of the notification of free legal advice) than of s 56, but, even if there were only such a breach of the Code, it is quite possible that the Court of Appeal would quash Billy's conviction as he was deprived of his fundamental right to legal advice as a result of the breach. In *Beycan* (1990), the Court of Appeal quashed a conviction based on a confession when the suspect had been arrested, taken to the station and asked: 'Are you happy to be interviewed in the normal way we conduct these interviews without a solicitor, friend or representative?' Billy's case is arguably stronger, as he has actually expressed a desire for advice and only proceeded reluctantly without it.

It may be possible to construe these events, in respect of Billy, in a way which shows him 'changing his mind' about taking legal advice. Thus, there could also be a possible breach of Code C, para 6.6(d):

> When the person who wanted legal advice changes his mind, the interview may be started without further delay provided the person has given his agreement in writing or on tape to being interviewed without receiving legal advice and that an officer of the rank of inspector or above has given agreement ...

In *Wadman* (1996), the defendant, having initially declined legal advice, changed his mind and then, while arrangements were being made, reverted to saying that he did not wish to have a solicitor. The police failed to comply with para 6.6(d) of Code C. The judge held that the Code was not 'mandatory' and admitted the evidence. On appeal, the conviction was quashed. The court ruled that the judge's approach to the Code was flawed; he confused the discretion he had on the *voir dire* – whether to admit the evidence – with the absence of discretion for police officers when complying with the Code: it was a disciplinary offence not to do so. It was not a case where the court should exercise its own discretion.

The appeals of both Pat and Billy could also be argued under s 76(2)(b), which permits the court not to allow the confession if it was gained in consequence of:

> ... anything said or done which was likely, in the circumstances existing at the time, to render unreliable any confession which might be made by him in consequence thereof.

The basis of argument would be the same as for s 78.

Question 28

After a serious assault on a old woman by a group of youths, PCs East and Wood stopped Peter in the street late at night. He had blood on his hands. When asked some simple routine questions, Peter became abusive and very hostile to the officers He told the officers that his name was 'Mickey Mouse' and refused to answer any questions.

The following day, Mary and Paul are arrested for taking part in the assault. During questioning by police, Mary sat with her boyfriend who is a law student. Before being cautioned, she answered some questions, but not others and, at her trial, the judge suggested to the jury that she 'might have remained silent to avoid incriminating herself'.

Paul remained silent after being cautioned, refusing to answer police questions and, at trial, the judge invited the jury to consider whether an innocent man would have behaved in such a manner.

Peter has been convicted of obstructing the police officers in the execution of their duty. Mary and Paul have now been convicted of the assault. Advise Peter, Mary and Paul about their possible grounds of appeal.

Answer plan

Advice to Peter

In advising Peter:

- apply *Rice v Connolly* (1966) – consider what constitutes 'obstruction';
- apply *Ricketts v Cox* (1982) – 'the manner of a person together with his silence';
- are the decisions distinguishable?

Advice to Mary

When advising Mary:

- apply *Davis* (1959) – improper directions to a jury;
- consider the rule in *Parkes* (1976), where people are speaking on equal terms;
- discuss the decision in *Chandler* (1976);
- evaluate which case is closer to the facts of the problem.

Advice to Paul

Your advice to Paul should include:

- the basis for an appeal – Criminal Appeal Act 1968;
- application of *Chandler* (1976).

Answer

Advice to Peter

Peter might have an appeal against his conviction for obstructing the police officers in the execution of their duty if he was not legally obliged to answer the questions put to him by the officers Normally, the citizen is entitled to remain silent in the face of police questions, without this being either the subject of a charge of obstructing the police in the execution of their duties, or of the silence being commented on adversely by the prosecution or judge at trial.

This rule is established by the important Divisional Court decision in *Rice v Connolly* (1966). The appellant was seen by officers at night in an area where burglaries had been committed. He refused to tell the police where he had come from or where he was going. He identified himself only by his surname and a street name where he said he lived. He refused to accompany the police to a police box to further verify his identity. His conviction for an offence under s 51(3) of the Police Act 1964 (resisting or wilfully obstructing a police officer in the execution of his duty) was quashed, as the Divisional Court said he had the right not to answer the questions. Lord Parker CJ stated that a proper conviction would require proof that the action was 'wilful', which means not only done intentionally, but also done without lawful excuse. Citizens, he said, had a moral duty and perhaps a social one to help the police with their inquiries, but there was no such legal duty.

The decision in *Rice v Connolly* was unanimous, but James J noted that he would not go so far as to say that silence combined with conduct could not amount to an obstruction. It would be a matter for the courts to decide on the facts of any particular case. In *Ricketts v Cox* (1982), on facts similar to those in question here, the defendant's appeal against a conviction under s 51(3) was dismissed. Two police officers questioned the defendant and another man in the early hours of the morning following a serious assault. The defendant was unco-operative and shouted in obscene language at the officers and then tried to walk away without answering any questions The court found that this was an instance where 'the manner of a person together with his silence' could amount to obstruction. This decision probably accounts for Peter's conviction, his obstreperous conduct coupled with the evidently false name he gave.

The decision in *Ricketts v Cox* has been widely criticised (Glanville Williams; Smith and Hogan; and Bailey, Harris and Jones) as flawed and at odds with *Rice v Connolly*. If a refusal to answer questions is lawful, which it clearly is, then how can this important constitutional right be cancelled merely because the questioned party is abusive? Peter's appeal could be based upon this point, inviting the Court of Appeal to deal with the confusion promoted by the two Divisional Court decisions by overruling *Ricketts v Cox*. Peter could possibly be acquitted if the facts of his case were governed simply by the decision in *Rice v Connolly*. Even though, unlike the appellant in the 1966 case, Peter had gone beyond simple reticence and told the officers his name was 'Mickey Mouse', this could perhaps be argued to be so self-evidently false as tantamount to saying, 'I shall not tell you my name'. The court agreed, in *Rice v Connolly*, that to tell a 'cock and bull' story to the police would, obviously, be an obstruction. This would clearly cover Peter had he said his name was Tom Smith and misled the police as to his true identity, but his sarcastic reference to a cartoon character could be regarded as not seriously misleading, and lawful, as he is not legally obliged to reveal his name. It does not look like Peter was under caution when he refused to answer police questions. If he was, then his failure to answer could be made the subject of comment (see below, under 'Advice to Mary') by the trial judge under s 34 of the CJPOA 1994.

Advice to Mary

Mary's conviction could be quashed if it can be shown that the trial judge's words to the jury amounted to a misdirection. Before the CJPOA 1994, the 'right to silence' was regarded as a well entrenched principle of law. The common law position is that everyone still has the right to remain silent in the same circumstances as they did before the 1994 Act; what *has* changed is the entitlement of the judge or prosecuting counsel to make adverse comment on such a silence. There are many reasons why a suspect might remain silent when questioned (for example, fear, confusion, reluctance to incriminate another person) and, generally, failure or refusal to answer questions does not amount to evidence against the person concerned, unless it can be said that the defendant was on 'equal terms' with the questioner. In *Parkes* (1976), the Privy Council ruled that a judge could invite the jury to consider the possibility of drawing adverse inferences from silence from a tenant who had been accused by a landlady of murdering her daughter. The landlady and tenant, for this encounter, were regarded as having parity of status, unlike a person faced with questions from the police. Failure to answer questions put by a police officer, or someone in a similar position, is unlikely to lead to adverse inferences being drawn at any trial. In *Chandler* (1976), the suspect, in the company of his solicitor, refused to answer some questions asked by a police officer before the caution. The judge told the jury that they should decide whether the defendant's silence was attributable to his wish to exercise his common law right, or because he might incriminate himself. The Court of Appeal thought the presence of Chandler's solicitor meant that the parties were on 'even terms' but, on the facts, quashed Chandler's conviction, since the judge had gone too far in suggesting that silence before a caution could be evidence of guilt.

The alleged advantage of the change of law is that ss 34–38 of the CJPOA 1994 helps convict criminals who, under the old law, used to be acquitted because they took advantage of the right to keep quiet when questioned, without the court or prosecution being able to comment adversely upon that silence. The dangers, however, entailed in undermining the right of silence are most acute in respect of police questioning scenarios. In *R v Condron* (1997), the Court of Appeal said that the guidelines set out in *R v Cowan* (1996), regarding the drawing of adverse inferences where the accused fails to testify, are equally applicable where the accused fails to answer questions when being interviewed by the police. More detailed guidance was given in *R v Argent* (1996), where the Court of Appeal set out the conditions which have to be satisfied before adverse inferences can be drawn from a person's failure to answer police questions (s 34 of the CJPOA 1994). The conditions include:

(a) the failure to answer had to occur before a defendant was charged;

(b) the alleged failure must occur during questioning under caution;

(c) the questioning must be directed at trying to discover whether and by whom the offence has been committed;

(d) the failure must be a failure to mention any fact relied on in the person's defence; and

(e) the fact the defendant failed to mention had to be one which this particular defendant could reasonably be expected to have mentioned when being questioned, taking account of all the circumstances existing at that time (for example, the time of day, the defendant's age, experience, mental capacity, state of health, sobriety, personality and access to legal advice).

Section 34(1), therefore, only applies in respect of questioning under caution. If no caution is administered, no inference can be drawn from failure to mention a fact in response to such questioning. A person must be cautioned where there are grounds to suspect him or her of an offence, before any questions are put to him regarding involvement or suspected involvement in that offence (Code C, para 10.1 of PACE 1984) and; a person must normally be cautioned on being arrested (Code D, para 10.3). A caution need not be administered if the questions are put for other purposes. Section 34 permits adverse inferences to be drawn from silence in situations that do not amount to 'interviews', as defined by Code C of PACE 1984, and, thus, which are not subject to the safeguards of access to legal advice and of contemporaneous recording which exist where a suspect is interviewed at a police station. An 'interview' is defined by Code C, para 11.1A, as being:

> ... the questioning of a person regarding his involvement or suspected involvement in a criminal offence or offences which by virtue of para 10.1 of Code C is required to be carried out under caution.

Sections 36 and 37 of the CJPOA 1994 permit inferences to be drawn from the failure of an arrested person to account for an object, substance or mark, etc, or to account for his presence at a particular place where he is found. The main differences between s 34 and ss 36 and 37 are that s 34 applies where the suspect has been cautioned, but ss 36 and 37 only apply where the suspect has been arrested; and ss 36 and 37 apply whether, or not, a fact is relied upon in a person's defence, whereas s 34 applies only in respect of failure to mention a fact relied upon in a person's defence.

Mary could appeal against her conviction if prosecution evidence is obtained as a result of unfair or unlawful police conduct, under ss 76 and 78 of PACE 1984. The questioning of Mary at the station prior to a caution being given may be in contravention s 34 of the CJPOA 1994 and the Codes of Practice in PACE 1984 (Code C, para 10 and Code D). Cautions need not be given if the questions put did not constitute an 'interview' and were 'questions put for other purposes', but these considerations would not be applicable here, as Mary was already arrested at the material time of being questioned. If Mary failed to answer questions subsequently, under caution or on being charged, s 34 applies only to facts which she later relies on in her defence. The section has no function if she makes no attempt to put previously undisclosed facts forward at trial.

The common law position continues to apply where the new statutory provisions do not apply. Mary could appeal against her conviction on the grounds that she was not on 'equal terms' with the officer who interviewed her, as, unlike the defendant in *Chandler*, she was not accompanied by a lawyer, but merely a law student.

Advice to Paul

Prior to 1996, the Court of Appeal would allow an appeal if they though that: (a) the conviction was unsafe and unsatisfactory; (b) that the judgment of the court trial should be set aside on a wrong decision on any question of law; and (c) that there had been a material irregularity in the course of the trial. The Criminal Appeal Act 1995 abolishes the three grounds of appeal, replacing them with a single test, namely, that the court thinks the conviction is unsafe. The Act does not contain any definition of the word 'unsafe'. Much of the former law will, therefore, be relevant in deciding what is liable to render a conviction unsafe. In particular, the court may still apply the 'lurking doubt' test enunciated in *R v Cooper* (1969):

> ... whether we are content to let the matter stand as it is, or whether there is not some lurking doubt in our minds which makes us wonder whether an injustice has been done.

As noted above, ss 34–38 of the CJPOA constitute a major curtailment of the 'right of silence'. Thus, although Paul retains his 'right' to remain silent both at the trial and the interrogation, 'proper' inferences may be drawn from his failure to mention certain facts when questioned under caution or on being charged (s 34).

Paul's appeal could succeed, if he can show that s 78 of PACE 1984 should have been used to exclude adverse inferences of his silence because of significant breaches of s 34 of the CJPOA 1994. If he simply contends that there is no case to answer, that he has no fact which he could have contributed and he does not rely on a particular defence, s 34 can have no effect. There can be no conviction on silence alone. Section 38 applies to all four provisions of the 1994 Act which operate to permit the drawing of inferences and stipulates that a defendant cannot be convicted or have a case to answer solely on the basis of an inference drawn from silence. There must, therefore, be some other evidence in addition to any inference to be drawn.

Question 29

After an armed robbery at the Upland Bank in Oldcastle, the police arrested Karl for his involvement in the crime. An hour later, having interviewed Karl at the police station, the police went to his parents' home to remove for forensic examination a car parked in his driveway. Tony, Karl's father, resisted the police attempts to remove the vehicle and punched PC Grit. Tony was eventually overpowered and PC Grit then searched the garage and found a collection of plastic bank cards with different names and a pile of correspondence about crimes, including some letters bearing advice from Karl's solicitor.

Karl has been charged with involvement in the bank robbery and crimes relating to the stolen bank cards. Tony has been charged with assaulting an officer in the execution of his duty. Advise Karl and Tony.

Answer plan

Advice to Karl

You should include:

- an explanation and application of s 78 of PACE 1984;
- an explanation and application of s 18 of PACE 1984;
- an explanation and application of s 32 of PACE 1984;
- an application of *Badham* (1987);
- consideration of Code B (revised) on searches and s 67(11) on exclusions;
- discussion of the ambit of s 19 of PACE 1984.

Advice to Tony

Include:

- an explanation of the effect of s 117 of PACE 1984 in the context of the legality of the searches under s 18 or s 20;
- discussion of s 51 of the Police Act 1964.

Answer

Advice to Karl

The police appear to have had sufficient evidence on which to arrest Karl before any examination of the car in his driveway. Nevertheless, the car seems to be very significant evidence as the police went back to get it. It is important to discover, therefore, whether the police were legally entitled to act as they did. If not then the evidence obtained might be excluded under s 78 of PACE 1984, if it is likely to have, in all of the circumstances, an adverse effect on the trial.

The answer to this particular question – whether the police search was lawful – will also determine whether Tony was legally justified in acting as he did, so we shall return to this matter again later.

Karl has been arrested for robbery which is an arrestable offence by virtue of the fact that Karl, if he was over 21 (even without previous convictions) could be sentenced to a term of imprisonment for five years or more upon conviction (s 24 of

PACE 1984). Section 18 of PACE 1984 empowers an officer to enter premises 'occupied or controlled by a person arrested for an arrestable offence' to search for evidence related to that or connected offences. He must, however, have 'reasonable grounds' for believing that there is evidence on the premises that relates to the offence in question or to some offence 'which is connected with or similar to that offence'. Searching for the vehicle suspected of being used in the armed robbery would be within the section's ambit, provided that Karl was an occupant of the address in the sense that he lived or stayed there. We know that letters to Karl from his solicitor were found in his father's garage, which suggests that Karl lived at that address. The search of the garage which results in the discovery of the cards and letters would also be within the section's scope if crimes relating to stolen bank cards can be regarded as 'similar to' the crime of bank robbery. The element of violence or its threat involved in robbery would probably, however, put it in a different class from matters of deception and fraud.

The section also states that any officer making such a search must have prior authorisation in writing from a fellow officer of at least the rank of inspector, or subsequent approval, if such is necessary for the 'effective investigation of the offence'. The authorising officer must make a record of the search and, if the search was authorised in advance, it must show the nature of the evidence that was sought, in order to avoid 'fishing expeditions'. Failure to conform with these rules courts the risk that evidence, thus obtained, will not be admissible in court. Many searches of this type are conducted some time after arrest, so the lapse of an hour before the police come to search Tony's premises and take the evidence does not appear to affect the lawfulness of the conduct.

It may be that Karl did not live with or stay with his parents, in which case the search would not be lawful under s 18. There is, however, the possibility that the search could have been lawful under s 32 which authorises the search, *inter alia*, of any premises on which the arrest took place. The search can be for anything relating to the offence for which a person has been arrested. If the search was made under this power, then it would be lawful in respect of the car (allegedly, used in the robbery), but not in respect of the bank cards or letters. We do not know where Karl was arrested, but, if he was arrested at his parents' home, then s 32 would legitimise the police search. The delay, though, might be more significant here. According to the decision in *Badham* (1987), a search of the home where the defendant lived with his father which took place three hours after the defendant's arrest was not lawful. The Act gave no time limit, but the section was headed 'Search upon arrest' and the power was an immediate one. The Crown Court held it would be wrong to permit an open ended right to go back to the premises where the arrest had taken place. Here, PC Grit goes to Tony's house only an hour after Karl's arrest, but the *ratio decidendi* of *Badham* would apply just as much to this shorter, but still considerable, delay. Section 32 might, perhaps, permit an officer escorting an arrested suspect back to the station to turn around after two minutes walking and return to search the premises where the arrest was made but not after an hour.

It is a requirement of the revised Code B (April 1995) that, when conducting a search, the police shall give to the occupier a written notice of powers and rights showing which powers have been exercised. This applies to searches made under several powers, including those under ss 18 and 32. The notice must specify under which power the search is being made. The notice must also explain the rights of the occupier and the owner of any property seized. The Codes of Practice are not technically 'law', although they have, as Zander has observed, been mistakenly attributed with such status by the Court of Appeal in *McCay* (1991). If Karl can show that evidence (that is, relating to the car) has been obtained in breach of the Code, then the trial judge or Appeal Court can be invited to exclude that evidence (s 67(11)).

There is no common law power to enter and search premises after an arrest, so any search not lawful under s 18 or 32 would be unlawful.

Under s 19, an officer who is lawfully searching any premises is authorised to seize any article (if it is not covered by legal professional privilege), if he, reasonably, believes that it is evidence relating to the offence which he is investigating or 'any other offence' and that it is necessary to seize it in order to prevent it from being 'concealed, lost, damaged altered or destroyed'. It would be possible for the police to make a convincing case for the car (if there was evidence connecting it to the robbery) and the bank cards to be seized. It seems likely, though, that the solicitor's letters would be protected within the status of professional legal privilege, as s 10(1)(a) defines items 'subject to legal privilege' as including 'communications between a professional legal adviser and his client made in connection with giving legal advice to the client'.

In sum, Karl might be able to show that any evidence obtained relating to the car should be excluded by s 78. The search might not be lawful under s 18 if: (a) Karl was not an occupant of his father's house; or (b) the search was not properly authorised in writing by an inspector; or (c) there were no reasonable grounds to believe that there was evidence at Tony's address which related to the robbery. Additionally, the search might not be lawful under s 32, if it was not the site of Karl's arrest. Furthermore, Karl might be able to show that the conduct of the search was not in accordance with Code B if, for example, the written notice of rights and powers was not given to Tony.

Advice to Tony

If the search of Tony's premises is lawful under either s 18 or s 32, then s 117 of PACE 1984 confers power on the police to use force in order to carry out their search, provided that the force used is reasonable and necessary. In such circumstances, PC Grit would have been acting in the execution of his duty and Tony would be guilty of an assault under s 51 of the Police Act 1964. If, however, PC Grit's search was unlawful, so that he was not acting in the execution of his duty, then Tony would be entitled to use force to resist the intrusion on to his premises. There are many decisions to vindicate Tony's actions, if the search was unlawful. The convictions of *Badham* (1987) and *Churchill* (1989), for obstructing a police officer in the execution of his duty and assault occasioning actual bodily harm, respectively, were quashed on appeal, because the searches in both cases were not justifiable within the provisions of PACE 1984. If the search was unlawful for the reasons discussed in the advice to Karl, then the prosecution of Tony for the assault might fail.

Question 30

Ben was walking home in the early hours of the morning. He was approached by two constables, PC Blue and PC Green and asked to stop. He then, reluctantly, answered some questions about who he was and where he had been. By now fed up, he started to walk away as PC Blue was checking his details over the radio. PC Green tired to stop Ben and was punched in the face.

Later, but before dawn, PC Blue saw Dodger, who appeared scruffy and panicked and whom he suspected was carrying a set of 'skeleton' keys to fit various types of household door. He stopped Dodger, asked, 'Okay if we have a look at what you have got on you?' and then, receiving no reply, searched him, very thoroughly. Dodger then protested and PC Blue replied: 'Look, this is quite legal, I am PC Blue of Fenwick Street station and I think you are up to no good.' PC Blue found 'skeleton keys' keys on Dodger, who has, as a result, now been convicted of 'going equipped to steal'.

Ben has been charged with assaulting a constable in the execution of his duty and Dodger wishes to appeal against his conviction. Advise Ben and Dodger.

Answer plan

Advice to Ben

Consider:

- whether PC Green was acting in the course of his duty;
- the *de minimus* rule;
- any application of *Bentley v Brudzinski* (1982).

Advice to Dodger

You should:

- explain the statutory setting: ss 1, 67 and 78 of PACE 1984 and revised Code A;
- apply this to the facts;
- discuss s 2 of PACE 1984 and the legality of the search;
- apply *Fennelley* (1989).

Answer

Advice to Ben

In order to discover whether Ben has assaulted the constable in the execution of his duty, we need to determine whether PC Blue was acting 'in the course of his duty'. If not, then Ben cannot be convicted of the crime charged, although it is worthy of note that had he been charged with common assault, he could have been found guilty, according to *obiter dicta* of Donaldson LJ in *Bentley v Brudzinski* (1982).

In *Kenlin v Gardiner* (1967), a police officer took hold of the arm of a boy whom he wanted to question about the latter's suspicious conduct. The boy did not believe the man was a policeman, despite having been shown a warrant card, and punched the officer in order to escape. The other boy behaved similarly and their convictions for assaulting an officer in the execution of his duty were quashed by the Divisional Court. The court held that the boys were entitled to act as they did in self defence as the officer's conduct in trying to physically apprehend them had not been legal. There is no legal power of detention short of arrest. As Lawton LJ observed in *Lemsatef* (1977), the police do not have any powers to detain somebody 'for the purposes of getting them to help with their enquiries'. This reasoning would assist Ben, assuming that PC Green was not, in fact, trying to stop Ben in order to arrest him.

It is important, however, to examine the precise circumstances of the detaining officer's conduct because there are cases to suggest that, if what the officer does amounts to only a *de minimus* interference with the citizen's liberty, then forceful 'self defence' by the citizen will not be justified. In *Donnelly v Jackman* (1970), an officer approached a suspect to ask some questions. The suspect ignored the request and walked away from the officer. The officer followed and made further requests for the suspect to stop and talk. He tapped the suspect on the shoulder and the suspect reciprocated by tapping the officer on the shoulder and saying, 'Now we are even, copper'. The officer tapped the suspect on the shoulder again which was replied to with a forceful punch. Mr Donnelly's conviction was upheld and the decision in *Kenlin v*

Gardiner was distinguished as, in the earlier case, the officers had actually taken hold of the boys and detained them. The court stated that:

> ... it is not every trivial interference with a citizen's liberty that amounts to a course of conduct sufficient to take the officer out of the course of his duties.

In *Bentley v Brudzinski*, the facts were very close to those in question. A constable stopped two men who had been running barefoot down a street in the early hours. He questioned them about a stolen vehicle, as they fitted the description of suspects in an earlier incident. They waited for about 10 minutes while the officer checked their details over a radio and then they began to leave. Another constable, who had just arrived on the scene, then said, 'Just a minute', and put his hand on the defendant's shoulder. The defendant then punched that officer in the face. Unlike the decision in *Donnelly v Jackman*, the Divisional Court held here that the officer's conduct was more than a trivial interference with the citizen's liberty and amounted to an unlawful attempt to stop and detain him. The respondent was, thus, not guilty of assaulting an officer in the execution of his duty. We know that PC Green 'tried to stop Ben'. If this attempt involved physical restraint, then the authorities suggest that Ben's resistance would not have amounted to the crime of assaulting an officer in the execution of his duty because the officer would not have been acting within his powers. Conversely, if the attempt amounted to nothing more than a tap on the shoulder, Ben would probably be guilty as charged.

Advice to Dodger

Under s 1 of PACE 1984, PC Blue is entitled to stop and search someone whom he reasonably suspects of carrying certain items, including an article 'made or adapted for use in the course of or in connection with ...' (s 1(7)(b)(i)) '... burglary' (s 1(8)(a)). 'Skeleton keys' would fall within such a category. It might be, however, that PC Blue is in breach of the rules in the Codes of Practice, in particular, Code A for the exercise by police officers of statutory powers of stop and search. The Codes are not technically law although, as Zander has observed, they were mistakenly labelled as having 'statutory authority' by Russell LJ in *McCay* (1991). A judge may, however, exclude evidence which has been obtained in breach of the rules and an appeal court may quash a conviction where the judge failed to do so (s 67(11)). Additionally, s 78 of PACE 1984 allows the exclusion of evidence which has been obtained in breach of the Act. The court, after considering all the circumstances, including the circumstances in which the evidence was obtained, will not admit evidence which would have 'an adverse effect on the fairness of the proceedings that the court ought not to admit it'.

What, if anything, has PC Blue done wrong? Did he have reasonable grounds for suspecting that Dodger was carrying 'skeleton keys'? Reasonable suspicion requires an objective basis. In favour of PC Blue's case is the fact that it was in the early hours and Dodger was 'panicked'. Code A states that reasonable suspicion may exist where 'a person is seen acting covertly or warily'. It would perhaps be difficult to bring 'panic' within the categories cited by the Code. The Code specifically states that 'hairstyle', 'manner of dress' and knowledge of 'previous convictions' cannot alone or in combination give grounds for suspicion.

The current Code A (May 1997) was amended to provide some clarification of police powers in relation to groups and gangs. The additional sections (Code A, para 1.6A and Code A, para 1.7AA) state that, where there is reliable information that members of a group or gang who habitually carry knives, weapons or controlled drugs and wear a distinctive item of clothing or other means of identification to indicate membership of it, then police officers may use that identifying item as the basis of their suspicion.

We are not informed as to what basis PC Blue thinks he has for his suspicions, but as he suspects Dodger to be carrying skeleton keys, in particular, we might infer that PC Blue knows Dodger from a previous encounter, perhaps one which resulted in Dodger's arrest and subsequent conviction. Even this, coupled with Dodger's scruffiness would not suffice as a reasonable ground. 'Time and place' and 'behaviour' are factors which can constitute the necessary reasonable grounds and it is just possible that the panic of Dodger in the early hours in the street would lend support to the officer's case, but he would still have to address the question of why he suspected Dodger of carrying 'skeleton keys'.

Under s 2 of PACE 1984, the police officer who proposes to carry out a search must state his name and police station (which PC Blue does, but only after the search has begun), the purpose of the search and the grounds for the search. PC Blue fails to comply with these latter rules. A failure to give grounds, as required by s 2(3)(c), will render the search unlawful (*Fennelley* (1989)) and, in view of the very generalised explanation given by PC Blue, 'I think you are up to no good', it seems the officer is in breach of the Act. The *Fennelley* decision shows that the courts are prepared to be quite strict in their interpretation of the rules. The defendant (F), a heroin addict, was seen by plain clothes police officers in the street. They believed they witnessed him selling drugs on the street. F was stopped, questioned and asked what he had in his pockets. He was searched and no drugs were found but, during a later strip search at the police station, some heroin was found in his underpants. F was charged with possession with intent to supply the drug, but the Crown Court decided that the evidence found by the police officers during the search should be excluded, using s 78 of PACE 1984, as the police officers had failed to abide by the Act and the Codes in a number of respects but, significantly, for our concerns here, they had failed to comply with the mandatory requirements of s 2(3), in that they had not informed F about their grounds for suspicion, nor about the purpose of their search. It was argued that these breaches affected the fairness of the trial, because F had not been given the chance to answer the suspicions of the police at the earliest opportunity. If he had, he might have been able to give an explanation which would have resulted in his being charged with mere possession rather than possession with intent to supply.

The Act also requires that a search in the street must be limited to outer clothing and gloves (s 2(9)). We know that Dodger has been searched 'very thoroughly' and, if that has entailed the removal of more than a coat, jacket or gloves in the street, then the rule has been broken.

The Act, however, does not apply to voluntary searches. If Dodger 'consents' to be stopped and searched, then PC Blue is not exercising any power. Dodger's protests come only towards the end of the search, so his acquiescence at the outset could be construed as consent. The revised Code A now states that juveniles or mentally handicapped people should not be subject to voluntary searches. If Dodger was in either category, then even a voluntary search would be in breach of the rules.

Thus, Dodger might be able to succeed on appeal, if he can show that key evidence leading to his conviction should have been excluded as having been obtained in breach of the Act or the Codes and in a way that had an adverse effect on the proceedings. The weak grounds for his original suspicions, the failures properly to inform Dodger about the grounds for, and the purpose of, the search and the nature of the search itself are all in question and could separately, or together, form the basis of an appeal. This, provided that the search was not by consent.

Question 31

Dozy went shopping at his local supermarket. He picked an apple from the shelf and ate it while doing his other shopping in the store. Dozy then paid for the items in his trolley and walked towards the exit. Before he left, Dozy was apprehended by Peter, a store detective, who said, 'You cannot leave this store'. Dozy asked why not and was informed that he was not being arrested, but that the store manager wished to see him. Dozy was then taken by force to the manager's office where he was made to wait for an hour until the manager returned from his lunch. When the manager arrived, he told Dozy that the store's policy was to always prosecute shoplifters and that the police would now be called to take Dozy away.

Dozy has now been acquitted on a charge of stealing the apple and he wishes to sue the supermarket. Advise Dozy.

Answer plan

You should consider:

- grounds for Dozy's civil action;
- the legal definition of an 'arrest';
- the lawfulness of the arrest;
- *Walters v WH Smith & Son Ltd* (1914);
- *Self* (1992);
- *John Lewis & Co Ltd v Tims* (1952).

Answer

Dozy might have an action for damages against Peter or the store (if vicarious liability applies) for false imprisonment. The answer to this question would largely depend upon whether the action of Peter was lawful.

There is no legal power to detain a suspect without arrest. 'Arrest', however, is a matter of fact, not a legal concept. In *Spicer v Holt* (1977), Lord Dilhorne said that:

> Whether or not a person has been arrested depends not on the legality of the arrest, but on whether he has been deprived of his liberty to go where he pleases.

Thus, Dozy may have been arrested, if he was prevented from leaving (the use of force on him to take him back to the manager's office helps support such an argument), but whether the arrest was lawful will depend on other matters, namely, the conditions specified in s 24 of PACE 1984. Aside from the technicalities of whether there has been an arrest, there seems clear *prima facie* evidence of false imprisonment. Having been forcibly taken to the manager's room, it seems likely that force or its threat was used to keep Dozy there, but, even if not, an action for false imprisonment would still exist. The claimant need not even know he has been restrained. In *Meering v Grahame White Aviation Co Ltd* (1919), Lord Atkin stated that a person could be 'imprisoned' within the terms of the tort, even if they were asleep or drunk at the time and, thus, remain unaware of their captivity.

Peter, though, may have arrested Dozy. If this was so, the question remains whether the arrest was lawful.

Dozy was evidently not informed of why he was being arrested. Section 28(3) of PACE 1984 states that an arrest is not lawful unless the person arrested is informed of the ground for the arrest at the time of, or as soon as practicable after, the arrest. It was, however, recognised in *Christie v Leachinsky* (1947), and remains good law today, that the rule does not apply where the arrest is by a private citizen and the ground of arrest is obvious. If Peter's actions, despite his words, do amount to an arrest, then it could be regarded as having taken place in circumstances which made it obvious why it was being carried out. Even if the arrest is regarded as unlawful for failure to inform of the relevant ground, the illegality will not operate retrospectively to vitiate the whole arrest. It will, according to the Divisional Court in *DPP v Hawkins* (1988), render the arrest unlawful, as from the moment when it would have been practicable for the arrestor to have given a reason. Thus, any damages which Dozy could claim would be limited to those reflecting his experience during the time in the office, from when he should have been informed about why he had been arrested, until the time he was told of the reason for his arrest by the police.

An arrestable offence is one for which the sentence is fixed by law or for which a person over 21 may be sentenced on the first occasion for at least five years' imprisonment (s 24 of PACE 1984). Theft, fitting in the second category, is an arrestable offence and ss 24 and 25 of PACE 1984 give a general power of arrest without warrant for 'arrestable offences'. The Act, however, preserves an old common law distinction in respect of the powers of constables and private individuals when making such arrests. Where an arrest is being made *after* an offence is thought to have been committed, then PACE 1984 confers narrower rights upon the private individual than on the police officer.

In *Walters v WH Smith & Son Ltd* (1914), the defendants had reasonably suspected that Walters had stolen books from a station bookstall. At his trial, Walters was acquitted as the jury believed his statement that he had intended to pay for the books. No crime had, therefore, been committed in respect of any of the books. Walters sued the defendants, *inter alia*, for false imprisonment, a tort which involves the wrongful deprivation of personal liberty in any form, as he had been arrested for a crime which had not, in fact, been committed. The Court of Appeal held that, to justify the arrest, a private individual had to show, not only reasonable suspicion, but also that the offence for which the arrested person was given over into custody had in fact been committed, even if by someone else. A police officer making an arrest in the same circumstances could legally justify the arrest by showing 'reasonable suspicion' alone, without having to show that an offence was, in fact, committed.

This principle is now incorporated into PACE 1984 and Peter appears to have fallen foul of the provision, because the *de facto* arrest takes place after the alleged crime of shoplifting but, as events fall, the criminal courts have acquitted Dozy of any crime. If there was no crime, then Peter could not rely on s 24(5) which only allows an individual to arrest a suspect whom he has reasonable grounds to believe has committed the offence 'where an arrestable crime has been committed'.

It is worthy of note that the less prudent arrestor who acts against a suspect when the latter is suspected of being in the act of committing an arrestable offence (s 24(4)) can justify his conduct simply by showing that there were 'reasonable grounds' on which to base the suspicion. They need not show that an offence was, in fact, being committed.

This analysis is supported by the recent decision of *Self* (1992) on facts very similar to the questions. The defendant was seen by a store detective in Woolworths to pick up a bar of chocolate and leave the store without paying. The detective followed him out into the street and, with the assistance of a member of the public, she arrested the suspect under the powers of s 24(5) of PACE 1984. The suspect resisted the arrest and assaulted both his arrestors. He was, subsequently, charged with theft of the chocolate and with offences of assault with intent to resist lawful apprehension or detainer, contrary to s 38 of the Offences Against the Person Act 1861. At his trial, he was acquitted of theft (apparently, for lack of *mens rea*), but convicted of the assaults. These convictions were quashed by the Court of Appeal on the grounds that, as the arrest had not been lawful he was entitled to resist it. The power of arrest conferred upon a citizen (s 24(5)) in circumstances where an offence is thought to *have been committed*, only applies when an offence *has* been committed, and, as the jury decided that Mr Self had not committed any offence, there was no power to arrest him.

We know that Dozy has been acquitted of any crime, so, it looks as if any arrest made by Peter (*de facto* and, therefore, in law) would be invalidated by virtue of s 24(5) of PACE 1984, which provides that the offence must have 'been committed'. However, despite Dozy's acquittal, it might be possible to contend that a crime had still 'been committed'. Such a contention was not possible in *Walters v WH Smith* because there Mr Walters had denied the *mens rea* of the offence of theft, a vital ingredient of the crime, and the jury had accepted this version, thus, denying that a crime had taken place. In different circumstances, perhaps, than those in the question, it might be that the defendant in any criminal proceedings (Dozy) was acquitted by way of a successful 'excusatory defence', for example, insanity, which would not deny that a crime had occurred, simply that the defendant could not be legally responsible. In such circumstances, the arrest would be lawful, as a crime would have 'been committed'.

A question would then arise as to the period of detention for over an hour. In *John Lewis & Co v Tims* (1952), Mrs Tims and her daughter were arrested by store detectives for shoplifting four calendars from the appellant's Oxford Street store. It was a regulation of the store that only a managing director or a general manager was authorised to institute any prosecution. After being arrested, Mrs Tims and her daughter were taken to the office of the chief store detective. They were detained there until a chief detective and a manager arrived to give instructions whether to prosecute. They were, eventually, handed over to police custody within an hour of arrest. In a claim by Mrs Tims for false imprisonment, she alleged that the detectives were obliged to give her into the custody of the police immediately upon arrest. The House of Lords held that the delay was reasonable in the circumstances, as there were advantages in refusing to give private detectives a 'free hand' and leaving the determination of such an important question as whether to prosecute to a superior official.

Dozy's case may be distinguishable (although, the distinction is not a compelling one) as here, the reason for the delay is concerned with the comfort the manager will enjoy by not interrupting his lunch, rather than any matter of company business. The evidence in the *John Lewis* case was that the manager came without any delay and listened to the evidence; any delay (which was evidentially in doubt) occurred while the accounts of the store detectives were being given in the presence of the suspects.

It is true that Dozy has not suffered any real damage to his person but, as Lord Porter observed in the *John Lewis* case, when 'the liberty of the subject is at stake, questions of the damage sustained become of little importance'.

Question 32

On the one hand, English law rightly presumes that everyone is innocent until proven guilty, so it would be wrong to keep anyone in custody (normally a punishment) unless they have been convicted. On the other hand, some of those charged with serious crimes are likely to try to abscond or interfere with witnesses or evidence unless they are kept secure until trial. Framing rules to govern this conflict is a question of balance.

In the light of recent changes to the principles of bail in the English legal system, discuss whether current law has the balance right.

Answer plan

Answers should incorporate:
- discussion of the background to key legal changes in 1993–94;
- explanation of the current legal framework;
- s 27 of the CJPOA 1994 – extension of police powers in relation to bail;
- the Bail Act 1976 and the presumption of bail;
- s 25 of the CJPOA 1994 and the denial of bail where there has been earlier conviction for murder, etc;
- appeals and repeated applications;
- the Bail (Amendment) Act 1993;
- conclusions.

Answer

Over recent years, the Government took the view that bail was too easily granted and that too many crimes were being committed by those on bail who deserved to be in custody while awaiting trial. The Bail (Amendment) Act 1993, and the CJPOA 1994 (ss 25–30) emanate from that philosophy, their aim being to restrict the granting of bail. A case which caught public sympathy for this view involved a young man who had many convictions for car crime and joyriding. Whilst on bail, he was joyriding in a vehicle when he smashed into a schoolgirl. She clung to the bonnet but he shook her off and, thus, killed her. The Home Secretary commented publicly that the new legislative measures would prevent such terrible events.

Each year (prior to the 1976 Acts), about 50,000 offences are committed by people on bail. A study by the Metropolitan police in 1988 indicated that 16% of those charged by that force were already on bail for another offence. Another study in 1993, from the same force, showed that of 537 suspects arrested in one week during a clamp down on burglary, 40% were on bail. Some had been bailed 10 or 15 times during the preceding year.

Before examining how recent legislation changes the law, it is appropriate to set out the general principles of bail. In the criminal process, the first stage at which bail is raised as an issue is at the police station. If a person is arrested on a warrant, this will indicate whether he is to be held in custody or released on bail. If the suspect is arrested without a warrant, then the police will have to decide whether to release the suspect after he has been charged. After a person has been charged, s 38(1)(a) of PACE 1984 states that a person must be released unless: (a) his name and address are not known; or (b) the custody officer, reasonably, thinks that his detention is necessary for his own protection, or to prevent him from injuring someone or damaging property; or (c) because he might abscond or interfere with the course of justice. Most arrested people are bailed by the police. In 1990, 83% of those arrested in connection with indictable offences and 88% of those arrested for summary offences (other than motoring offences) were released. This area has been amended by s 28 of the 1994 Act. A custody officer can now, in the case of an imprisonable offence, refuse to release an arrested person after charge if the officer has reasonable grounds for believing that the detention of that person is necessary to prevent him from committing *any* offence. Previously, many cases were caught by (b) (above), and the police officer was able to keep a dangerous person in custody, but some sorts of conduct that the arrested person was likely to go out and commit (for example, drink driving) were not the sort of thing that the police were entitled to use to refuse bail.

Section 27 of the 1994 Act amends ss 38 and 47 of PACE 1984, so as to allow the police to grant conditional bail to persons charged. The conditions can be whatever is required to ensure that the person surrenders to custody, does not commit an offence while on bail, or does not interfere with witnesses or otherwise obstruct the course of justice. The new powers of the custody officer, however, do not include a power to impose a requirement to reside in a bail hostel. By amending Pt IV of PACE 1984, s 29 of the 1994 Act gives the police power to arrest without warrant a person who, having been granted conditional police bail, has failed to attend at a police station at the appointed time.

The Bail Act 1976 created a statutory presumption of bail. It states (s 4) that, subject to Sched 1 and amendments made by s 25 of the 1994 Act about murder, manslaughter, etc (see below), bail shall be granted to a person accused of an offence in a magistrates' court or a crown court and to convicted people who are being remanded for reports to be made. The court must, therefore, grant bail (unless one of the exceptions apply), even if the defendant does not make an application. Schedule 1 provides that a court need not grant bail to a person charged with an offence punishable with imprisonment, if it is satisfied that there are substantial grounds for believing that, if released on bail, the defendant would: (a) fail to surrender to custody; (b) commit an offence while on bail; or (c) interfere with witnesses, or otherwise obstruct the course of justice. The court can also refuse bail if it believes that the defendant ought to stay in custody for his or her own protection, or if it has not been practicable 'for want of time to obtain sufficient information to enable the court to make its decision on bail'.

When the court is considering the grounds stated above, all relevant factors must be taken into account, including the nature and seriousness of the offence, the character, antecedents, associations and community ties of the defendant and his record for satisfying his obligations under previous grants of bail.

If the defendant is charged with an offence not punishable with imprisonment, Sched 1 provides that bail can only be withheld if he has previously failed to surrender on bail and if the court believes that, in view of that failure, he would fail again to surrender if released on bail.

Section 25 of the CJPOA 1994 provides that, in some circumstances, a person who has been charged with or convicted of murder, attempted murder, manslaughter, rape or attempted rape must not be granted bail. The circumstances are simply that the conviction must have been within the UK and that, in the case of a manslaughter conviction, it must have been dealt with by way of a custodial sentence. The term 'conviction' is given a wide meaning and includes anyone found 'not guilty by way of insanity'.

There has been debate about whether the changes wrought by s 25 are justifiable. A Home Office minister, defending the section, stated that it would be worth the risk if it prevented just one murder or rape, even though there might be a few 'hard cases', that is, people eventually acquitted of crime who were remanded in custody pending trial. As Card and Ward have remarked in a commentary on the Act (*Criminal Justice and Public Order Act 1994*), the Government, when pushed, was unable to cite a single case where a person released on bail in the circumstances covered by s 25 re-offended in a similar way. There is no time limit on the previous conviction and there is no requirement of any connection between the previous offence and the one in question. Card and Ward suggest that there is a world of difference between a person who was convicted of manslaughter 30 years ago on the grounds of complicity in a suicide pact and who is now charged with attempted rape (of which he must be presumed innocent), and the person who was convicted of rape eight years ago and now faces another rape charge. The first person is not an obvious risk to society and it is, they argue, regrettable that bail will be denied to him. There is, also, argument to be had with the contents of the s 25 list. Why should some clearly dangerous and prevalent crimes like robbery be omitted from it? In any case, it may have been better had the offences in the list raised a strong presumption against bail as opposed to an absolute ban, as the former could be rebutted in cases where there was, on the facts, no risk.

Bail can be granted as conditional or unconditional. Where it is unconditional the accused must simply surrender to the court at the appointed date. Failure to appear without reasonable cause is an offence under s 6 of the Bail Act 1976 and can result, if tried in a crown court, in a sentence of up to 12 months' imprisonment or a fine. Conditions can be attached to the granting of bail where the court thinks that it is necessary to ensure that the accused surrenders at the right time, does not interfere with witnesses, or commit further offences. There is no statutory limit to the conditions the court may impose and the most common include requirements that the accused reports daily or weekly to a police station, resides at a particular address, surrenders his passport or does not go to particular places or associate with particular people.

Section 7 of the 1976 Bail Act gives the police power to arrest anyone on conditional bail whom they reasonably suspect is likely to break the conditions, or that he has already done so. Anyone arrested in these circumstances must be brought before a magistrate within 24 hours. The magistrate may then reconsider the question of bail.

Personal recognisances, by which the suspect agreed to pay a sum if he failed to surrender to the court, were abolished by the 1976 Act, except in cases where it is believed that he might try to flee abroad. The Act did retain the court's right to ask for sureties as a condition of bail. By putting sureties in a position where they can have large sums of money 'estreated', if the suspect does not surrender to the court, a significant pressure (not using the resources of the criminal justice system) is put on the accused. The proportion of those who do not answer to bail is very small – consistently about 4% of those given bail. Section 9 of the Act strengthens the surety principle by making it a criminal offence to agree to indemnify a surety. This sort of thing could happen, for example, if the accused agreed to reimburse the surety in the event that the accused skipped bail and the surety was requested to pay.

The rules which govern how someone who has been refused bail might re-apply and appeal have also been framed with a view to balancing the interests of the accused with those of the public and justice. The original refusal should not be absolute and final but, on the other hand, it is seen as necessary that the refusals are not reversed too easily.

If the court decides not to grant the defendant bail, then s 154 provides that it is the court's duty to consider whether the defendant ought to be granted bail at each subsequent hearing. At the first hearing after the one at which bail was first refused, he may support an application for bail with any arguments, but at subsequent hearings the court need not hear arguments as to fact or law which it has heard before. The Criminal Justice Act 1982 enables a court to remand an accused in his or her absence for up to three successive one week remand hearings, provided that he consents and is legally represented. Such repeated visits are costly to the State and can be unsettling for the accused, especially if he has to spend most of the day in a police cell only to be told the case has been adjourned again without bail. If someone does not consent, they are prevented from applying for bail on each successive visit if the only supporting arguments are those that have been heard by the court before (*Nottingham JJ ex p Davies* (1981)).

To avoid unproductive hearings, that is, to promote courts being able to adjourn a case for a period within which reasonable progress can be made on a case, s 155 of the Criminal Justice Act 1988 allows for adjournments for up to 28 days provided the court sets the date for when the next stage of the proceedings should take place. What began as an experiment under this section has now, by statutory order (SI 1991/2667), been extended to all courts.

The interests of the accused are also served by the variety of appeals he may make if bail has been refused. If bail has been refused by magistrates, then, in limited circumstances, an application may be made to another bench of magistrates. Applications for reconsideration can also be made to a judge in chambers (through a legal representative), or to the Official Solicitor (in writing). Appeal can also be made to a Crown Court in respect of bail for both pre-committal remands and where a defendant has been committed for trial or sentence at the Crown Court.

Section 3 of the Bail Act 1976 allows for an application to vary the conditions of court bail to be made by the person bailed, or the prosecutor or a police officer. Application may also be made for the imposition of conditions on unconditional court bail. As amended by the CJPOA 1994, s 3 of the Bail Act 1976 now allows for the same thing in relation to police bail, although the new provisions do not allow the prosecutor to seek reconsideration of the decision to grant bail itself. Under the Bail (Amendment) Act 1993, however, the prosecution does now have a right to appeal against the grant of bail by a court. This right applies to offences which carry a maximum sentence of imprisonment of five years, or more, and to offences of taking a vehicle without consent (joyriding). When this right of appeal is exercised, the defendant will remain in custody until the appeal is heard by a Crown Court judge who will decide whether to grant bail or remand the defendant in custody within 48 hours of the magistrate's decision. Parliament was concerned that this power could be abused and has stated that it should be reserved 'for cases of greatest concern, when there is a serious risk of harm to the public' or where there are 'other significant public interest grounds' for an appeal.

Although this area of law was subject to a comprehensive revision after a Home Office special working party reported in 1974, and has been legislatively debated and modified four times since the 1976 Act, it is still a matter of serious concern, both by those civil libertarians who consider the law too tilted against the accused, and by the police and some commentators who believe criticism of the law from both sides to the debate might indicate a desirable state of balance reached by the current regulatory framework.

It is still worrying that, for example, in 1990, of those dealt with summarily after being remanded in custody, 50% received non-custodial sentences and a further 25% were acquitted. There are wide variations in the local policies of different courts; one study has shown, for instance, that the number of indictable custodial remands per 1,000 indictable proceedings was 111 in Brighton, as against 313 in Bournemouth. The last decade has seen a disturbing rise in the remand prison population. In 1980, it accounted for 15% of the average prison population. By 1990, it had risen to over 10,000 prisoners, 22% of the average prison population. Conversely, there are arguments which point to the numbers of people who commit offences whilst out on bail. Whether the level of such crime drops significantly as a result of the new legislation remains to be seen.

Question 33

What difficulties are involved in designing rules to govern plea bargaining and how successful is the English system in this respect?

Answer plan

Any answer on this theme should take account of the research findings presented to the Royal Commission on Criminal Justice and the recommendations made by the Commission:

- definition of terms;
- explanation of the guidelines in *Turner* (1970);
- difficulties in applying the *Practice Direction (Turner Rules)* (1976);
- discussion of the points in *Pitman* (1991);
- whether the Court of Appeal can attract proper guilty pleas whilst not engaging in injudicious disclosure of possible sentence;
- Runciman Commission recommendations;
- conclusion.

Answer

'Plea bargaining' has been defined as 'the practice whereby the accused enters a plea of guilty in return for which he will be given some consideration that results in a sentence concession' (Baldwin and McConville, *Negotiated Justice*, 1977). In practice, this can refer to a situation either where there has been a plea arrangement for the accused to plead guilty to a lesser charge than the one with which he is charged (charge bargaining), or where there is simply a sentencing discount available on a plea of guilty by the accused (sentence bargaining).

For a guilty defendant and for the prosecution, such a negotiated settlement represents a mutually valuable compromise because the prosecution has gained a guilty plea and the defendant a sentence concession. Additionally, there will have been a significant saving to the State in the cost of a trial. Such bargains, however, are fraught with legal difficulties, chiefly because they can be construed as circumstances where undue pressure has been put on the accused to plead guilty. Many convictions have been quashed for just such a reason.

Research conducted by Professor Zander for the Royal Commission on Criminal Justice (Runciman Report, Cm 2263, 1993) found that, in a study of 900 Crown Court cases, 90% of barristers and two thirds of judges were in favour of formalising plea bargaining based on sentence discounts. The study suggests that 11% of those who pleaded guilty, in fact, maintained their innocence but wanted to secure a reduction in sentence.

A plea of guilty by the accused must be made freely. He must only be advised to plead guilty if he has committed the crime in question. In *Turner* (1970), Lord Parker CJ set out guidelines on plea bargaining. He stated that:

(a) it may sometimes be the duty of counsel to give strong advice to the accused that a plea of guilty with remorse is a mitigating factor which might enable the court to give a lesser sentence;

(b) the accused must, ultimately, make up his own mind as to how to plead;

(c) there should be open access to the trial judge and counsel for both sides should attend each meeting, preferably in open court; and

(d) the judge should never indicate the sentence which he is minded to impose, nor should he ever indicate that on a plea of guilty he would impose one sentence, but that on a conviction following a plea of not guilty he would impose a more severe sentence. The judge could say what sentence he would impose on a plea of guilty (where, for example, he has read the depositions and antecedents), but without mentioning what he would do if the accused were convicted after pleading not guilty. Even this would be wrong, however, since the accused might take the judge to be intimating that a more severe sentence would follow upon conviction after guilty plea. The only exception to this rule is where a judge says that the sentence will take a particular form, following conviction, whether there has been a plea of guilty or not guilty.

These guidelines were subsequently embodied in the Court of Appeal's *Practice Direction (Turner Rules)* (1976). A number of difficulties have been experienced in applying these principles. Perhaps the greatest problem has resulted from the fact that, although the principles state (d) that a judge should never say that a sentence passed after a conviction would be more severe than one passed after a guilty plea, it is a generally known rule that guilty pleas lead to lesser sentences. In *Cain* (1976), it was stressed that, in general, defendants should realise that guilty pleas attract lesser sentences. Lord Widgery said: 'Any accused person who does not know about it should know about it.' The difficulty is that the trial judge must not mention it, otherwise he could be construed as exerting pressure on the accused to plead guilty.

In *Turner*, the defendant pleaded not guilty on a charge of theft. He had previous convictions and, during an adjournment, he was advised by counsel in strong terms to change his plea; after having spoken with the judge, which the defendant knew, counsel advised that in his opinion a plea of guilty would result in a non-custodial sentence, whereas, if he persisted with a not guilty plea and, thereby, attacked police witnesses, there was a real possibility of receiving a custodial sentence. The defendant changed his plea to not guilty and then appealed, on the ground that he did not have a free choice in changing his plea. His appeal was allowed on the basis that he might have formed the impression that the views being expressed to him by his counsel were those of the judge, particularly, as it was known by the accused that counsel had just returned from seeing the judge when he gave his advice to the accused.

The advantages for the prosecution in gaining a guilty plea are obvious but, as the *Code for Crown Prosecutors* notes, administrative convenience in the form of a rapid guilty plea should not take precedence over the interests of justice. Justice demands that the court should be able to pass a proper sentence, consistent with the gravity of the accused's actions and, if a plea is accepted, then the defendant can only be sentenced on the basis of the crime that he has admitted. It is noteworthy that the judge is not bound to accept a plea arrangement made between the sides. The Farquharson Committee on the Role of Prosecuting Counsel thought that there is a general right for the prosecution to offer no evidence in respect of any particular charge, but that, where the judge's opinion is sought on whether it is desirable to reassure the public at large that the right course is being taken, counsel must abide by the judge's decision. Where the judge thinks that counsel's view to proceed is wrong, the trial can be halted until the Director of Public Prosecutions (DPP) has been consulted and given the judge's comments. In the notorious case of *Sutcliffe* (1981) (the 'Yorkshire Ripper' case), the prosecution and defence had agreed that Sutcliffe would plead guilty to manslaughter on the grounds of diminished responsibility, but the trial judge rejected that agreement and, after consultations with the DPP, Sutcliffe was eventually found guilty of murder.

The extent of the difficulties in framing rules on plea bargaining which achieve clarity and fairness can be judged by the remark of Lord Lane CJ in the case of *Pitman* (1991):

> There seems to be a steady flow of appeals to this court arising from visits by counsel to the judge in his private room. No amount of criticism and no amount of warnings and no amount of exhortation seems to be able to prevent this from happening.

In this case, on counsel's advice, the appellant pleaded not guilty to causing death by reckless driving. On cup final day in 1989, he had driven, having been drinking all afternoon, in a car without a rear view mirror. He had crashed into another car, killing one of its passengers, whilst having double the permitted level of alcohol in his blood.

During the trial, the judge called both counsel to his room and stated that he did not think there was a defence to the charge. Counsel for the appellant explained that, although the appellant had admitted that his carelessness caused the accident, the advice to plead not guilty was based on the fact that the prosecution might not be able to prove the necessary recklessness. The trial judge replied that the appellant's plea was a matter for the appellant himself and not counsel and that, if the appellant accepted responsibility for the accident, he ought to plead guilty and if he did so he would receive 'substantial credit' when it came to sentencing.

Counsel for the appellant then discussed this with the appellant who changed his plea to guilty and was sentenced to nine months' imprisonment and was disqualified for four years. His appeal was allowed as the judge had put undue pressure on the appellant and his counsel to change his plea to guilty and his remarks had suggested that his chances of acquittal were slight if he pleaded not guilty and that, if he was found guilty, having pleaded not guilty, he would certainly be sentenced to imprisonment. Lord Lane CJ emphasised that a judge should not initiate discussions in private and that where, at the behest of counsel, they are absolutely necessary, they should be recorded by shorthand or on a recording device.

Another problem here concerns framing the guidelines so that they are sufficiently permissive to allow counsel access to the judge in his private room in cases in deserving instances but avoiding the problems of confidentiality. As Mustill LJ said in *Harper-Taylor and Bakker* (1988):

> The need to solve an immediate practical problem may combine with the more relaxed atmosphere of the private room to blur the formal outlines of the trial.

There is a risk that counsel and solicitors may hear something said to the judge which they would rather not hear, putting them into a state of conflict between their duties to their clients and their obligations to maintain the confidentiality of the private room. Reviewing the current state of the law, Curran has written that the effect of cases like *Bird* (1977) and *Agar* (1990) (the latter not a plea bargaining case but one which hinged on a judge's ruling in his private room as complied with by counsel to the appellant's detriment) is that defence counsel has a duty to disclose to his client any observations made by the judge in his room which significantly affect the client's case, whether or not the judge expresses them to be made confidentially (see [1991] Crim LR 79).

The difficulties in this area of law stem, largely, not from deficient rules but, rather from the wish that the rules should achieve diverse aims. As Zander has observed, the fundamental problem is that the Court of Appeal wants to have it both ways:

> On the one hand it wants defendants to appreciate that if they plead guilty they will receive a lesser sentence. On the other hand, it does not want judges to provide defendants with solid information as to how great the discount will be [*Cases and Materials on the English Legal System*, 7th edn, 1996].

The Royal Commission on Criminal Justice, chaired by Viscount Runciman, reported in July 1993. It recommended (pp 156–59) a clearly articulated system of sentence discounts, with earlier pleas attracting higher discounts. Lord Runciman pointed out that this was not 'plea bargaining' in the American sense, in which the prosecution can suggest the appropriate sentence. The proposal was supported by law enforcement officers, like the DPP, who regard it as a way to tackle 'cracked trials': those which abort at the last minute through a change of plea to guilty. In 1994, 83% of defendants who elected for trial at the Crown Court changed their plea to guilty. The proposal was, however, opposed by groups like Liberty and Justice who believe that these changes might pressurise innocent people, intimidated by the system, into a guilty plea. It can be seen as subtly undermining the presumption of innocence and the requirement that the prosecution proves its case.

Sanders and Young (*Criminal Justice*, 1994) have argued that it is artificial and unrealistic for the law to encourage guilty pleas through the sentence discount, whilst, simultaneously, denying the defence the opportunity to discover exactly what, if anything, is on offer from the judge in a particular case. They contend that, in practice, both defence counsel and judges have abused their right to meet in private and have, despite the Court of Appeal's guidance, engaged in sentence bargaining on a wide scale.

The Court of Appeal has consistently indicated that the information should not be given to defendants because that might put undue pressure on them to plead guilty, but sentence discounts are legally recognised (see Thomas, DA, in *Current Sentencing Practice*, para A8 2(b)), a guilty plea attracts a lighter sentence, the extent of the reduction is usually between one quarter and one-third of what would have otherwise been the sentence. Moreover, Lord Widgery has stated (above) that defendants should know about them. The pressure could scarcely be increased by informing a defendant with details rather than leave it to his or her general knowledge. If anything, Zander has argued, it would diminish the pressure by making it clear that the defendant's fears about the penalty for pleading not guilty are exaggerated.

There is, though, reason for anxiety with such a call for more openness. Sanders and Young regard it as 'an idealistic notion' that one can improve the effectiveness of the system in convicting the guilty without also increasing its effectiveness in convicting the innocent (*Criminal Justice*, 1994). In one Home Office study (1992), Hedderman and Moxon found that 65% of those pleading guilty in Crown Court cases said that their decision had been influenced by the prospect of receiving a discount in sentence. Even the Royal Commission recognised that not all those pleading guilty are, in fact, guilty; some may have just capitulated to the pressure of taking the reduced sentence, rather than run the risk of the full sentence. As Sanders and Young contend, this issue goes to the heart of constitutional principles. Only if the State acts properly in collecting and presenting evidence can punishment be justified, according to commonly accepted principles. Even the guilty are entitled to due process of law. A system of plea bargaining may undermine such principles since it allows the State to secure convictions based on unproven allegations.

Question 34

Critically evaluate the approach to custodial sentencing in the criminal justice system. What role does public opinion play in this area?

Answer plan

You should:
- set the social, legal and political context;
- introduce the sentencing procedure;
- provide the context for a discussion on prisons;
- explain the relevance of public opinion;
- articulate what judges are supposed to do when sentencing;
- refer to Lord Bingham CJ's 1997 speech;
- refer to the Crime and Disorder Act 1998 and sentencing provisions;
- conclude on the need for a Royal Commission and the future.

Answer

With crime and punishment rapidly rising on the pre-election political agenda, Lord Woolf, the Lord Chief Justice, takes a cautious attitude to the use of custody. In December, 2000, he urged politicians not to play the 'prison card' and to introduce policies that would result in fewer custodial sentences. He said: 'Politicians don't approve of playing what is called the race card. I wish they took the same view with regard to the prison card.'

It was revealed in January 2001 that the number of children being remanded into prison custody has more than doubled in the last 10 years. It is, therefore, critically important to ask the question: is prison working?

One cardinal purpose of the prison service today was first articulated in the Prison Rules of 1949. It states that the purpose of prison is 'to encourage and assist the inmate to lead a good and useful life'. There are several ways, however, in which the custodial system can be seen as failing to meet its objectives. The prison population now stands at around 66,000 with 11,500 prisoners under the age of 21 – this makes the prison population, as a proportion of the general population, one of the highest in Western Europe. It costs an average of £25,792 to keep someone in prison for a year, but 57% of all persons released in 1996 were reconvicted of an offence within two years.

When one looks at the figures for young male offenders, the reconviction rate (within two years of a young person being released) rises to 76%. During the period 1990–99, 606 people committed suicide in British prisons.

If the dramatic rise in the prison population during the last 50 years was associated with a significant reduction in crime, then, naturally, there would be a reasonably convincing case for the unhesitating use of imprisonment as a crime reduction policy. But, cramming more offenders into prison cannot be seen to reduce crime. Despite an inexorably rising prison population during the last 50 years, crime has grown exponentially. In fact, whereas throughout the 1950s the number of recorded offences in England and Wales hovered around the 200,000 mark, the scale of crime had increased tenfold by the 1980s, with annual recordings coming in, as they still are, at around five million offences.

Oddly, in the face of all the evidence, the courts seem increasingly disposed to sentence people to custody, even though the evidence suggests that it will, in most cases, neither make them into law-abiding citizens nor chasten any significant number of others into not committing crime. In 1997, 25% of adults convicted of indictable offences were sentenced to immediate custody compared to only 16% in 1992.

Contrary to a popular myth, British prisons are not packed to the rafters with people who have been sentenced for violent or sexual offences. Home Office data reveals that about 70% of people sentenced to immediate custody in 1997 had committed non-violent offences. In fact, this sort of profile has been the case for a long time – a prison census of 1776 found that 59.7 per cent of the prison population was made up of debtors. Clearly, society does not require a massive punitive infrastructure in order to restrain the relatively small number of clinically violent and sexually delinquent offenders detected each year.

Following conviction, the magistrate or judge will decide upon the most appropriate sentence for an offender. In making this decision, account will be taken of the facts of the case (for example, in theft, stealing a milk bottle will attract a different sentence from stealing the wages van at the dairy) and the circumstances of the offender. In 1997, 1.5 m offenders were sentenced for all offences. In the magistrates' courts, four out of 10 people sentenced for an indictable offence were given a fine, two were given a conditional or absolute discharge, two were given a community sentence and two were sentenced to immediate custody.

There is, though, considerable evidence that the system does not work in the way it is supposed to. Contrary to popular belief, for example, most inmates are not violent criminals. In fact, over 80% of prisoners entering prison are doing so for property offences. Apart from this, many people enter prison as a result of not paying a fine: in 1997, over 20,000 people were imprisoned for such an offence.

Following the opinion columns of certain (mostly tabloid) newspapers, there has been a growth in public opinion favouring more severe sentencing for criminals. This has taken place during an era when recorded crime has doubled since 1980 and the agencies of the criminal justice system have been publicly regarded as progressively unable to cope with the problem of rising crime. How far, if at all, should judges respond to public opinion when sentencing criminals? This question raises important issues concerning the role of the judiciary.

In a very significant speech in 1997, Lord Bingham, the former Lord Chief Justice, gave an authoritative articulation of the principles that should be used by judges when giving sentences to convicted offenders. As the most senior judge in the criminal justice system, the Lord Chief Justice can exert influence over sentencing policy.

Lord Bingham identified an unusual problem, what he called 'the extraordinary paradox' that judges and magistrates have been roundly criticised for overlenient sentencing during a period when they have been sending more defendants to prison for longer periods than at any time in the last 40 years. The increase in the prison population is not explained by any recent increase in sentencing powers. Lord Bingham stated that he had no doubt that it is related to 'the pressure of public opinion'.

Lord Bingham said this was not necessarily wrong, because judges should be alive to the views of their fellow citizens. Nevertheless, he argued, it was only a few years ago since the judiciary was being criticised for being too severe in its sentencing, so it should take care not to 'be blown hither and thither by every wind of political or penal fashion'. Going into more detail, he said that, in determining the sentence in any given case, the judge should 'close his or her ears to public and media clamour concerning the case'. He said it would, for example, be 'an abdication of the rule of law' for a judge to take into account a newspaper campaign designed to encourage him to increase a particular sentence. This confirms a House of Lords' decision (*Thompson and Venables* (1997)) which ruled that it was wrong for a Home Secretary to take into account a public campaign organised by a popular newspaper (including a mass petition) to recommend a high sentence tariff in respect of two children who had killed a toddler.

Lord Bingham stated that, in addition to the three traditional purposes of sentencing (retribution, deterrence, and rehabilitation), there should now be recognised two others:

incapacitation (putting it out of the power of the offender to commit further offences) and the maintenance of public confidence.

In an interesting interpretation of these principles, the former Lord Chief Justice said that the different types of sentence served the various purposes of sentencing in different measure and that a sentence of imprisonment was 'very largely retributive' and not usually passed with a view to rehabilitating the offender.

A trial judge is currently supposed to decide upon an appropriate sentence in the following stages:

(a) the judge should note the nature and circumstances of the crime, and the precise crime for which the defendant falls to be sentenced. It is the wrongness of the defendant's act or omission which is critical, rather than how dire were the consequences of such behaviour. Sometimes, a bad but not heinous mistake could lead to death (as in a traffic accident involving neither drunkenness nor excessive speed or recklessness), but it is not the judge's function to simply equate the loss of life with a certain number of years or months in prison;

(b) the judge should consider the personal circumstances of the offender. Prompt guilty pleas and previous good character are relevant in mitigation of sentence. Nevertheless, the character of the offence always has to be kept in mind. In minor offences like shoplifting, there would come a point at which a repeat offender's sentence should not be increased any more because it would then become disproportionate to the gravity of the offence;

(c) the effect of the crime on the victim should be considered. Contrary to common misconception, it has always been the custom of prosecution counsel to tell the court of the effects of the crime on the victim, but it would be contrary to the interests of justice to accord the victim any significant say in determining the appropriate level of sentence: the passing of sentence must be governed by reason and guided by precedent, not coloured by emotion or by a desire for revenge;

(d) the sentencer must always have regard to the wider public interest in order to maintain public confidence. If informed public opinion perceived that sentences failed to match the gravity of crimes, then the public may be tempted to take justice into its own hands and resort to private vengeance.

New measures to improve the consistency of sentencing by the courts are contained in the Crime and Disorder Act 1998. Under the provisions, the Court of Appeal will be producing sentencing guidelines when appropriate cases come before them. They will also review existing guidelines. Detailed guidance already exists in relation to some offences and the intention now is to build and improve upon them.

In drawing up the guidelines, the Court of Appeal will be required to consider:

(a) the need to ensure greater consistency;
(b) the cost and effectiveness of different sentences;
(c) the need to promote public confidence in the criminal justice system;
(d) the weight that should be given to previous convictions.

A sentencing advisory panel has been established by the Lord Chancellor to provide advice to the Court of Appeal. The panel will consult with representatives of the police, the probation service and victims.

The Home Secretary has the power to refer particular offences to the panel for examination. When the panel receives a referral, it must then provide advice to the Court of Appeal, who will consider producing sentencing guidelines when a suitable case arises.

These new measures will help to produce greater public confidence in judicial sentencing, but it is, arguably, high time that we had established a Royal Commission on Crime and Punishment. As the annual cost of crime in the UK is in the region of £20 bn, the Government might be persuaded to spend some resources on researching this issue.

Prison is a relatively recent penal institution having not existed for more than three quarters of the last millennium. Until the 18th century, prisons, dungeons and gaols were owned by municipal and private bodies and were used to hold debtors or people awaiting trial at quarterly sittings of the criminal court. Serious offences were punished by execution or transportation, and lesser offences were dealt with by the stocks (reportedly favoured as ripe for revival by William Hague), floggings or fines. It was not until the beginning of the 19th century that prisons were seen as places which could be used to reform criminals and make them penitent. The birth of the penitentiary was part of a wider young family of institutions – with the sibling asylums, orphanages, workhouses and hospitals – which were seen as being able to deal with the large scale social problems being thrown up by the development of modern capitalism.

Will prisons be a feature of the social landscape in 200 years? In 1993, the Home Secretary, Michael Howard, said resolutely that 'prison works'. Since then the prison population has grown from 44,000 to 66,000, but the annual crime figure has moved from 5.2 m offences to 5.3 m. More people imprisoned does not mean Britain is safer. Worryingly, the apparently extravagant and ineffective policy looks set to expand. According to the latest long term projections of the prison population published by the Home Office, UK prisons will house between 70,000 and 80,000 prisoners by 2007.

CHAPTER 6

CIVIL PROCESS AND
LEGAL SERVICES

Since 1999, the civil process and the provision of legal services have undergone major change. The new Civil Procedure Rules (CPR), the most fundamental changes in civil process for over a century, have radically altered the operation of civil justice. Part of the rationale of the new rules was to expedite the way cases were dealt with and to allow more cases to be settled early, through negotiation between the parties or alternative dispute resolution (ADR). In this respect there is some evidence of success.

The overriding objective of the CPR is to enable the court to deal justly with cases. The first rule reads:

1.1(1) These rules are a new procedural code with the overriding objective of enabling the court to deal with cases justly.

This objective will include ensuring that the parties are on an equal footing and saving expense. When exercising any discretion given by the CPR, the court must, according to r 1.2, have regard to the overriding objective and a checklist of factors, including the amount of money involved, the complexity of the issue, the parties' financial positions, how the case can be dealt with expeditiously and by allotting an appropriate share of the court's resources, while taking into account the needs of others. In future, as Judge John Frenkel observes ('On the road to reform' (1998)): 'The decisions of the Court of Appeal are more likely to illustrate the application of the new rules to the facts of a particular case, as opposed to being interpretative authorities that define the meaning of the rules.'

Another area of change concerns Conditional Fee Arrangements (CFAs). In the first version of CFAs, only people who expected to win money from their case could benefit from conditional fees. This was the only way that most people could afford to pay the success fee. But, it meant that a successful litigant would not receive all the money he or she had been awarded. So in 2000, the Government took the power, in the Access to Justice Act 1999, to make it possible for the winning party to recover the success fee and any insurance premium, from the losing party. This will ensure that it is the person or organisation that has committed the legal wrong who pays, and it will allow defendants and claimants (other than in family law cases), whose case is not about money, to use CFAs.

Legal services have also undergone very significant change in recent times. Expanded rights of advocacy for solicitors and others (including patent agents) have changed the traditional picture of the courts as the domain of barristers. The introduction of the Legal Services Commission (LSC) and the Community Legal Service (CLS) marks a sea-change in the delivery of publicly funded law and the impending change, to a public defender system, carries the potential for far-reaching implications for both the legal system and for the public, as consumers of its services.

You should be familiar with:

- the main provisions of the 1996 Woolf Report on Civil Justice;
- the purpose and main provisions of the new CPR;
- the arguments both for and against the proposition that the reforms can, and have, worked well in practice;
- the main provisions of the Access to Justice Act 1999;
- the role and purpose of the LSC and the CLS;
- CFAs;
- the nature and purpose of the proposed Salaried Defence Service and critical commentary on this system;
- recent changes concerning rights of audience and legal liability of the legal professions.

Question 35

Describe the defects that were seen as blighting the old civil justice process, and explain how the strategic changes of the Woolf reforms seek to improve the system.

Answer plan

- Background and defects in the old system.
- Cost, delay and complexity of the old system.
- The Civil Procedure Act 1997 and the new CPR.
- Active case management.
- Pre-action protocols.
- Alternative dispute resolution.

Answer

The CPR 1998 came into force in April 1999. Since then, to April 2001, they have undergone much adaptation (21 updates). They are part of a strategy formulated by Lord Woolf to radically overhaul the operation of the civil justice system.

A survey by the National Consumer Council, in 1995, found that three out of four people in serious legal disputes were dissatisfied with the civil justice system (*Seeking Civil Justice: A survey of people's needs and experiences*, 1995, NCC). Of the 1,019 respondents, 77% claimed the system was too slow, 74% said it was too complicated, and 73% said that it was unwelcoming and outdated.

According to the Civil Justice Review (CJR) 1988, delay in litigation 'causes continuing personal stress, anxiety and financial hardship to ordinary people and their families. It may induce economically weaker parties to accept unfair settlements. It also frustrates the efficient conduct of commerce and industry.' Despite some of the innovations in the five years following that CJR, the problems continued. In 1994, the Lord Chancellor set up the Woolf Inquiry to look at ways of improving the speed and accessibility of civil proceedings, and of reducing their cost.

Defects in the system were also identified by the The Heilbron Hodge Report, *Civil Justice on Trial: The Case for Change* (1993). The Report resulted from an independent working party set up in 1992 by the Bar Council and The Law Society. The 39 member working party was chaired by Hilary Heilbron QC; its vice chair was solicitor Henry Hodge OBE. The Report called for a 'radical reappraisal of the approach to litigation from all its participants'. The Report painted a depressing picture of the civil justice system, where delays are endemic and often contrived and procedures are inflexible, rule-ridden and often incomprehensible to the client. It noted that, incongruously for a multimillion pound operation, technology scarcely featured. All High Court and county court records, for example, were kept manually. The main plank of the Report was concerned with making the operation of the courts more 'litigant-friendly'. It said that judges, lawyers and administrators should develop a culture of service to the litigant.

When Lord Woolf began his examination of the civil law process, the problems facing those who used the system were many and varied. His *Interim Report* published in June 1995 identified these problems. He noted, for example, that: '... the key problems facing civil justice today are cost, delay and complexity. These three are interrelated and stem from the uncontrolled nature of the litigation process. In particular, there is no clear judicial responsibility for managing individual cases or for the overall administration of the civil courts.' (*Access to Justice: Interim Report*, 1995.) He noted that, just as the problems are interrelated, so, too, should be the solutions. The Report suggested that, in many instances, the failure of previous attempts to address the problem stemmed, not from the solutions proposed, but from their partial, rather than their complete, implementation.

In the system that Lord Woolf examined, the main responsibility for the initiation and conduct of proceedings rested with the parties to each individual case and it was normally the plaintiff (now claimant) who set the pace. Thus, Lord Woolf also noted that, without effect judicial control, the adversarial process is likely to encourage an adversarial cultural and to degenerate into an environment in which the litigation process is, too often, seen as a battlefield where no rules apply. His Report states:

> In this environment, questions of expense, delay, compromise and fairness have only a low priority. The consequence is that the expense is often excessive, disproportionate and unpredictable; and delay is frequently unreasonable [*Access to Justice: Interim Report*, 1995, p 7].

Historically, the system degenerated in a number of other respects. Witness statements, a sensible innovation aimed at a 'cards on the table' approach began, after a very short time, to follow the same route as pleadings, with the draftsman's skill often used to obscure the original words of the witness.

The use of expert evidence under the old system left a lot to be desired. Woolf noted that the approach to expert evidence exhibited a range of difficulties: instead of the expert assisting the court to resolve technical problems, delay was caused by the unreasonable insistence on going to unduly eminent members of various professions (civil engineers, medical experts, dental experts, mechanical experts, etc) and evidence was undermined by the partisan pressure to which the parties' experts were subjected.

Historically, change has come very slowly, and gradually, to the legal system. The report of the CJR was largely ignored and, with the exception of a shift in the balance of work from the High Court to the county court (under the Courts and Legal Service Act 1990), no major changes came from its recommendations. The whole process began again with the Woolf Review of the Civil Justice System. In March 1994, Lord Woolf was invited by the Government to review the work of the civil courts in England and Wales. He began from the proposition that the system was 'in a state of crisis ... a crisis for the government, the judiciary and the profession'. The recommendations he formulated, after extensive consultation, in the UK and in many other jurisdictions, form the basis of major changes to the system that came into effect in April 1999. David Gladwell, head of the Civil Justice Division of the Lord Chancellor's Department (LCD), stated (*Civil Litigation Reform*, 1999, p 1) that these changes represent 'the greatest change the civil courts have seen in over a century'.

Following the Civil Procedure Act 1997, the changes are effected through the new CPR 1998. These have been supplemented by new practice directions and pre-action protocols. There are three main aspects to the reforms.

The first principle is one of judicial case management. The judge is a case manager in the new regime. The new system allocates cases to one of three 'tracks' depending upon the complexity and value of the dispute. The small claims track deals with the simplest cases; the fast track deals with more weighty disputes; and the multitrack system allows a court to use a variety of procedures. The judge will be centre stage for the whole action, and not just someone who is brought in for the final triumphal scene. Litigation proceeds on a court controlled timetable. Parties can no longer agree extensions with each other. Previously, lawyers from either side were permitted to wrangle, almost endlessly, with each other about who should disclose what information and documents to whom and at what stage.

Now, the judge is under an obligation 'actively' to manage cases. This includes: encouraging parties to co-operate with each other; identifying issues in the dispute at an early stage; disposing of summary issues which do not need full investigation; helping the parties to settle the whole or part of the case; fixing timetables for the case hearing and controlling the progress of the case; and considering whether the benefits of a particular way of hearing the dispute justify its costs.

If the parties refuse to comply with the new rules, the practice directions or the protocols, the judge will be able to exercise disciplinary powers. These include:

(a) using costs sanctions against parties (that is, refusing to allow the lawyers who have violated the rules to recover their costs from their client or the other side of the dispute);

(b) 'unless' orders;

(c) striking out;

(d) refusal to grant extensions of time; and

(e) refusal to allow documents not previously disclosed to the court and the other side to be relied upon.

One of the greatest changes, however, concerns the spirit of the law. The new style of procedure, which is intended to be brisk, will be of paramount importance. The courts will, it is intended, become allergic to delay or any of the old, ponderous, long winded techniques previously used by many lawyers. David Gladwell (p 2) has noted that: 'Strict observance of the black letter of the rules, so beloved of procedural lawyers, will no longer be enough. The courts will be adopting a more creative approach.'

The second major element of the new strategy is the introduction of the 'pre-action protocol'. Part of the problem in the past arose from the fact that the courts could only start to exercise control over the progress of a case, and the way it is handled, once proceedings had been issued. Before that stage, lawyers were at liberty to take inordinate amounts of time to do things related to the case, to write to lawyers on the other side of the dispute and so forth. Now, a mechanism allows new pre-action requirements to be enforced. Various protocols have been drawn up, to apply in the largest areas of litigation, for example in clinical negligence (including actions against doctors, nurses, dentists, hospitals, health authorities, etc); and personal injury (road accidents, work accidents, etc).

The protocols aim to achieve a number of things: to encourage greater contact between the parties at the earliest opportunity; to encourage a better exchange of information; to encourage better pre-action investigation; to put parties in a position to settle cases fairly and early; and to reduce the need for the case going all the way to court.

Another part of the new strategy is the development of alternatives to going to court. Rule 4.1 requires the court as a part of its 'active case management' to encourage and facilitate the use of ADR and r 26.4 allows the court to stay proceedings (that is, halt them), to allow the parties to go to ADR, either where the parties themselves request it or where the court 'of its own initiative' considers it appropriate.

It will, clearly, take time before the strategy of the Woolf reforms becomes fully effectual. There is some evidence, for example, that the attempt to impose a new unified system of rules of procedure across all civil courts is being troubled by diverse interpretations of rules by different judges and courts. A letter to *The Times* ((2000) 19 September), for example suggests that 'under the Woolf reforms and Civil Procedure Rules each individual judge interprets the rules in a different way rather than in any uniform manner', and the writer adduces evidence related to various claims he has brought in a local county court. In a similar vein, Richard Burns, a barrister and recorder, has written that: '... the Lord Chancellor's foot has made a worrying reappearance with the same rules being interpreted very differently from one area to another.' ((2000) 150 NLJ 1830.) It should be remembered, however, that all the great social institutions that are respected today – on the scale comparable to that of the CPR – including, say the BBC, the blood donor system, etc, were once young, developmental and subject to various teething problems.

Question 36

What pressures have been found to encourage litigants to settle claims, even against their best interests, and what approach to this issue is taken by the new CPR?

Answer plan

- The nature of settlement.
- Fear of costs and uncertainty of outcome.
- Part 36 payments.
- The CPR and limiting costs.
- Active case management.

Answer

A settlement is a compromise. In the context of litigation, it involves the parties deciding to resolve their dispute out of court rather than go to a full hearing and have the matter decided by a judge, or even a civil jury. If a litigant is being pushed into giving in, when he has a sound legal case and his rights should be vindicated, then a compromise is undesirable. Where, however, a dispute is evenly balanced and would involve a great deal of time, anxiety and resources to resolve in a full trial, then a compromise might well represent a trilateral relief: relief for both sides and the tax payers, who support the legal system.

Most civil disputes are settled out of court. Less than 10% of cases, where a claim form is issued, actually go to court and, even of those which do go to trial, many are settled before judgment. Evidence presented by the London Passenger Transport Board to the Winn Committee on Personal Injury Litigation (1968), for example, showed that, of about 5,000 claims made against it a year, about 4,900 were settled without proceedings. Of the 100, or so, cases which were commenced, only about one-quarter were taken to full judgment.

The largest study of this sort was conducted by the Oxford Centre for Socio-Legal Studies (Harris *et al*, *Compensation and Support for Illness and Injury*, 1984) which examined a random sample of 1,711 accident victims who had been incapacitated for a minimum of two weeks. Of this group, only 26% had considered claiming damages, only 14% had consulted a solicitor and only 12% were awarded damages. The study looked at the level of damages obtained by the small group (8%), who gained them without the use of solicitors, and concluded that these people appeared to be undercompensated. In the 182 cases (from 1,711 in the sample) in which damages were obtained, the claimant accepted the first offer made in 104 cases. See Genn, *Hard Bargaining: Out of Court Settlements in Personal Injury Claims* (1987).

Many factors combine to persuade disputants to settle out of court and the fear of prohibitive costs can be a serious deterrent to taking proceedings. This is particularly so, when it is remembered that the basic rule is that 'costs follow the event', that is, the successful party can expect the judge to order the loser to pay some or all of his or her solicitor's bill. Costs, however, are a discretionary matter, so the whole process is beset with uncertainties. Another gamble the claimant is faced with is the procedure of 'payment into court' (now known as a 'Pt 36 payment') where, at any stage after the commencement of proceedings, the defendant may make a payment into court in satisfaction of the claimant's claim. The claimant may accept the payment, or continue the action. If they choose to continue, and the damages obtained are not greater than the amount paid in by the defendant, the claimant will be liable for the defendant's taxed costs (that is, costs which are authorised by a court official – a taxing master) from the time of payment in, even though he or she has won the action. When the judge makes an award of damages, he will not know the amount of any payment into court, so he cannot influence the matter of whether the claimant has to suffer under the rule.

There were 80 cases in the Oxford study which involved abandoned claims and, of these, 16% were abandoned because of fear of legal expenses. Where a claimant is not legally aided, the lawyer may try to persuade him or her to accept a settlement offer, plus costs, rather than risk a legal action which could fail. This is better for the lawyer, as it assures the payment of costs but, arguably, not in the best interest of many claimants because settlement awards are generally lower than damages awarded by courts for the same types of case.

A study of High Court personal injury cases by Zander (1973–74) ((1975) Law Soc Gazette, 25 June, p 680) showed that, while costs were a relatively low proportion of damages in large claims, they were, proportionately, very high in small claims. Where the damages were under £1,000, 86% of cases had claimed costs for one side amounting to three-fifths of the damages or more. In 33% of cases, the total costs of both sides amounted to more than the amount in dispute. The CJR found that the average cost to the claimant in High Court personal injury actions in 1984 was £6,830 in London and £2,480 outside London. In the county court, costs were an average of 99% of the claimant's damages recovered, as opposed to about one-quarter in the High Court. When the costs of both sides were combined, it was estimated that, in the county court, they amounted to 125% of damages and between 50 and 75% in the High Court.

Research conducted for the Woolf Report on the civil justice system threw further light on this area. The Final Report (*Access to Justice*, 1996) includes a survey of Supreme Court Taxing Office taxed bills conducted by Professor Hazel Genn of University College, London. Genn found alarming data on costs. Her findings indicate the average costs among the lowest value claims, consistently, represented more than 100% of the claim value. They also showed that, in cases worth between £12,500 and £25,000, average costs ranged from 40% to 95% of the value of the claim. The system provided higher benefits to lawyers than to their clients.

In the Oxford study, delay was another significant factor influencing people to discontinue claims; 6% of those who abandoned their actions cited it as affecting their decision. Cane (in Atiyah's *Accidents, Compensation and the Law* (1993)) has shown evidence that delay and its attendant anxiety can cause a recognisable state of 'litigation neurosis', a complaint which ceases upon the resolution of the dispute. Delay generally assists the defendant and is, sometimes, used as a deliberate tactic against weaker opponents, or to alleviate the cash flow problems of the smaller insurance companies.

Another factor putting pressure on litigants to settle is that of the risks and uncertainties entailed in the claim. If the case goes to trial, then the claimant will, to succeed, have to prove his or her case on the balance of probabilities. The process is beset with legal uncertainties. Is the defendant liable at law for the claimant's loss or injury? Even where the law is clear, there may be evidential difficulties. Genn (*Hard Bargaining: Out of Court Settlement in Personal Injury Claims* (1987)) has presented material to suggest that, in many cases, a claimant's solicitor either does not have sufficient resources to undertake proper factual investigations, or does not seek out all available reports. It is also very difficult to contact all relevant witnesses and to assess how persuasive their courtroom evidence would be. Defendants, including or assisted by insurance companies, will often have resources which place them in a good position fully to investigate the circumstances of accidents. Assessing the quantum of damages is another very problematic part of litigation. In an American experiment, 20 pairs of practising lawyers negotiated on identical information about a case and were instructed to negotiate a settlement. Their resultant settlements ranged from the highest of US$95,000 to the lowest of US$15,000 with an average of just over US$47,000.

The Oxford study found that many other factors contributed to the discontinuation of claims, including the fear of affecting a continuing relationship and arguments that the victim's own fault caused the accident. The most cited reason (mentioned by 45% of respondents) was problems over obtaining evidence. There have been some legal changes since the Oxford study in 1984 and it will be interesting to see if future studies detect any significant consequential changes in claimants' behaviour.

The LCD committed itself (in the CJR's General Issues Paper) to the use of new technology, especially for improving the system of county court debt business. The Production Centre has operated since early 1990, since when, relying on new technology, it has issued over 1.5 m summonses. Dealing more expeditiously with this sort of work could free the courts and, thus, reduce delays for other types of case.

The courts have made some progress in this area since 1996, although the challenges in the UK are considerable. Lord Justice Brooke, a leading proponent of the use of information and communications technology (ICT) in the courts, has noted that, in England, there is no Ministry of Justice, with masses of resources at its command and the LCD, which supports the courts, is a small department, and, over the last 10 years, its credibility with the Treasury was damaged because of the way that unbudgeted legal aid expenditure went on soaring. Lord Justice Brooke believes that expenditure on ICT has suffered as a result:

> We have certainly not seen any of the imaginative forward investment in IT which other comparable countries have experienced. In America, for instance, the federal judiciary run the federal courts, and, in 1990, the Senate voted them US$70 m to undertake a programme of computerisation in the court process [Lord Justice Brooke, *The Changing Jurisdiction, IT and the English and Welsh Courts: the Next 10 Years*, keynote speech to the 13th Bileta Conference, Dublin, 28 March 1998].

In 2001, there are only about 140 judges using computers in court, but the number is rising steadily with consequential improvements in the efficiency of the courts.

Under the new CPR, there is a greater incentive for parties to settle their differences. The court now takes into account any pre-action offers to settle when making an order for costs. Thus, a side which has refused a reasonable offer to settle will be treated less generously, in the issue of how far the court will order their costs to be paid by the other side. For this to happen, the offer, though, must be one which is made to be open to the other side for at least 21 days after receipt (to stop any undue pressure being put on someone with the phrase: 'Take it or leave it, it is only open for one day then I shall withdraw the offer.'). Also, if the offer is made by the defendant, it must be an offer to pay compensation and to pay the claimant's costs.

Several aspects of the new rules encourage litigants to settle rather than take risks in order (as a claimant) to hold out for, unreasonably, large sums of compensation, or try to get away (as a defendant) with paying nothing rather than some compensation. The system of Pt 36 payments, or offers, does not apply to small claims, but, for other cases, it seems bound to have a significant effect. Thus, if at the trial a claimant does not get more damages than a sum offered by the defendant in what is called a Pt 36 payment (that is, an offer to settle or a payment into the court), or obtain a judgment more favourable than a Pt 36 offer, the court will order the claimant to pay any costs incurred by the defendant, after the latest date for accepting the payment or offer. The court now has a discretion to make a different order for costs than the normal order.

District Judge Frenkel has given the following example: claim, £150,000 – judgment, £51,000 – £50,000 paid into court. The 'without prejudice' correspondence shows that the claimant would consider nothing short of £150,000. The claimant may be in trouble. The defendant will ask the judge to consider overriding principles of Pt 1: 'Was it proportional to incur the further costs of trial to secure an additional £1,000?'. Part 44.3 confirms the general rule that the loser pays, but allows the court to make a different order to take into account offers to settle, payment into court, the parties, conduct including pre-action conduct and exaggeration of the claim ((1999) 149 NLJ 458).

Similarly, where, at trial, a defendant is held liable to the claimant for more money than the proposals contained in a claimant's Pt 36 offer (that is, where the claimant has made an offer to settle), the court may order the defendant to pay interest on the award, at a rate not exceeding 10% above the base rate, for some or all of the period starting with the date on which the defendant could have accepted the offer.

Active case management imposes a duty on the courts to help parties settle their disputes. A 'stay' is a temporary halt in proceedings and an opportunity for the court to order such a pause arises at the stage when the defence to a claim has been filed. Parties can indicate that they have agreed on a stay to attempt to settle the case and, provided the court agrees, can have an initial period of one month to try to do this. In order to avoid the stay being used as a delaying tactic, the order granting the stay will require the parties to report back to the court within 14 days of the end of the period of the stay to: (a) inform the court if the matter has been settled either wholly or partly; or (b) asking for more time for settlement; or (c) reporting that the attempt to settle has failed, so that the process of allocation of court track can take place.

The court will always give the final decision about whether to grant the parties more time to use a mediator, or arbitrator, or expert to settle, even if the parties are agreed they wish to have more time. A stay will never be granted for an indefinite period.

In the Final Report on *Access to Justice*, Lord Woolf recognised the importance of witness statements in cases, but observed that they had become problematic because lawyers had made them excessively long and detailed in order to protect against leaving out something which later proved to be relevant. He said 'witness statements have ceased to be the authentic account of the lay witness; instead, they have become an elaborate, costly branch of legal drafting' (para 55). Under the new rules, witness statements must contain the evidence that the witness will give at trial, but they should be briefer than those drafted under the previous rules: they should be drafted in lay language and should not discuss legal propositions. Witnesses are now allowed to amplify on the statement, or deal with matters that have arisen since the Report was served, although this is not an automatic right and a 'good reason' for the admission of new evidence will have to be established.

Overall, it seems likely that as a result of the introduction of the new CPR, fewer of the annually settled cases will have been settled for the 'wrong reasons' (that is, because parties are frightened of the possible delays, costs, and uncertainties of proceeding to a full judgment) and more disputants will settle in the truer spirit of compromise, facilitated by an improved legal system.

Question 37

> The Civil Procedure Rules introduced in 1999 have been an unqualified success in changing the legal system.

Discuss.

Answer plan
- Background to the new Rules.
- Burton J's criticisms.
- The assessment of Burns J.
- Concealed delays under the new system.
- The Eversheds' study.
- Judges and lawyers struggling with the new system.

Answer

The new CPR, the most fundamental changes in civil process for over 100 years, have radically altered the operation of civil justice. Since the new Rules came into force (26 April 1999), they have been regularly reformed. The 21st update came into force in 2001.

Part of the rationale of the new rules was to expedite the way cases were dealt with and to allow more cases to be settled early through negotiation between the parties or ADR. In this respect, there is some evidence of success. During the May to August period 1999, there was a 25% reduction in the number of cases issued in the county courts compared with the same period the previous year. By the end of January 2000, the was a further fall to 23%. There is also evidence (speech by David Lock MP, Parliamentary Secretary to the LCD, 15 October 1999) that changes to pre-action behaviour, as a result of the pre-action protocols, have been partly responsible for the reduction in the number of cases going all the way through to trial.

An interesting assessment of the new rules was presented by Mr Justice Burton of the Queen's Bench Division. Speaking at the city law firm Kennedys, he outlined five benefits of the reforms, five problems and what he referred to as 'one big question mark' ((2000) Law Soc Gazette, 10 February).

The five problems with the reforms were: the courts' inflexibility in not allowing parties to agree extensions of time between themselves; the danger of the judiciary pushing time guillotines onto parties; the risk that lawyers and clients could exploit 'standard' disclosure to conceal important documents; single joint experts possibly usurping the role of judges; and summary assessments of costs leading to judges making assumptions replacing detailed costs analysis. He itemised the benefits as: pre-action protocols, emphasis on encouraging settlement, judicial intervention, Pt 24 strike-out provisions and Pt 36 offers to settle.

Mr Justice Burton said there had been three options for reforming appeals: (1) to extend the present system in order to discourage more than one appeal; (2) to refuse appeals without leave; or (3) to abolish the present system, giving no right to rehearings, only appeals. He said he regretted that all three had been adopted (in the Access to Justice Act 1999). The consequence will be pressure on judges 'to get it right first time' and higher costs for parties.

Richard Burns, a barrister and recorder sitting in the county court, and, thus, someone who has experienced the new Rules from both sides of the Bench, has made some interesting observations about the new system ('A view from the ranks' (2000) 150 NLJ 1829, pp 1829–30). On the positive side, Judge Burns says that 'the transition has been far smoother than many had anticipated and there have been a number of very worthwhile gains'. He notes, however, that, set against the ambitious aims Lord Woolf had set for the reforms, they were a 'relative failure'. Among the gains, the judge lists the unified system of procedure in all civil courts, awareness that the costs of litigation should bear a 'passing resemblance to the value of the claim', vastly improved pre-action co-operation, more sensible and open pleadings which force the parties to define the issues at an early stage, in the wider use of jointly instructed (and, therefore, impartial) experts and, in CPR Pt 36, rules cunningly devised to encourage the parties to settle.

One way in which the system is not working properly, according to Richard Burns, is in relation to costs. He argues that the system is, in fact, proving more expensive than the old system for many litigants as the timetable imposed usually compels the parties 'to spend time and money progressing claims to trial whether or not they expect to settle. Paradoxically, the procedures encouraging as they do, the front-end loading of expenditure on cases may lead to more trials – certainly, this appears to have been happening in some of the court centres where I appear'.

Another difficulty concerns the system of case management which Lord Woolf envisaged would be the engine to drive forward the litigation cheaply and expeditiously. Burns regards this as a system which is 'excessively bureaucratic and makes too many demands on the parties'. It is also, he argues, very poorly resourced as the Court Service received very little extra money to finance the sort of increases in judicial staffing and information technology Woolf had seen as essential.

Concealed delays are also blighting the system, according to Judge Burns. While recognising that, on the whole, cases come to trial more quickly than they did, he notes that:-

The overall delay experienced by litigants is much the same as it ever was. This is because solicitors, feeling daunted by the demands made on them by the CPR and lacking the time and resources to manage more than a certain quota of cases through the system, are delaying the issue of proceedings. The delay frequently runs into years.

Eversheds, the corporate law claims firm, has conducted an 'access to justice' survey for five years. It canvasses the opinions and experiences of lawyers and those using the legal system. Results published in 2000, after one year of the Woolf reforms, showed that of its respondents, 54% said that the civil litigation process had improved in the past year, a big increase on 1998's 15%. Some 52% of respondents believed that litigation was quicker, but only 22 per cent thought costs were lower.

John Heaps, head of litigation at Eversheds, has stated ((2000) *The Times*, 2 May) that: 'The UK legal system historically has been plagued by unsatisfactory delays and expense. The style of dispute resolution is changing as a result of the Woolf reforms; people no longer seek aggressive uncompromising lawyers, but those who look for commercial solutions.'

The survey sought the views of heads of legal departments of UK companies and public sector bodies; 70% of respondents were in the private sector, with 30% in London. The replies suggest that a change in culture is emerging. Nearly two-thirds of respondents did not think the reforms would make them less likely to start proceedings, but 43% said they were settling cases earlier and almost half said their lawyers were handling disputes differently. Mediation, or ADR, is also becoming more popular: 41% have used it, compared with 30% in 1998.

There is, however, concern that, while judges are managing cases more effectively, the courts do not have adequate resources. (This was expressed by 50% of respondents.) Only 24% believed that litigants were now getting better justice; 44% said they were not.

On the matter of costs, opinions were sharply divided. Nearly half did not believe costs to have been affected by the introduction of the new rules. Disturbingly, however, 19% said costs had risen, particularly in the regions. But, a conference on Woolf, held by CEDR found that, although costs had increased at the start of litigation (front-loading), overall they were down as settlements came sooner.

Conditional or 'no win, no fee' work is attractive in principle, but little used: 48% of respondents said they would pay lawyers a higher fee for winning, if they could pay a lower fee, or none, if the case was lost. But, only 24% had discussed such a deal.

Litigation may be quicker and less likely to go to court, but 52% of respondents expected to have the same number of business disputes in the following year, with as many being resolved through litigation. One in five was more optimistic and thought fewer disputes would be resolved in court.

John Heaps argues that, overall the findings are positive. He has said: 'Over half the respondents feel the speed of resolving disputes has improved. But there are concerns that the aims and aspirations are not matched by court resources.'

A survey carried out by the City Research Group of the firm Wragge & Co obtained similar findings ((2000) *The Times*, 2 May). It suggests that, among in-house lawyers from FTSE 1000 companies, a lack of resources has become 'a major stumbling block'. Some 81% of respondents thought courts did not have the resources to process claims quickly enough and some complained of 'inconsistent interpretation' between courts. But 89% of respondents backed the changes and said litigation was quicker with fewer 'frivolous claims'. Some 41% thought costs had been cut and there was strong backing for ADR, with 80% saying it had proved popular. Nine in 10 lawyers thought clients were more involved in the management of the dispute, but 38% believed that the reforms had compromised justice at the expense of cost-cutting. As with the CEDR survey, the change singled out for the biggest impact is that which allows either party to make a formal settlement offer at any stage – or, potentially, face cost penalties.

A senior litigation partner at Wragge and Co, Andrew Manning Cox, observed that the survey mirrored the firm's experiences. Among surprise findings, was the low awareness of Woolf among businesses. Their lawyers were apparently not using the new rules to the best tactical advantage of their companies.

Another City law firm, Lovells, found 71% of respondents now treating litigation as a last resort, with 72% willing, voluntarily, to exchange documents with the other side. Where litigation is unavoidable, it is quicker, with 66% saying that judges now set tighter timetables. Two-thirds found the court 'rubber stamped' joint requests by the parties to move back dates in the timetable, but this flexibility did not extend to trial dates.

One of the findings that will be very disappointing for many involved with the project of the Woolf reforms is the, apparently, low use of a jointly appointed expert. According to the survey, only 7% of respondents were involved in cases with such an expert.

The survey also highlights a low level of case management. Only 9% found that the court monitored case progress and chased lawyers to meet deadlines; 42% found the court had sought to narrow the issues as early as it could. The commercial court, Lovells found, was managing cases better than other High Court divisions. And courts did not penalise parties who failed to comply with the new rules. This certainly ties in with the experience of the barrister and county court judge Richard Burns. He has noted that the burden of work on many civil judges is so heavy that they cannot properly manage each case:

> Their burden in the busier courts is so huge that all they can do is skim the surface of files that cross their desks. It is rare, in my experience, for the same judge to be able to deal with all the interlocutory stages of even the bigger cases and so there is little or no continuity. [(2000) 150 NLJ 1830.]

Asked for the worst aspect of the reforms, respondents chose the rule on summary assessment of costs in preliminary hearings, criticised as a lottery. In fact, the main deficiency in the new system seems to be one of variable application according to the style or interpretation of them favoured in any given court or region. This, though, may well become more uniform over time, and, if that occurs, then the new rules really can claim to have radically and successfully altered the civil process in England and Wales.

Question 38

How far is it true to say that society is becoming more litigious, and is a move in that direction a socially healthy development?

Answer plan
- Society becomes more legalistic.
- The scale of the problem.
- The experience of the USA.
- What can be inferred from booming litigation.
- The area of clinical negligence and what it can teach us.

Answer

Today, society seems much more tilted towards the legalistic settlement of disputes than it was in previous eras.

Nowadays, a person will be asked to sign solemn legal declarations, if he or she is about to receive hospital treatment, hand in a university assignment, join a company, leave a company or even send a child to school or on a school trip. It is possible to buy confectionery nut bars bearing the label 'this product may contain nuts' and a cup of coffee with the warning 'this product is hot'.

Certainly, the range of behaviours for which people are being sued and the sorts of duties which are, allegedly, being breached have expanded in recent times — schools for failing to identify dyslexia, *Phelps v Hillingdon LBC* (2000), for example, or employers for exposing employees to unbearable stress *Beverley v Birmingham CC* (1999). The headlines of recent newspaper reports indicate a similar phenomenon: 'Parents sue over exam failure' ((2000) *The Independent*, 1 August); 'Insurer sues boy who 'failed to stop accident' ((2000) *The Independent*, 19 December); 'Girl, 16, sues father over payment of school fees' ((2000) *The Guardian*, 7 November); 'Service veterans seeking millions for combat stress' ((2000) *The Independent*, 22 April).

According to an investigation conducted by *The Independent* ((2000) 10 October), compensation *payouts* are running at about £12 bn a year, with the brunt of the bill being borne by the taxpayer. This is a different index, of course, from the number of cases being brought, but it is, nonetheless, an important indicator of the scale of compensation. Compensation payouts in 2000 required £9 bn from the public purse. This, therefore, changes the issue into one of public importance as the £9 bn is the equivalent to 4 p on the basic rate of income tax. The money would pay for four new hospitals or 3,000 new schools or put £2.50 on the basic weekly pension. The Treasury, however, does not know the full scale of the problem because the compensation claims from public bodies being found liable (which need to be paid from the public purse) are not recorded or tracked.

Eight out of 10 Whitehall departments could not say how much compensation cost them or the extent of their liabilities. The Ministry of Defence, one of the two departments that does monitor payouts, stated to *The Independent* that compensation claims by service personnel have trebled in the past five years.

The problem is so serious that the National Audit Office (NAO) is pressing the Government to establish risk management taskforces to reduce 'financial loss and impropriety'. This is at a time when the Government faces a wave of new compensation claims. Miners suffering from coal dust related lung disease are likely to get a record industrial payout of £2 bn to £3 bn. A Department of Trade and Industry spokeswoman said claims were being received at an 'unprecedented' rate of about 600 a week, some dating back to the 1930s.

The Ministry of Agriculture, Fisheries and Food is fighting a compensation battle with victims of CJD, the human form of mad cow disease, which, combined with the amount already paid out to farmers who were forced to cull their cattle, is expected to top £4 bn. The Home Office is facing a legal challenge by the former directors of Matrix Churchill – who were wrongly accused of selling arms to Iraq – which could open the floodgates for hundreds of people convicted of crimes but subsequently exonerated to sue the Home Office.

The NHS is the biggest single target for compensation claims. According to the Medical Defence Union, negligence claims in some areas of practice are outstripping those in the USA. The NAO says negligence claims are exposing the NHS to 'potential liabilities' now running at £2.4 bn a year, an increase of £600 m on the previous year, with a further £1 bn worth of claims going unreported. The annual cost of medical negligence compensation would pay for 40,000 patients to receive dialysis treatment.

Behind the rise, is a series of court rulings that have created costly potential liabilities dating back many years. Claims are also being stimulated by a burgeoning compensation industry, which attracts clients by prime time television advertising.

Councils are facing hundreds of 'failure to nurture' cases due to alleged negligence in schooling or childcare and about 4,000 claims are being brought by emergency services staff for stress suffered in dealing with incidents such as the Dunblane school massacre.

The rise in litigation is seen by many as emanating from the USA, which is generally regarded as the most litigious society in the world. It will soon become the first country in the world to boast one million lawyers. Litigation in the USA is an immensely important phenomenon, as the decision in the Florida tobacco case (July 2000) illustrates. A jury issued a 'death penalty' to the big tobacco companies, ordering them to pay record punitive damages of $145 bn (£96 bn) to 500,000 sick smokers in Florida. The case will now go to a long and expensive appeal but would bankrupt the companies, if the decision is upheld. In 1999, a jury in Los Angeles awarded a $4.9 bn judgment against General Motors for the negligent production of a dangerous car, although the award was later reduced to $1.2 bn by a judge.

Curiously, official figures for England and Wales tell the story of a decline in litigation in England and Wales. According to *Judicial Statistics*, published by the LCD, 153,624 writs and originating summonses were issued in 1995 in the Queen's Bench Division of the High Court – the place where all the main wrongs against people and property are heard. That represented a 2% drop on the previous year's figures. The LCD reported a further fall in its 1997 Report, with the figure dropping to 121,446. During 1998, only 114,986 writs and originating summonses were issued, 5% fewer than in 1997. The pattern is also reflected in county court summonses.

It might well be that the number of actions formally commenced has fallen, while social litigiousness has risen. This could happen if many more actions were being threatened, but were being settled by solicitors before actions went to court.

Intriguingly, the phenomenon of a more litigious society can be interpreted in two quite antithetical ways. It can be seen as a desirable development because more people are asserting their rights and are testing new claims to improve the legal protection afforded to consumers, voters, drivers, students, patients, employees, and so forth. By contrast, though, it can be seen as an undesirable development because the law is putting more people into arms-length, mistrustful relationships and, thereby, pervading communities with formal and confrontational styles of dispute settlement.

At the American Bar Association conference in London in 1999, one of the sessions was entitled 'Products over the pond – is US style litigation invading the UK?'. In one event, the legal consequences of a fabricated accident were played out as a drama – starting with recorded television mock news coverage of the incident. Real lawyers and judges from the USA and UK then acted out all the parts, including client interviewing and advocacy, to show how the two systems would deal with the case. The incident under discussion was fraught with detailed uncertainties. A woman was killed when her car crashed under the rear of a large lorry she was following. The rear bumper of the lorry was possibly defective, the lorry had made an emergency stop because the van it was following had lost its load and the reason for the shed load might have been a door left open by a worker, as part of a union dispute.

In some ways, the approach of the two legal systems is very similar, in respect, for example, of the principles of establishing negligence or strict liability, but there are also key differences. The American court would hear this case with a jury, whereas in the UK, it would be heard by a judge alone. One consequence of this is that it is a judge who decides the quantum of damages, so our awards have not spiralled into the ionosphere, as in the USA.

If the American influence of litigation practice continues to develop in the UK, what shall we see next? Some lawyers are considering suits against the alcoholic beverage industry, which they would hold liable for drink driving deaths and other alcohol-related losses, using the same 'negligent marketing' allegations that have been lodged against gunmakers. An action, however, that won't be brought here is one against MacDonald's by anyone who spills cold milkshake on himself while driving a car, gets a shock and crashes his vehicle. Such an action was brought in America, recently, but failed.

Since the 1960s, there has been an exponential growth in people suing for alleged clinical negligence – indeed, this new term is now to replace 'medical negligence', so as to include the dental surgeons, nurses and other practitioners who are commonly facing the growth in litigation. The Medical Protection Society, the doctors' insurance body, receives over 1000 inquiries a week, regarding incidents that could be followed by legal action.

For lawyers, clinical staff, politicians and the public, one critically important question is whether surrounding health care with the threat of litigation is a socially healthy option. Do lawyers help keep clinicians on their toes, or is the net effect the promotion of distrust between patients and the health service?

In May, 1999 a conference in London, attended by the Health Minister Baroness Hayman, was told that more than 800 medical accidents happen in NHS hospitals every day. Arnold Simanowitz, a prominent medical injury lawyer, and president of the charity Action for Victims of Medical Accidents (AVMA) said that the number of medical accidents, annually, in the NHS was about 300,000, of which about 82,000 arose from incidents of actionable negligence. Of these, though, only 15,000 resulted in legal action. This calculation takes no account of the 9.8 m new attendances in A & E in the period April to December 1998.

The NAO reported in 1999 that the NHS was operating under the shadow of a £2.8 bn bill for negligence claims. Mr Simanowitz observed that the bill would be for a great deal more were everyone entitled to compensation to take legal action.

The mission of AVMA is to ensure that medical accidents are reduced to the barest minimum and that 'when such accidents take place, all patients' resulting needs and those of their families, including that for compensation, are dealt with speedily, fairly and thoroughly'. Along with many other experienced professionals in this field, Mr Simanowitz is convinced that patients are not primarily interested in money when things go wrong. They want be to be told the truth, they want an apology, where that is appropriate, and they want changes of practice to prevent others suffering in future.

One of the greatest challenges here, however, is the absence of hard data about how many cases there are of medical negligence each year. The figure of 80,000 cases of negligence is based upon the most reliable large scale study, the Harvard Medical Practice Study, conducted in America. It was found that 3.7% of a sample of 30,000 hospital patients had been victims of medical accidents, and, of these, 27% had resulted from negligence. It is when these percentages are transposed into the UK raw figures that the figure of 82,000 cases of negligence emerges. When in April, 1999, Jacqui Smith MP asked in Parliament how many claims have been brought against the NHS, and how many were successful, she was told by John Denham: 'The information is not available in the format requested.'

At another conference in London entitled 'The Influence of Litigation on Medical Practice' (1999), very divergent views were expressed by lawyers and clinicians as to whether the new litigious environment was desirable.

Adrian Whitfield QC, a widely respected specialist in the field of medical litigation, identified three areas in which there have been improvements in medical practice as a result of it having come, more generally, under legal attention during the last 20 years. Medical record-keeping has, he argues, become more detailed, accurate and reliable. Communication with patients, especially over issues like consent to treatment, has become much better, and, in areas like obstetrics, where there has often been much dispute about whether certain procedures have caused injury, much epidemiological and neurological research seems to have been prompted by the volume of legal claims in this area.

One problem for clinicians is rising patient expectations of what medicine can achieve. In the 1950s, there were relatively few tests that could be carried out on patients to assist diagnosis. Much medical insight was gained from what was discovered after death, when patients were subject to post mortem examinations. By contrast today, there are scores of possible tests that can be conducted on patients presenting with various syndromes. One fear is that, faced with the tide of litigation, many doctors are ordering an unwarranted range of tests on all patients in order to safeguard against being accused of not having considered a possible diagnosis.

Margaret Brazier, director of Manchester University's Institute of Medicine, Law and Biotechnics, has referred to the 'spectre of defensive medicine' in *Street on Torts*, which has followed the rise in medical litigation. The idea is that fearful of being sued some doctors will recommend treatments which have been generally least likely to attract litigation rather than the treatment which might in their better judgment be more appropriate for any given patient. As Professor Brazier points out, however, there is very little evidence that such conduct is anything other than extremely rare.

Technically, it has recently become easier in some respects to sue health care professionals. The House of Lords has declared that, in order to vindicate any treatment, it will now take more than doctors in court giving evidence that, in their clinical judgment, a defendant doctor had acted reasonably. Clinical opinion with no 'logical basis' can be discounted by a judge. How far the queue of medical negligence claimants is allowed to grow will now depend in no small part on governmental legal aid policy.

Question 39

Explain the circumstances in which an advocate can be held liable for courtroom negligence and assess the public policy arguments in this area.

Answer plan
- The decision in *Arthur JS Hall v Simons* (2000).
- The brief historical background.
- The advocate's divided loyalty.
- The 'cab rank' rule.
- The witness analogy.
- Collateral attack.
- The need for public confidence in the system.

Answer

In *Arthur JS Hall & Co v Simons* (2000), the House of Lords made a bold change in this area of law. It imposed a duty of care upon courtroom advocates that had not been previously supported in law.

Lawyers are, for the general public, the most central and prominent part of the English legal system. They are, arguably, to the legal system, what doctors are to the health system. For many decades, a debate has grown about why a patient injured by the negligence of a surgeon in the operating theatre can sue for damages, whereas a litigant whose case is lost because of the negligence of his advocate cannot sue. It all seemed very unfair. Even the most glaringly obvious courtroom negligence was protected against legal action by a special advocates' immunity. The claim that this protection was made by lawyers (and judges who were lawyers) for lawyers was difficult to refute. In this House of Lords' decision, the historic immunity has been abolished in respect of both barristers and solicitor-advocates (of whom there are now over 1,000 with higher courts' rights of audience) and for both civil and criminal proceedings.

In three cases, all conjoined on appeal, a claimant raised a claim of negligence against a firm of solicitors and, in each case, the firms relied on the immunity attaching to barristers and other advocates from actions in negligence. At first instance, all the claims were struck out. Then, on appeal, the Court of Appeal said that claims could have proceeded. The solicitors appealed to the Lords and two key questions were raised: should the old immunity rule be maintained and, in a criminal case, what was the proper scope of the principle against 'collateral attack'? A 'collateral attack' is when someone convicted in a criminal court tries to invalidate that conviction outside the criminal appeals process by suing his trial defence lawyer in a civil court. The purpose of such a 'collateral attack' is to win in the civil case, proving negligence against the criminal trial lawyer, and, thus, by implication, show that the conviction in the criminal case was unfair.

The House of Lords held (Lord Hope, Lord Hutton and Lord Hobhouse dissenting in part) that, in the light of modern conditions, it was now clear that it was no longer in the public interest in the administration of justice that advocates should have immunity from suit for negligence for acts concerned with the conduct of either civil or criminal litigation.

Lord Hoffmann (with Lord Steyn, Lord Browne-Wilkinson and Lord Millett delivering concurring opinions) said that over 30 years had passed since the House had last considered the rationale for the immunity of the advocate from suit, in *Rondel v Worsley* ([1969] 1 AC 191). Public policy was not immutable and there had been great changes in the law of negligence, the functioning of the legal profession, the administration of justice and public perceptions. It was, once again, time to re-examine the whole matter. Interestingly, Lord Hoffmann chose to formulate his opinion in a creative mode to reflect public policy, rather than in the tradition of what can be seen as slavish obedience to the details of precedent:

> I hope that I will not be thought ungrateful if I do not encumber this speech with citations. The question of what the public interest now requires depends upon the strength of the arguments rather than the weight of authority.

The point of departure was that, in general, English law provided a remedy in damages for a person who had suffered injury as a result of professional negligence. It followed that, any exception which denied such a remedy, required a sound justification. The arguments relied on by the court in *Rondel v Worsley* as justifying the immunity had to be considered. One by one these arguments are evaluated and rejected.

Advocate's divided loyalty

There were two distinct versions of the divided loyalty argument. The first was that the possibility of being sued for negligence would actually inhibit the lawyer, consciously or unconsciously, from giving his duty to the court priority to his duty to his client. The second was that the divided loyalty was a special factor that made the conduct of litigation a very difficult art and could lead to the advocate being exposed to vexatious claims by difficult clients. The argument was pressed, most strongly, in connection with advocacy in criminal proceedings, where the clients were said to be more than usually likely to be vexatious.

There had been recent developments in the civil justice system designed to reduce the incidence of vexatious litigation. The first was rule 24.2 of the new CPR which provided that a court could give summary judgment in favour of a defendant. if it considered that 'the claimant had no real prospect of succeeding on the claim'. The second was the changes to the funding of civil litigation. introduced by the Access to Justice Act 1999. which would make it much more difficult than it had been in the past to obtain legal help for negligence actions which had little prospect of success.

There was no doubt that the advocate's duty to the court was extremely important in the English justice system. The question was whether removing the immunity would have a significantly adverse effect. If the possibility of being held liable in negligence was calculated to have an adverse effect on the behaviour of advocates in court, one might have expected that to have followed, at least in some degree, from the introduction of wasted costs orders (where a court disallows a lawyer from being able to claim part of a fee for work which is regarded as unnecessary and wasteful). Although the liability of a negligent advocate to a wasted costs order was not the same as a liability to pay general damages, the experience of the wasted costs jurisdiction was the only empirical evidence available in England to test the proposition that such liability would have an adverse effect upon the way advocates performed their duty to the court and there was no suggestion that it had changed standards of advocacy for the worse.

The 'cab rank'

The 'cab rank' rule provided that a barrister could not refuse to act for a client on the ground that he disapproved of him or his case. The argument was that a barrister, who was obliged to accept any client, would be unfairly exposed to vexatious actions by clients whom any sensible lawyer with freedom of action would have refused to act for. Such a claim, however, was, in the nature of things, intuitive, incapable of empirical verification and did not have any real substance.

The witness analogy

The argument started from the well established rule that a witness was absolutely immune from liability for anything that he said in court. So were the judge, counsel and the parties. They could not be sued for libel, malicious falsehood or conspiring to give false evidence. The policy of the rule was to encourage persons who took part in court proceedings to express themselves freely. However, a witness owed no duty of care to anyone in respect of the evidence he gave to the court. His only duty was to tell the truth. There was no analogy with the position of a lawyer who owed a duty of care to his client. The fact that the advocate was the only person involved in the trial process who was liable to be sued for negligence was because he was the only person who had undertaken such a duty of care to his client.

Collateral attack

The most substantial argument was that it might be contrary to the public interest for a court to retry a case which had been decided by another court. However, actions for negligence against lawyers were not the only cases that gave rise to a possibility of the same issue being tried twice. The law had to deal with the problem in numerous other contexts. So, before examining the strength of the collateral challenge argument as a reason for maintaining the immunity of lawyers, it was necessary to consider how the law dealt with collateral challenge in general.

The law discouraged re-litigation of the same issues except by means of an appeal. The Latin maxims often quoted were *nemo debet bis vexari pro una et eadem causa* and interest *rei publicae ut finis sit litium*. The first was concerned with the interests of the defendant: a person should not be troubled twice for the same reason. That policy had generated the rules which prevented relitigation when the parties were the same: *autrefois acquit* (someone acquitted of a crime cannot be tried again for that crime), *res judicata* (a particular dispute decided by a civil court cannot be re-tried) and issue estoppel (a person cannot deny the fact of a judgment previously decided against him).

The second policy was wider: it was concerned with the interests of the state. There was a general public interest in the same issue not being litigated over again. The second policy could be used to justify the extension of the rules of issue estoppel to cases in which the parties were not the same, but the circumstances were such as to bring the case within the spirit of the rules. Criminal proceedings were in a special category because, although they were technically litigation between the Crown and the defendant, the Crown prosecuted on behalf of society as a whole. So, a conviction had some of the quality of a judgment *in rem*, which should be binding in favour of everyone.

Not all re-litigation of the same issue, however, would be manifestly unfair to a party, or bring the administration of justice into disrepute. Sometimes, there were valid reasons for re-hearing a dispute. It was, therefore, unnecessary to try to stop any re-litigation by forbidding anyone from suing their lawyer. It was 'burning down the house to roast the pig; using a broad-spectrum remedy without side effects could handle the problem equally well'.

The scope for re-examination of issues in criminal proceedings was much wider than in civil cases. Fresh evidence was more readily admitted. A conviction could be set aside as unsafe and unsatisfactory when the accused appeared to have been prejudiced by 'flagrantly incompetent advocacy': see *R v Clinton* ([1993] 1 WLR 1181). After conviction, the case could be referred to the Court of Appeal, if the conviction was on indictment, or to the crown court, if the trial was summary, by the Criminal Cases Review Commission.

It followed that it would, ordinarily, be an abuse of process for a civil court to be asked to decide that a subsisting conviction was wrong. That applied to a conviction on a plea of guilty, as well as after a trial. The resulting conflict of judgments was likely to bring the administration of justice into disrepute. The proper procedure was to appeal, or if the right of appeal had been exhausted, to apply to the Criminal Cases Review Commission. It would, ordinarily, be an abuse because there were bound to be exceptional cases in which the issue could be tried without a risk that the conflict of judgments would bring the administration of justice into disrepute.

Once the conviction has been set aside, there could be no public policy objection to an action for negligence against the legal advisers. There could be no conflict of judgments. On the other hand, in civil, including matrimonial, cases, it would seldom be possible to say that an action for negligence against a legal adviser or representative would bring the administration of justice into dispute. Whether the original decision was right or wrong was, usually, a matter of concern only to the parties and had no wider implications. There was no public interest objection to a subsequent finding that, but for the negligence of his lawyers, the losing party would have won.

But, again, there might be exceptions. The action for negligence might be an abuse of process on the ground that it was manifestly unfair to someone else. Take, for example, the case of a defendant who published a serious defamation which he attempted, unsuccessfully, to justify. Should he be able to sue his lawyers and claim that, if the case had been conducted differently, the allegation would have been proved to be true? It seemed unfair to the claimant in the defamation action that any court should be allowed to come to such a conclusion in proceedings to which he was not a party. On the other hand, it was equally unfair that he should have to join as a party and rebut the allegation for a second time. A man's reputation was not only a matter between him and the other party. It represented his relationship with the world. So, it might be that, in such circumstances, an action for negligence would be an abuse of the process of the court.

Having regard to the power of the court to strike out actions which had no real prospect of success, the doctrine was unlikely, in that context, to be invoked very often. The first step in any application to strike out an action alleging negligence in the conduct of a previous action had to be to ask whether it had a real prospect of success.

Lord Hope, Lord Hutton and Lord Hobhouse delivered judgments in which they agreed that the immunity from suit was no longer required in relation to civil proceedings, but dissented to the extent of saying that the immunity was still required in the public interest in the administration of justice in relation to criminal proceedings.

This decision is of major and historic importance in the English legal system for several reasons. It can be seen as a bold attempt by the senior judiciary to drag the legal profession (often a metonymy for the whole legal system) into the 21st century world of accountability and fair business practice. In his judgment, Lord Steyn makes this dramatic observation:

> ... public confidence in the legal system is not enhanced by the existence of the immunity. The appearance is created that the law singles out its own for protection no matter how flagrant the breach of the barrister. The world has changed since 1967. The practice of law has become more commercialised: barristers may now advertise. They may now enter into contracts for legal services with their professional clients. They are now obliged to carry insurance. On the other hand, today we live in a consumerist society in which people have a much greater awareness of their rights. If they have suffered a wrong as the result of the provision of negligent professional services, they expect to have the right to claim redress. It tends to erode confidence in the legal system if advocates, alone among professional men, are immune from liability for negligence.

The case raises and explores many key issues of the legal system, including the proper relationship between lawyers and the courts, the proper relationship between lawyers and clients, the differences between criminal and civil actions, professional ethics, the nature of dispute resolution and the circumstances under which the courts should make new law. Above all, however, the case has one simple significance: 'It will', in the words of Jonathan Hirst QC, Chairman of the Bar Council, 'mean that a claimant who can prove loss, as the result of an advocate's negligence, will no longer be prevented from making a claim. We cannot really say that is wrong' ((2000) *Bar News*, August, p 3).

Question 40

The White Paper *Modernising Justice: The Government's Plans for Reforming Legal Services and the Courts* (1998) proposed fundamental changes in the delivery of publicly funded justice. Why did it propose the changes it recommended, and how far has the reform achieved its aims?

Answer plan

- The nature of the problems – expense and complexity of legal processes.
- The CLS.
- Why replace the old legal aid system?
- The provision of contracted services from law firms.
- The Criminal Defence Service (CDS).
- Apparent decline in the use of the courts – a good or bad sign?

Answer

The changes proposed in the White Paper and the reforms implemented since then amount to the largest scale change in the delivery of publicly funded services since the Second World War. The White Paper stated:

> A fair and efficient justice system is a vital part of a free society. The criminal justice system exists to help protect us from crime, and to ensure that criminals are punished. The civil justice system is there to help people resolve their disputes fairly and peacefully. This Government has a radical programme of reform for the whole country. The justice system cannot be left out. We want a clearer, fairer, better system, that will make justice available to all the people.

The Paper argued that many people are put off getting help with legal problems because the legal system is slow, expensive and difficult to understand. It proposed a new CLS to ensure that 'people's needs are properly assessed, and that public money is targeted on the cases that need help most'.

Providing value for money in law is identified as a key aim of reform. The Paper argued that taxpayers have, year on year, been paying heavily for legal aid, while fewer people have been helped. By introducing contracting for legal services (the franchise system) and abolishing restrictive practices, the Government aims to increase competition among lawyers and help keep costs down. It says it will create new avenues to justice by extending conditional fees and modernising court procedures.

The CLS

About £800 m a year is spent on lawyers' fees under the civil legal aid system. Another £150 m a year from local government, central Government, charities and businesses is spent on the voluntary advice sector, including Citizens' Advice Bureaux, law centres and other advice centres. The Government has now set up the LSC to take the lead in establishing a CLS to co-ordinate the provision of legal services in every region. The plan is to achieve control over the legal aid budget and gradually to change over to a system in which the governmental spending on legal aid and voluntary sector advice is managed from one fund.

The LSC manages the CLS fund, which will replace legal aid in civil and family cases.

Why replace civil legal aid?

The Government argues as follows. Taxpayers spend £800 m a year through the civil legal aid system on buying legal services from lawyers for those who cannot afford to pay for themselves and this system now needs radical change. The old system was too heavily biased towards expensive court based solutions to people's problems. Despite a merits test, legal aid was, sometimes, used to fund cases that appeared to be undeserving. It was also not possible to control spending effectively. From 1992–93 to 1997–98, spending on civil and family legal aid grew by 35% from £586 m to £793 m; but, at the same time, the number of cases funded actually fell by 31% from 419,861 to 319,432. Lawyers were paid according to the amount of work claimed for, so there was no incentive to handle cases quickly or work efficiently.

Who will do the work and who will qualify for help?

The LSC buys services for the public under contracts. Only lawyers and other providers with contracts are able to work under the new scheme. This enables budgets to be strictly controlled, helps to ensure quality of service, and provides a basis for competition between different providers. The fund targets those people who are most in need of help and on high priority cases. There is no absolute entitlement to help and the fund will not be spent on cases which could be financed by other means, such as conditional fees. The Government does, however, intend to increase the number of people potentially eligible for advice and assistance under the scheme, to bring this into line with eligibility for representation. At the same time, those who can afford to contribute towards their legal expenses will be required to do so.

How will the Government help people who do not qualify for help from the CLS fund? It is clear that not everyone will benefit under the new scheme. In this context, the Government states that it will work with the insurance industry to widen cover (it says that 17 m people are already covered by one sort of legal insurance or another, although this figure includes people entitled to legal services in respect of only one type of situation like a traffic accident or holiday disasters). It is also intended to widen the scope of the conditional fee system. In 2000, for example, the scheme was extended to include some forms of institutional action like those involving trade unions.

The CDS

The Government states that it will maintain the fundamental principle that those facing a criminal trial should not be afraid that lack of resources and proper representation might lead to their wrongful conviction. However, serious weaknesses in the current criminal legal aid system are identified. The cost has risen from £507 m in 1992–93 to £733 m in 1997–98 – an increase of 44%. At the same time, the number of cases dealt with has increased by only 10%. Although standard fees are now paid in many cases, the most expensive cases are paid in the traditional way, by calculating the bill after the event. This gives lawyers an incentive to boost their fees by dragging cases out, and these cases take up a disproportionate amount of money. The system for means testing defendants to see whether they should contribute to the costs of their case is a waste of time and money. The test has not stopped some, apparently, wealthy defendants from receiving free legal aid and 94% of defendants in the Crown Court pay no contribution.

The Government intends to replace the current criminal legal aid scheme with a new CDS. To begin with, the CDS will be run, by the LSC, but it will be an entirely separate scheme from the CLS, with a separate budget. The Commission will develop contracts for different types of criminal defence services and implement them following pilot schemes. All contracts for criminal defence services will include quality requirements and, wherever possible, prices for the contracts will be fixed in advance. Fixed prices create an incentive to avoid delay and reward efficient practice. Eventually, contracts with solicitors firms will cover the full range of defence services, from advice at the police station to representation in court. If a case requires the services of a specialist advocate in the Crown Court, this is likely to be covered by a separate contract. Opponents of this move argue that fixed price work is not conducive to justice, as such a system of payment encourages corner-cutting and work of an inferior standard.

Very complex and expensive cases – where the trial is expected to last 25 days or more – will not be covered by ordinary contracts. A defendant's choice of solicitor will be limited to firms on a specialist panel and a separate contract will be agreed in each case.

Pressing questions here are whether the Government will introduce a salaried defender service and, if so, whether client choice will be limited? The Government has stated that it believes that the CDS should be free, in principle to employ lawyers directly to offer services to the public, as well as contracting with lawyers in private practice. The CDS will be expected to take account of the current pilot scheme involving public defence solicitors in Scotland. The Government has also said that, 'in most cases', suspects and defendants will be able to choose any lawyer who has a current contract with the CDS. The fact that lawyers have a contract will also be a guarantee that they have met the relevant quality standards. In very expensive cases, where special skills and experience are often needed, the defendant's choice will be limited to those lawyers who are on a special CDS panel and have demonstrated their ability to handle cases of this type.

Lawyers, however, have expressed fear at this proposal. The Law Society has said that famous campaigning lawyers such as Gareth Peirce (who helped release the Guildford Four and the Birmingham Six) and Jim Nicol (who represented the appellants in the Carl Bridgewater case) might be shunned by the CDS.

Who will decide whether to grant criminal representation and how? As now, it will be for the court to decide whether to grant a defendant representation at public expense, according to the interests of justice. But the current requirement for a means test will be abolished. Instead, after a case is over, a judge in the Crown Court will have the power to order a convicted defendant to pay some or all of the costs of his defence. This will mean that assets frozen during criminal proceedings, and any assets which only come to light during proceedings, will be taken into account, so some wealthy criminals will pay much more than they do now.

Plans for the new Salaried Defence Service (SDS) are now under way. In December 2000, adverts were placed in the legal press seeking six lawyers to be the 'pioneers of a radical far-reaching initiative', and the LSC began to make appointments in 2001.

The Service in its pilot stage will comprise six offices with at least three opening in April 2001. The proposals are causing some concern in the solicitors' branch of the legal profession, especially among those smaller firms, which currently pay their lawyers in private practice to do criminal defence work. The worry is that, if the SDS became established nationally, then criminal defence lawyers in private practice would be lured into the large institution – which looks like paying more than private practice. The SDS salaries are set to go up to £50,000 and, in practice, many people currently on £25,000 in a private firm look like being able to make a £10,000 leap in their salary by joining the SDS. Peter Binning, a former Crown Prosecutor, has identified a problem in this area – that of working for public organisations such as the Crown Prosecution Service. He says that, 'the professional integrity of the individual lawyer is subsumed to the organisation's priorities' ((2000) Law Soc Gazette, 16 November, p 29). There are other objections, in principle, to the Public Defenders Scheme. The State arrests, prosecutes and sentences individuals involved in the criminal justice system. For the state to purport to defend that individual will allow a breeding ground for miscarriages of justice, according to the Criminal Courts Solicitors Association. Some solicitors have been wary about the development of a 'canteen culture', where deals are struck between Crown Prosecutors and Public Defenders over a coffee in the morning. Both lawyers would be on a salary and a pension and neither would want to rock the boat.

By February 2001, over 5,000 contracts had been awarded to law firms and advice agencies in the first key stage of the reforms which will, eventually, see the almost complete replacement of the legal aid system as it was previously known.

Since 2000, only contract holders have been allowed to provide publicly funded advice and assistance and only providers with proven expertise and experience will be able to hold such contracts. The Legal Aid Board has awarded around 5,000 general civil contracts to solicitors firms and a further 330 to not-for-profit agencies (such as Citizens' Advice Bureaux) for civil advice and assistance work (the old Green Form scheme).

The Government has argued that these contracting arrangements will improve the quality of legal services and achieve two other key objectives: control costs and target priority needs.

The contracting system sets a range of controls, such as specifying the number of new advice and assistance cases a solicitor can undertake in a year, although a flexible approach is being adopted so the number of cases could be increased if demand warranted. The LSC will be retaining a reserve fund for such cases. By the same token, the number of cases funded could be reduced if a firm's average case costs are exceeding their budget terms. Further contracts for other types of legal assistance – such as legal representation in civil cases and criminal legal aid – will be phased in, until everything covered by the current legal aid fund will be subject to contracting from April 2001.

The LSC and its Regional Committees will establish priorities (in many respects locally set) for publicly funded legal advice and assistance. Since 2000, ordinary personal injury claims have not been publicly funded as the Government believes that such cases are best conducted by way of conditional fee (no win, no fee) agreements. The quality of such agreements has, however, been called into question. Michael Gould, a solicitor and legal academic, wrote to *The Times* on this issue (23 November 1999). He noted:

I was recently asked for advice by a student on behalf of a friend who was being asked to enter into [a no win, no fee] agreement. The friend had been injured in an accident while a passenger in a car. The agreement provided for a charging rate of £165 per hour, whatever level of fee earner handled the case, and that the client would be responsible for payment of the fees if he ended the agreement early. It authorised the solicitors to retain one quarter of the damages recovered.

The implications of these provisions appeared to me to be that if the client became dissatisfied with the way the office cleaner was handling his claim and took his business elsewhere he would pay at the rate referred to above. If he waited until damages were recovered (as they almost inevitably would be in these circumstances) he would hand over a quarter of his damages to his solicitors in addition to the costs they would recover from the defendant.

If this sort of arrangement is common (and that is difficult to tell), then it is clear that many clients are clearly not getting a fair deal.

The official figures tell of a decline in litigation in England and Wales. The *Judicial Statistics* (LCD) released at the end of July 2000, show that there was an 11% drop in county court claims during the previous year. In 1999, there were 2,000,337 claims, a fall of 244,987 cases on the 1998 figure. Actions in the High Court saw an even more dramatic drop – a 37% fall in actions last year down to 72,161. This could show that, as a result of the new reforms, many of the sort of undeserving cases which some commentators allege were being brought under the old legal aid system are not now being brought. That would indicate a successful reform has been well implemented. Alternatively, the figures could be used to argue that the new system replacing the older legal aid schemes has excluded many deserving people from the legal process.

It might well be that the number of actions formally commenced has fallen while social litigiousness has risen. This could happen if many more actions were being threatened but were being settled by solicitors before actions went to court. The phenomenon of a more litigious society can be interpreted in two antithetical ways. You can see it as a good thing because more people are asserting their rights and are testing new claims to improve the legal protection afforded to consumers, voters, drivers, students, patients, employees and so forth. By contrast, though, you can see it as a bad thing because the law is putting more people into arms-length, mistrustful relationships and thereby pervading communities with formal and confrontational styles of dispute settlement.

The latest governmental proposals in this area appear in a Consultation Paper (*Community Legal Service: Financial Conditions for Funding by the Legal Services Commission*, LCD, July 2000). The new plan requires currently eligible people to pay a larger contribution, and one proposal requires a person with more than £3,000 equity in his house (if someone sells his house, the *equity* is the money he would have remaining after he paid off his mortgage) to make a contribution to his CLS-funded case. Currently, homeowners with up to £100,000 equity are eligible to receive full funding provided they meet the other criteria of disposal income and disposable capital. Richard Miller, acting director of the Legal Aid Practitioners Group said ((2000) Law Soc Gazette, 3 August): 'These rules will demand money from people who quite clearly have no realistic means of contributing to costs, thus effectively preventing them from pursuing valid cases.'

CHAPTER 7

ALTERNATIVE DISPUTE RESOLUTION

Introduction

This part of the English legal system has undergone significant development in recent times. English legal system courses tend to focus too much attention on the operation of the traditional court system. Whilst the courts are of fundamental importance, one should not overlook the increasing importance of alternative methods of deciding disputes. It should never be forgotten that tribunals actually deal with more cases than the county courts and High Court combined. The use of specialist tribunals to decide problems has a long history in England, but it has to be realised that the huge growth in the number of tribunals is a product of the growth of the interventionist/Welfare State and represents, at one level, an attack on the traditional legal system. These alternative mechanisms may also be seen as highlighting the weaknesses in the adversarial court system, in that they emphasise conciliation over conflict and, to that extent at least, they may well represent an advance on the traditional system of dispute resolution. It should also be borne in mind, however, that such informal procedures themselves are not without weaknesses.

Litigation is an extremely costly procedure. This is so not just for the parties concerned in any action who have to pay the costs of their legal representatives, but also for the State which has to provide the legal framework within which the action is taken, that is, courts, judges and other staff. This has been a great impetus for potential litigants to resort to alternative dispute resolution (ADR) and, in particular, to mediation – the use of a neutral third party to assist the disputants to reach a compromise. Most civil cases are settled at the door of the court, but, by the time they arrive there, most parties have spent much time and money. Mediation aims to encourage disputants to reach such an agreement earlier.

One private mediation company, Mediation UK, already mediates in over 5,000 neighbour disputes a year.

Checklist

You should:

- have at least a minimal understanding of the social historical process that saw the substantial development of tribunals;
- have particular knowledge of the operation of a substantial number of tribunals;
- be able to compare the advantages and disadvantages of alternative dispute resolutions, as against traditional court mechanisms;
- be able to distinguish and write about arbitration, mediation and conciliation;
- be prepared to answer a specific question relating to the Arbitration Act of 1996;
- be prepared to answer a question on the county court small claims procedure (this may stand you in good stead for questions on court structure or civil procedure as well).

Question 41

Critically evaluate the advantages and disadvantages that flow from the use of administrative tribunals, as opposed to ordinary courts.

Answer plan

This question invites a straightforward comparison of tribunals and courts and the answer should include at least some of the following points:

- consideration of the usual *advantages* cited for tribunals – cheapness, speed and informality;
- consideration of the foregoing, in the light of the *disadvantages* of the system;
- some note of the fact that the same areas can be cited as advantages and disadvantages, at one and the same time;

- comparison of the operation of tribunals with that of the courts;
- a conclusion suggesting whether, and if so how, the operation of tribunals can be improved (mention should be made of the review of tribunals being conducted by Sir Andrew Leggatt).

Answer

The reason generally put forward for the establishment and growth of tribunals in Britain since 1945 is the need to provide a specialist forum to deal with cases involving conflicts between an increasingly interventionist welfare State, its functionaries, and the rights of private citizens. It is arguable, however, that the large scale development of this special area of dispute resolution marks a diminishment in the general rule of law, to the extent that it has led to a transfer of power from the ordinary courts.

A number of advantages are usually cited in favour of the use of tribunals, rather than the ordinary court system. These advantages relate to the cost, speed, efficiency, privacy and the lack of formality involved in such proceedings. It is important, however, that these supposed advantages are not simply taken at face value for, although they do, no doubt, represent significant improvements over the operation of the ordinary court system, it is at least arguable that some of them are not, necessarily, as advantageous as they appear at first sight and that others represent potential (if not actual) weaknesses in the tribunal system.

The ordinary system of courts, with the important exception of the magistrates' courts, are staffed by people who have had a specifically legal education and training, as may be seen from the requirement for judges to be qualified legal practitioners of some standing. With regard to the tribunal system, however, this is not the case. Tribunals are usually made up of three members, only one of whom, the chair, is expected to be legally qualified. The other two members require no specific legal qualification or expertise. The lack of legal training is not considered a drawback given the technical administrative, as opposed to specifically legal, nature of the provisions they have to consider. Indeed, the fact of there being two lay representatives on tribunals provides them with one of their perceived advantages over courts; for, to the extent that the non-legal members may provide specialist knowledge, they enable the tribunal to base its decision on actual practice as opposed to abstract legal theory and, thus, enable decisions to be taken on practical grounds rather than on the basis of mere legal formalism.

An example of this can be seen in respect of the tribunals responsible for deciding matters relating to employment under the Employment Rights Act 1996. In practice, such tribunals are normally made up of a legally qualified chairperson, a representative of employers and a representative of employees. As a consequence, the tribunal has access to the practical experience of the lay members together with knowledge of the circumstances involved in any particular dispute from both sides of the employment relationship. Such practical experience and expertise provides a basis for the decisions of the tribunal and gives such decisions a degree of pragmatic legitimacy.

A lack of formalism is also evident in the general procedure of tribunals with the intention of making them less intimidating than full-blown court cases. Informality is shown in the fact that the strict rules relating to evidence, pleading and procedure, which apply in courts, are not binding or applied in tribunal proceedings. An example of this relaxation of strict court procedure is evident in the fact that tribunals are not bound by the strict rules of precedent. Of equal importance, is the perhaps conflicting, if not contradictory, need for consistency of treatment, which is one of the major justifications of the system of precedent.

When these matters relating to the lack of formality are linked with the fact that tribunal proceedings tend not to be accusatorial, they, generally, lead to the conclusion that complainants do not need to be represented by a lawyer in order to present their grievance. They may represent themselves or be represented by a more knowledgeable associate, such as a trade union representative or a friend.

The fact that complainants do not have to rely on legal representation, in turn, makes the tribunal procedure less expensive than using the traditional court system and this reduction in expense is further enhanced by the additional facts that there are no court fees involved in relation to tribunal proceedings and that costs are not normally awarded against a party who loses the case.

A further perceived advantage of the tribunal system is the speed of its operation, together with the certainty that it will be heard on a specific date.

The final advantage usually cited is the fact that proceedings can be taken before a tribunal without necessarily triggering the publicity that might follow from a court case.

All of these factors, making the use of the tribunal system less intimidating as well as much less expensive than using the normal court system, serve to encourage individuals to pursue their grievances in circumstances where they might not be willing to take action in the courts and, thus, they can be seen as serving the praiseworthy function of increasing access to the law and legal remedies.

Having examined the supposed advantages of the tribunal system, it remains to consider the its shortcomings. The first of these arises with regard to the uncertainty and lack of uniformity that exists in relation to appeals from tribunals. Rights of appeal from decisions of tribunals and the route of such appeals, depend on the provision of the statute under which a particular tribunal operates and, where they exist, may be exercised variously, to a further tribunal, a minister or a court of law. Prior to the Franks Committee Report (Cmnd 218, 1957), tribunals were not required to provide reasons for their decisions and this prevented appeals in most cases. Subsequent to the Franks Report, however, most tribunals, although still not all of them (and this remains a major bone of contention), are required to provide reasons for their decisions under s 12 of the Tribunals and Inquiries Act 1971. The importance of this provision is that, in cases where a tribunal has erred in its application of the law, the claimant can appeal to the High Court for an application for judicial review to have the decision of the tribunal set aside for error of law on the face of the record.

Secondly, it has generally been accepted that the lack of publicity in relation to the majority of tribunal proceedings is an advantage, but the alternative possibility has to be considered; that such lack of publicity is, in fact, a distinct disadvantage because it has the effect that cases involving issues of general public importance are not given the publicity and consideration that they might merit.

The major weakness as regards the operation of tribunals, however, is that except for Land Tribunals and the Commons Commissioners, people pursuing cases before tribunals were not entitled to legal aid to finance their cases. The effect of the replacement of legal aid by the Community Legal Service fund under the Access to Justice Act 1999 remains to be seen. It is probably accurate to say, however, that, in this particular area, it certainly can't make matters worse and that the establishment of Community Legal Service Partnerships may well improve the availability of quality advice for those with problems to be decided by tribunals.

The foregoing has stated that the major advantages of the tribunal system are to be found in its lack of formality and its non-legal atmosphere, but research has shown that individual complainants fare better where they are, in fact, represented by lawyers. Additionally, it is, perhaps, one of the unintended consequences of the Franks Report that the appointment of legally qualified chairpersons has led to an increase in the formality of tribunal proceedings. As a consequence, non-law experts find it increasingly difficult, in practice, to represent themselves effectively. This difficulty is compounded when the body which is the object of the complaint is itself legally represented, for, although the parties to hearings do not have to be legally represented, equally, there is nothing to prevent them from being so represented, no doubt to their advantage.

If tribunals are becoming increasingly important in determining individual rights and are, at the same time, becoming formalistic, then the refusal of assistance to fund legal representation to those seeking to use tribunals is tantamount to refusing them access to justice.

In May 2000, Lord Irvine appointed Sir Andrew Leggatt to review the current operation of the Tribunal system and the attendant consultation paper stated that:

> There are signs ... that the complexity of the system (if indeed it amounts to a system at all), its diversity, and the separateness within it of most tribunals, may be creating problems for the user and an overall lack of coherence.

Sir Andrew's task is to review the delivery of justice through tribunals other than ordinary courts of law. There are listed 130 bodies subject to the review which is due to be submitted in March 2001.

In conclusion, it is possible to argue that the provision of a forum for resolving disputes which is cheap, quick and informal represents a significant advance on the traditional court system, but, on the other hand, it is at least somewhat disconcerting to consider that these tribunals, as a consequence of the fact that they are cheap, quick and informal, actually represent an attack on legal standards and provide merely a second rate system of justice for those who cannot afford to pay for legal representation to ensure that they operate effectively and justly.

Question 42

Critically consider the role of the Parliamentary Commissioner for Administration.

Answer plan

The Parliamentary Commissioner for Administration (PCA) is better known as the Ombudsman, whose function, under the Parliamentary Commissioner Act 1967, is to investigate complaints relating to maladministration. The PCA deals with problems in relation to central Government, but other ombudsmen have been appointed to oversee the administration of local government in England and Wales, under the Local Government Act 1974. In dealing with this question, the following points should be addressed:

- a brief history of the concept of ombudsmen;
- the statutory basis of the PCA's powers;
- the meaning of maladministration;
- the filter role of MPs;
- the powers of the PCA;
- criticisms/limitations of the system;
- the spread of the system to other areas.

Answer

The actual concept of the ombudsman is Scandinavian in origin and the function of the office holder is to investigate complaints of *maladministration*; that is, situations where the performance of a Government department has fallen below acceptable standards of administration.

As with tribunals, so the institution of the ombudsman reflects the increased activity of the contemporary State. As the State became more engaged in everyday social activity it increasingly impinged on and, on occasion, conflicted with, the rights of individual citizen. Courts and tribunals were available to deal with substantive breaches of particular rules and procedures, but there remained some disquiet as to the possibility of the effect of the implementation of general State policy on individuals. If tribunals may be categorised as an alternative procedure of dispute resolution to the ordinary court system in relation to *decisions taken in breach of rules*; the institution of ombudsman represents a procedure for the redress of complaints about *the way in which those decisions have been taken*. It has to be admitted, however, that the two categories overlap to a considerable degree. The ombudsman procedure, however, is not just an alternative to the court and tribunal system; it is based upon a distinctly different approach to dealing with disputes. Indeed, the Parliamentary Commissioner Act 1967, which established the position of the first ombudsman, provides that complainants with rights to pursue their complaints in either of those fora will not be able to make use of the ombudsman procedure. This prohibition is subject to the discretion of the ombudsman and, in practice, it is interpreted it in a generous manner in favour of the complainant, so as to allow investigations.

The first ombudsman, appointed in 1967 under the aforementioned legislation, operated – and the present PCA, Michael Buckley , still operates – under the title of the PCA and was empowered to consider central Government processes only. Since that date, a number of other ombudsmen have been appointed to oversee the administration of local government in England and Wales, under the Local Government Act 1974. Scotland and Northern Ireland have their own local government ombudsmen fulfilling the same task. There is also a Health Service Ombudsman for England, Wales and Scotland, whose duty it is to investigate the administration and provision of services in the Health service. This role is, actually, assumed by the PCA, Michael Buckley. In 1994, an ombudsman for the Prison Service was appointed to cover that area. Additionally, the ombudsman role has proved popular in commercial areas and ombudsmen have been appointed in relation to legal services, banking, building societies, insurance and pensions. This proliferation of ombudsmen has led to some confusion as to which one any particular complaint should be taken to. This can be especially problematic where the complaint concerns more than one public body. In order to remedy this potential difficulty a Cabinet Office review recommended, in April 2000, that access be made easier through the establishment of one new Commission bringing together the ombudsmen for central government, local government and the health service.

The procedure for making use of the various ombudsmen, and their powers, differs, according to the particular field they cover and the manner in which they were established, that is, under statutory authority or purely as a voluntary procedure under commercial codes of conduct. As regards the PCA, the following points are worthy of mention.

Although maladministration is not defined in the Parliamentary Commissioner Act 1967, it has been taken to refer to an error in the way a decision was reached rather than an error in the actual decision itself. Indeed, s 12(3) of the Parliamentary Commissioner Act expressly precludes the PCA from questioning the merits of particular decisions taken without maladministration. Maladministration, therefore, can be seen to refer to procedure used to reach a result, rather than the result itself. In an illuminating, and much quoted, speech introducing the 1967 Act, Richard Crossman, the then leader of the House of Commons, gave an indicative, if non-definitive, list of what might be included within the term maladministration, and included within it: bias, neglect, inattention, delay, incompetence, ineptitude, perversity, turpitude and arbitrariness.

Members of the public do not have the right to complain directly to the PCA, but must channel any such complaint through an MP. Complainants do not have to provide precise details of any maladministration. They, simply, have to indicate difficulties they have experienced as a result of dealing with an agency of central Government. It is the function of the PCA to discover whether the problem arose as a result of maladministration. There is a 12 month time limit for raising complaints, but the PCA has discretion to ignore this.

The powers of the PCA to investigate complaints are similar to those of a High Court judge to require the attendance of witnesses and the production of documents; and wilful obstruction of the investigation is treated as contempt of court.

On conclusion of an investigation, the PCA submits reports to the MP who raised complaint and to the principal of the Government office which was subject to the investigation. The PCA has no enforcement powers, but, if his recommendations are ignored and existing practices involving maladministration are not altered, he may submit a further report to both Houses of Parliament, in order to highlight the continued bad practice. The assumption is that, on the submission of such a report, MPs will exert pressure on the appropriate minister of State to ensure that any necessary changes in procedure are made. Annual reports are laid before Parliament and a Parliamentary Select Committee exists to oversee the operation of the PCA.

Two reports from the PCA are worthy of particular consideration. The first one, issued in January 1995, related to the much criticised Child Support Agency (CSA) which was established in an attempt to ensure that absent parents, essentially fathers, would have to accept financial responsibility for the maintenance of their children as determined by the agency. The PCA's report followed complaints referred to him by 95 MPs, covering the time from when the CSA started its operations until the end of 1994. Although the PCA investigated 70 complaints, the report focused on seven of those as being representative of the whole. These complaints highlighted a number of failures on the part of the CSA: mistakes as to the identity of individuals subject to the determinations of the CSA; failure to answer correspondence; delay in assessing and reviewing maintenance assessments and delays in actually securing payments due; and the provision of incorrect or misleading advice. The conclusion of the PCA was that the CSA was liable for maladministration, inexcusable delays and slipshod service. In response to the report, the chief executive of the CSA wrote to the PCA, informing him that steps were being taken to deal with the problems highlighted in the report; and, pre-empting a significant alteration in the operation of the CSA implemented subsequently, the Junior Minister for Social Security promised alterations to improve quality, accuracy and customer service.

The second report, issued in February 1995, related to the effect of the delays in determining the route for the Channel Tunnel rail link. As a consequence of the four year delay on the part of the Department of Transport in deciding on a route, the owners of properties along the various possible routes found the value of their properties blighted, not to say unsaleable. The situation was not finalised until the Department announced its final selection in 1994. According to the PCA:

> The effect of the Department of Transport's policy was to put the project in limbo, keeping it alive when it could not be funded.

As a consequence, he held that the Department:

> ... had a responsibility to consider the position of such persons suffering exceptional or extreme hardship and to provide redress where appropriate. They undertook no such considerations. That merits my criticism.

The unusual thing about this case, however, was the reaction of the Department of Transport, which rejected the findings of the PCA and refused to provide any compensation. It was this refusal which led the PCA to issue his special report, consequent upon a situation where an 'injustice has been found which has not or will not be remedied'. Even then, the Department of Transport did not give way, until pressured to do so by the Parliamentary Select Committee on the PCA. Eventually, payments of £5,000 were made to those owners whose houses had suffered from property blight.

In offering an evaluation of the ombudsman procedure, it may be claimed that, all in all, the system appears to operate fairly well within its restricted sphere of operation, but there are major areas where it could be improved. The more important of the criticisms levelled at the PCA relate to:

(a) the retention of MPs as filters for complaints. It is generally accepted that there is no need for such a filter mechanism. At one level, it represents a sop to the idea of parliamentary representation and control. Yet, at the practical level, PCAs have referred complaints made to them directly on to the constituent's MP, in order to have them referred back in the appropriate form. It is suggested that there is no longer any need or justification for this fiction;

(b) the restrictive nature of the definition of maladministration. It is possible to argue that any procedure that leads to an unreasonable decision must involve an element of maladministration and that, therefore, the definition as currently stated is not overly restrictive. However, even if such reverse reasoning is valid, it would still be preferable for the definition of the scope of the PCA's investigations to be clearly stated and be stated in wider terms than at present;

(c) the jurisdiction the PCA. This criticism tends to resolve itself into the view that there are many areas that should be covered by the PCA but which are not. For example, as presently constituted, the ombudsman can only investigate the *operation* of general law. It could be claimed, and not without some justification, that the process of *making* law, in the form of delegated legislation, equally could do with investigation;

(d) the lack of publicity given to complaints. It is, sometimes, suggested that insufficient publicity is given either to the existence of the various ombudsmen or to the results of their investigations. The argument is that if more people were aware of the procedure and what it could achieve, then more people would make use of it, leading to an overall improvement in the administration of Governmental policies;

(e) the reactive role of the ombudsman. This criticism refers to the fact that the ombudsmen are dependent upon receiving complaints before they can initiate investigations. It is suggested that a more pro-active role under which the ombudsmen would be empowered to initiate investigation on their own authority would lead to an improvement in general administration, as well as an increase in the effectiveness of the activity of the ombudsmen. This criticism is related to the way in which the role of the ombudsmen is viewed. If they are simply a problem solving dispute resolution institution then a reactive role is sufficient; if, however, they are seen as the means of improving general administrative performance, then a more proactive role is called for.

Question 43

Explain the content and effect of the Arbitration Act 1996.

Answer plan

This question is very straightforward and simply tests the candidate's knowledge of this important piece of legislation. In answering it, candidates should be aware of the changes introduced by the Act; essentially, the shift from a court based system to a voluntary, party based system, and should be able to provide a clear analysis of the major statutory provisions. An explanation of the reasons for the change and its origin would also be beneficial. The following structure would provide a framework for answering the question adequately:

- introduction – principles behind and reasons for the Act;
- freedom of the parties to chose what suits them best;
- arbitrators and their powers;
- role and powers of the court.

Answer

The Arbitration Act 1996 was given royal assent in June 1996 and the majority of its provisions were brought into force by January 1997. The Act repeals Pt 1 of the Arbitration Act 1950 and the whole of the Arbitration Acts of 1975 and 1979. The Act follows the Model Arbitration Law adopted in 1985 by the United Nations Commission on International Trade Law (UNCITRAL).

Section 1 of the Act states that it is founded on the following principles:

(a) the object of arbitration is to obtain the fair resolution of disputes by an impartial tribunal without necessary delay or expense;

(b) the parties should be free to agree how their disputes are resolved, subject only to such safeguards as are necessary in the public interest;

(c) in matters governed by this part of the Act the court should not intervene except as provided by this part.

This statement of general principles, which should inform the reading of the later detailed provisions of the Act, is unusual for UK legislation, but may be seen as reflecting the purposes behind the Act. One major purpose was to ensure that London did not lose its place as a leading centre for international arbitration. As a consequence of the demand driven nature of the new legislation, it would seem that court interference in the arbitration process has had to be reduced to a minimum and replaced by party autonomy. Under the Act, the role of the arbitrator has been increased and that of the court has been reduced to the residual level of intervention where the arbitration process either requires legal assistance, or else is seen to be failing to provide a just settlement.

In analysing the operation of the Act, and contrasting it with the way in which the previous legislation operated, it is useful to consider it in three distinct parts: (a) autonomy of the parties; (b) powers of the arbitral panel; and (c) court powers.

Autonomy

As has been stated already, the main thrust of the Act is to empower the parties to the dispute and to allow them to decide how the matter is to be best decided. In pursuit of this aim, the mandatory parts of the Act only take effect where the parties involved do not agree otherwise. It is even possible for the parties to agree that the dispute should not be decided in line with the strict legal rules, but rather in line with commercial fairness, which might be a completely different thing altogether.

Whilst it is possible for there to be an oral arbitration agreement at common law, s 5 provides that Pt 1 of the Act only applies to agreements in writing. What this means in practice, however, has been extended by s 5(3), which provides that, where the parties agree to an arbitration procedure which is in writing, that procedure will be operative, even though the agreement between the parties is not itself in writing. An example of such a situation would be where a salvage operation was negotiated between two vessels at sea on the basis of Lloyd's standard salvage terms. It would be unlikely that the actual agreement would be reduced to written form but, nonetheless, the arbitration element in those terms would be effective.

Section 6 provides that an arbitration agreement means an agreement to submit to arbitration present or future disputes, whether contractual or not.

Arbitrators and their powers

The arbitration tribunal may consist of a single arbitrator, or a panel, as the parties decide (s 15). If one party fails to appoint an arbitrator, then the other party's nominee may act as sole arbitrator (s 17).

Under s 20(4), where there is a panel and it fails to reach a majority decision, then the decision of the chair shall prevail.

Section 28 expressly provides that the parties to the proceedings are jointly and severally liable to pay the arbitrators such reasonable fees and expenses as appropriate. Previously, this was only an implied term. And s 29 provides that arbitrators are not liable for anything done or omitted in the discharge of their functions, unless the act or omission was done in bad faith.

It is also for the tribunal to decide all procedural and evidential matters. Section 30 provides that, unless the parties agree otherwise, the arbitrator can rule on questions relating to its own jurisdiction, that is, in relation to:

(a) whether there actually is a valid arbitration agreement;

(b) whether the arbitration tribunal is properly constituted;

(c) what matters have been submitted to arbitration in accordance with the agreement.

Parties may be represented by a lawyer or any other person, and the tribunal may appoint experts or legal advisors to report to it.

Section 33 provides that the tribunal has a general duty:

(a) to act fairly and impartially between the parties, giving each a reasonable opportunity to state their case; and

(b) to adopt procedures suitable for the circumstances of the case, avoiding unnecessary delay or expense.

Section 35 provides that, subject to the parties agreeing to the contrary, the tribunal shall have the following powers:

(a) to order parties to provide security for costs (previously, a power reserved to the courts);

(b) to give directions in relation to property subject to the arbitration;

(c) to direct that a party or witness be examined on oath and to administer the oath. The parties may also empower the arbitrator to make provisional orders (s 39).

Section 46 states that the arbitral tribunal must decide the dispute:

(a) in accordance with the law chosen by the parties; or

(b) in accordance with such other considerations as the parties have agreed.

Section 48 again states that, unless agreed otherwise, the tribunal shall have the following powers:

(a) to make a declaration about any matter to be determined in the proceedings;

(b) to order payment of money;

(c) to order a party to refrain from doing anything;

(d) to order specific performance of a contract;

(e) to order rectification, setting aside or cancellation of a deed or any other document.

Section 49 empowers the awarding of interest, either simple or compound, and s 50 allows for the extension of the time for making an award.

Section 58 provides that any award made is final and binding on the parties and s 66 provides that any such award can be enforced in the same manner as a court judgment.

Role of the court

Where one party seeks to start a court action, in contradiction to a valid arbitration agreement to the contrary, then the other party may request the court to stay the litigation in favour of the arbitration agreement under ss 9–11 of the Act. Where, however, both parties agree to ignore the arbitration agreement and seek recourse to the litigation then, following the party consensual nature of the Act, the original agreement may be ignored.

Under s 12, the courts may grant an extension to any set time limit for starting proceedings, but only on the limited exceptions stated: that is, what is reasonable and in the interests of justice.

The courts may order a party to comply with an order of the tribunal and may also order parties and witnesses to attend and to give oral evidence before tribunals (s 43).

Under s 18, the court has power to revoke the appointment of an arbitrator, on application of any of the parties, where there has been a failure in the appointment procedure, and it also has powers to revoke authority under s 24, on the application of one of the parties, where the arbitrator:

(a) has not acted impartially;
(b) does not possess the required qualifications;
(c) does not have either the physical or mental capacity to deal with the proceedings;
(d) has refused or failed:
    (i)   to conduct the proceedings properly; or
    (ii) has been dilatory in dealing with the proceedings or in making an award,

to the extent that it will cause substantial injustice to the party applying for their removal.

Section 32 allows any of the parties to raise, in court, preliminary objections to the substantive jurisdiction of the arbitration tribunal, but provides that they may only do so on limited grounds, which requires either the agreement of the parties concerned, or the permission of the arbitration tribunal and the agreement of the court. Leave to appeal will only be granted where the court is satisfied that that the question involves a point of law of general importance.

Under s 45, the court may, on application by one of the parties, decide any preliminary question of law arising in the course of the proceedings.

Once the decision of the arbitral panel has been made, there are only limited grounds for appeal to the court. The first ground arises under s 67, in relation to the substantive jurisdiction of the arbitral panel, although this right may be lost if the party attempting to make use of it took part in the arbitration proceedings without objecting to the alleged lack of jurisdiction.

The second ground for appeal to the courts is on procedural grounds, under s 68, on the basis that some serious irregularity affected the operation of the tribunal. By serious irregularity is meant:

(a) failure to comply with the general duty set out in s 33;
(b) failure to conduct the tribunal as agreed by the parties;
(c) uncertainty or ambiguity as to the effect of the award;
(d) failure to comply with the requirement as to the form of the award.

Under s 69, parties may also appeal on a point of law arising from the award. However, the parties can agree beforehand to preclude such a possibility and, where they agree to the arbitral panel making a decision without providing a reasoned justification for it, they will also lose the right to appeal.

The foregoing sets out the main provision of the Arbitration Act 1996 in such a way as to demonstrate the shift from a court based system to a voluntaristic arbitration based system, in line with the expressed wishes of commercial enterprises.

Question 44

Explain what is meant by 'ADR' paying particularly attention to the following types:

(a) arbitration;
(b) mediation; and
(c) conciliation.

Answer plan

This question is more general than the previous ones, in that it introduces arbitration and asks for a consideration of the processes of mediation and conciliation. Detail is necessarily less, but the question still requires a substantial understanding of the processes. The following structure might prove satisfactory:

- consider the operation of arbitration as compared to the ordinary courts (refer specifically to the Arbitration Act 1996);
- consider the distinction between mediation and conciliation, as well as detailing how and when they are likely to be used;
- conclude by placing these various ADR mechanisms within the framework of the general legal system.

Answer

It is generally recognised that the formal atmosphere of the ordinary courts is not necessarily the most appropriate one in which to determine all disputes which might need adjudication. In recognition of this fact, various alternatives have been developed specifically to avoid the perceived shortcomings of court procedure.

The first and oldest of these alternative procedures is arbitration. Arbitration is the procedure whereby parties in dispute refer the issue under contention to a third party for resolution, rather than institute legal proceedings in the courts. This practice is well established in commerce and industry; its legal effectiveness has long been recognised by the court. In contemporary business usage, it is a matter of common practice for commercial contracts to contain express clauses referring any future disputes to arbitration.

Arbitration proceedings are now governed by the Arbitration Act 1996, which repeals previous legislation. This Act (which is dealt with in detail in Question 43, above) significantly alters the relationship between the parties, the arbitrator and the courts. Whereas, previously, the courts ultimately dominated the procedure, now their role has been reduced to providing safeguards against improper actions on the part of the arbitrator, and the determination of points of law. So, now the parties to any dispute are at liberty to provide their procedures for resolving it. Under the Act, arbitrators have a general duty to act fairly and impartially between the parties, giving each a reasonable opportunity to state their case; and to adopt procedures suitable for the circumstances of the case, avoiding unnecessary delay or expense. Section 46 states that the arbitral tribunal must decide the dispute:

(a) in accordance with the law chosen by the parties; or
(b) in accordance with such other considerations as the parties have agreed.

The court does have power, under s 24, to revoke the appointment of an arbitrator where the arbitrator has not acted impartially; does not possess the required qualifications; does not have either the physical or mental capacity to deal with the proceedings; or has failed to conduct the proceedings properly.

Once the decision of the panel has been made, there are only limited grounds for appeal to the court in relation to the substantive jurisdiction of the panel, or on procedural grounds, on the basis that some serious irregularity affected the operation of the tribunal. Under s 69, parties may also appeal on a point of law arising from the award. However, the parties can agree, beforehand, to preclude such a possibility and, where they agree to the arbitral panel making a decision without providing a reasoned justification for it, they will also lose the right to appeal.

It is possible for arbitration agreements to specify in advance who will act as arbitrator in the event of any dispute. Such a person may be a legal practitioner, or an expert in the particular field of commerce to which the contract relates. There are also specialist institutions which deal with arbitration and it is quite common for the agreement simply to refer the dispute to such an institution to select an appropriate arbitrator.

There are numerous advantages to be gained from using arbitration rather than the court system. First, arbitration tends to be a private procedure and this has the twofold advantage that outsiders do not get access to any potentially sensitive information and, further, the parties to the arbitration do not run the risk of any damaging publicity arising out of reports of the proceedings.

Secondly, the use of arbitration lessens the likelihood of protracted litigation, although it has to be admitted that, where one of the parties makes use of the available grounds to challenge an arbitration award, the prior costs of the arbitration will have been largely wasted.

This previous point leads to a consideration of the actual costs of the arbitration process. It is generally asserted that arbitration is a much cheaper procedure than taking a case to the normal courts, but the costs of arbitration and the use of specialist arbitrators should not be underestimated, for they can in themselves be considerable.

Cost is usually in direct proportion to the time taken to decide a case and, here again, the arbitration procedure has distinct advantages over the usual court procedure, for it is distinctly quicker in delivering a decision on the case in point. It has to be admitted, however, that delays may be inevitable where there is any doubt as to the application of a point of law and the arbitration procedure may have to be stalled in order for the arbitrator to get the definitive opinion of the ordinary courts on a particularly contentious aspect of law.

A further point which follows from the use of a specialist arbitrator is that the parties to the arbitration can rely on that person having a expert knowledge of the actual practice within the area that constitutes the ground of the dispute and count on the arbitrator delivering a decision in line with accepted practice.

The type of arbitration scheme considered above tends to relate to large business contracts,, but it should be noted that, since 1973, an arbitration service has been available within the county court specifically for the settlement of small claims. Any dispute involving a sum of £3,000 or less was automatically referred to this procedure and claims involving more than £3,000 could be referred to the procedure with the approval of the parties involved. As with arbitration, the aim of this procedure was to provide a cheap, informal, mechanism for dealing with small claims and, specifically, consumer complaints, usually under the supervision of a district judge. In pursuit of those ends, the county court rules actually provided that, in relation to the arbitration process, any such hearing should be informal and that the strict rules of evidence should not apply.

This previous procedure has been replaced following Pt 27 of the Civil Procedure Rules 1998. Under the new rules the concept of an 'arbitration' disappears and is replaced by a small claims hearing, although there is no longer any 'automatic' reference to the small claims track. Other consequential changes to the handling of small claims include:

- an increase in the jurisdiction from £3,000 to no more than £5,000, with the exception of claims for personal injury and for housing disrepair where the limit remains at £1,000;
- where a judge thinks that paper adjudication may be appropriate, that is, without the parties having to attend, then they will be asked to say whether or not they have any objections within a given time period. If a party does object, the matter will be given a hearing in the normal way;
- parties need not attend the hearing, but the court will take into account any written evidence that party has sent to the court;
- parties, with the court's approval, can consent to use the small claims track, even if the value of their claim exceeds the normal value for that track;
- parties will also be restricted to a maximum one day hearing.

Aspects of the old small claims procedure which are retained, include their informality, the interventionist approach adopted by the judiciary, the limited costs regime and the limited grounds for appeal (misconduct of the district judge, or an error of law made by the court).

Although the use of legal representation is not forbidden, it is, effectively, discouraged by the fact that the normal rule as to costs following the event is not applicable under the arbitration process; this no costs rule provides that expenses are not awarded to the successful party in such a case. The general attempt to provide an informal atmosphere is further encouraged by the wide discretion afforded to the courts as to the manner in which they pursue the arbitration procedure, to the extent that they can assume an inquisitorial approach to the hearings before them in order to elicit information on which to base their decisions.

Mediation and conciliation are the most informal of all ADR procedures. Mediation is the process through which a third party acts as the conduit through which two disputing parties communicate and negotiate in an attempt to reach a common resolution of a problem. Mediation has an important part to play in family matters, where it is felt that the adversarial approach of the traditional legal system has tended to emphasise, if not increase, existing differences of view between individuals and has not been conducive to amicable settlements. Thus, in divorce cases, mediation has, traditionally, been used to enable the parties themselves to work out an agreed settlement rather than having one imposed on them from outside by the courts. It is important to realise there are potential problems with mediation. The assumption that the parties freely negotiate the terms of their final agreement in a less than hostile manner may be deeply flawed, to the extent that it assumes equality of bargaining power and knowledge between the parties to the negotiation. Mediation may well ease pain, but, unless the mediation procedure is carefully and critically monitored, it may gloss over and perpetuate a previously exploitative relationship, allowing the more powerful participant to manipulate and dominate the more vulnerable, and force an inequitable agreement. Establishing entitlements on the basis of clear legal advice may be preferable to apparently negotiating those entitlements away in the non-confrontational, therapeutic, atmosphere of mediation. Much emphasis was placed on mediation in the Family Law Act 1996, which was introduced by the previous Conservative Government under the stewardship of the then Lord Chancellor Lord Mackay. The Act was designed to introduce 'no fault' divorce, backed by systems allowing for 'cooling off', reflection and mediation. The provisions of the Act were not introduced immediately, rather mediation, as an alternative to court hearings, was tried in some pilot schemes. The results of the pilot schemes were not good and in June 1999 the current Lord Chancellor, Lord Irvine, announced that the Act would not be implemented during the year 2000. In December of that year, a further report that mediation had produced no savings over the traditional method of using lawyers, was thought to signal the demise of the Family Law Act 1996 and, in January 2001, the Lord Chancellor announced the Government's intention to repeal Pt II of the Act.

Conciliation takes mediation a step further and gives the mediator the power to suggest grounds for compromise and the possible basis for a conclusive agreement. Both mediation and conciliation have been available in relation to industrial disputes, under the auspices of the government-funded Advisory Conciliation and Arbitration Service, and have an important part to play in family matters. The essential weakness in these two procedures, however, lies in the fact that, although they may lead to the resolution of a dispute, they do not necessarily achieve that end. Where they operate successfully, they are excellent methods of dealing with problems, as, essentially, the parties to the dispute determine their own solutions and, therefore, feel commitment to the outcome. The problem is that they have no binding power and do not always lead to an outcome.

In conclusion, the foregoing has considered a variety of alternative mechanisms for dealing with legal problems which have been developed in response to particular shortcomings in the ordinary court system and, perhaps, they point to a fundamental need to reform the operation of those law courts and to regularise the whole provision of dispute resolution devices under the law.

CHAPTER 8

THE RULE OF LAW, JUDICIAL REVIEW AND HUMAN RIGHTS

Introduction

The questions in this chapter may not appear in all English legal system syllabuses. It is true that this chapter touches on material that will, traditionally, be considered more fully in other courses, such as public or constitutional and administrative law; civil liberties options; or, indeed, some legal theory courses. The fact is, however, that the English legal system simply cannot be fully understood or placed in its contemporary context without a consideration of the points raised hereafter; and many syllabuses look to students to have at least a passing acquaintance with the matters that are considered in this chapter.

The English legal system cannot be treated as static; it is continuously responding to changes that take place in society as a whole. As was stated in the introduction to Chapter 1 of this text, to deny the relevance of European law in an English legal system course would not only be restrictive, it would be wrong to the extent that it ignored an, increasingly, important factor in the formation and determination of UK law. The same can be said of the change in the form and content of law that has taken place in the course of the 20th century and which can be linked to the emergence of the interventionist State. Equally, the same can be said with regard to the increase in applications for judicial review. Arguably, this may be seen as the judges fighting a reactionary rearguard action against the forces of the all-encompassing State, or it can be seen as the judges valiantly endeavouring to curtail excesses of that State in the defence of individual liberties. In either case, it represents a political struggle between the judiciary and the executive and one that has fundamental implications for, not only the English legal system, but also the constitution of the UK.

The incorporation of the European Convention on Human Rights (ECHR) into UK law through the Human Rights Act (HRA) 1998 has profound implications for the operation of the English legal system and the relationship of the judiciary to the legislature and executive. Although how it finally works out remains to be seen, it can already be seen to have had a substantial effect since its implementation in October 2000.

Checklist

- What is actually meant by the term 'the rule of law'?
- Does everyone agree as to the meaning?
- To what extent has the meaning changed over time?
- Is there an identifiable core meaning to 'the rule of law'?
- What is judicial review and what remedies does it offer?
- Why have applications for judicial review increased so remarkably?
- Is law an end in itself, or simply a means to an end?
- What does the HRA 1998 provide?
- What are the implications of the HRA 1998?

Question 45

What is meant by 'the rule of law' and of what relevance is it in contemporary society?

Answer plan

This question asks for a general consideration of the rule of law and, importantly, questions its relevance in contemporary times. Candidates must understand what is understood by the concept and must offer an opinion as to its continued relevance; but they must be careful to substantiate any opinion and not resort to mere assertion and amorphous waffle. One way (and it is only one of many ways) to answer this question is as follows:

- offer a general definition of the rule of law, before going on to examine particular versions of the idea;
- explain AV Dicey's understanding of the concept;

- outline historical criticisms of Dicey;
- give an account of Friedrich von Hayek's view of the rule of law;
- describe Raz's critique of Hayek and his version of the rule of law;
- conclude by considering the possibility of there being some core meaning within the idea of the rule of law.

Answer

The rule of law has been described by DM Walker, in *The Oxford Companion to Law* (1980), as a 'concept of the utmost importance but having no defined, nor readily definable, content'. Although there is certainly an element of truth in what Walker states, it is suggested that it is possible to establish a core meaning in relation to the idea of the rule of law, although the complete meaning of the concept does tend to be more ambiguous and subject to change depending on the political outlook of the person using the term and the time period in which it is being considered.

In considering the meaning of the concept, 'the rule of law', one is immediately drawn into a consideration of the work of the late 19th century writer on the English constitution, AV Dicey, whose *Law of the Constitution* was first published in 1885. According to the chauvinistic Dicey, the rule of law was one of the key features which distinguished the English constitution from its continental counterparts. (The other essential element in the English constitution was the sovereignty of Parliament; an idea not completely compatible with the rule of law, for the idea that Parliament is sovereign and recognises no restraint is in conflict with a notion of the rule of law which sees it as primarily about controlling executive power.)

Whereas foreigners were subject to the exercise of arbitrary power, the Englishman was secure within the protection afforded him by the rule of law. In setting out what was actually meant by the rule of law, Dicey considered three distinct elements. First, it involved an absence of arbitrary power on the part of the Government. Under the rule of law, the extent of the State's power and the manner in which it exercises such power is limited and controlled by law. This control is aimed at preventing the state from acquiring and using wide discretionary powers, because Dicey recognised that, inherent in discretion, is the possibility of its being used in an arbitrary manner.

The second of Dicey's elements related to equality before the law; the fact that no person is above the law, irrespective of rank or class, together with the related fact that functionaries of the State are subject to the same law and legal procedures as private citizens. Thus, the law, as represented in Dicey's version of the rule of law, ignores *substantive* differences and treats everyone as *formally* equal. In other words, the law is blind to real, concrete differences between people, in terms of wealth or power or connection, and treats them all the same as possessors of abstract rights and duties.

The third component of the rule of law, for Dicey, related to the fact that the rules of the English constitution were the outcome of the ordinary law of the land and were based on the provision of remedies by the courts, rather than on the declaration of rights in the form of a written constitution.

It is essential to recognise that Dicey was writing not just at a particular historical period, but, perhaps more importantly, he was writing from a particular political perspective. He was a committed believer in the free operation of the market and was opposed to any increase in State activity, particularly with regard to any attempt by the State to regulate the economy. It is at least arguable that, at the time Dicey wrote his *Law of the Constitution*, he was misrepresenting changes that had already occurred in the UK polity, in a desire to curtail the burgeoning activity of the State and, at the same time, to justify that political stance on the basis of a spurious constitutional history. Certainly, by 1933, and in the light of the increased role that the State had assumed in organising society, in general, and the economy, in particular, Sir Ivor Jennings, in his book *The Law and the Constitution* (5th edn, 1959), could express the view that, if Dicey's version of the rule of law:

> ... means that the State exercises only the functions of carrying out external relations and maintaining order, it is not true. If it means that the State ought to exercise these functions only, it is a rule of policy for Whigs (if there are any left). [Whigs were a former political party.]

If there were no Whigs as such, their attitudes towards the free market lived on in the work of such social thinkers as FA von Hayek. Although Hayek's work has become increasingly influential with the coming to power of the Thatcher Conservative Government in 1979, it has to be said that, in 1944, when his *The Road to Serfdom* was first published, he was almost a lone voice crying in the wilderness. As regards the rule of law, it is not surprising that Hayek followed Dicey in emphasising its essential component as the absence of arbitrary power in the hands of the State. According to Hayek:

> Stripped of all technicalities, the rule of law means that government in all its actions is bound by rules fixed and announced beforehand.

Hayek, however, went further than Dicey in setting out the actual form and, at least in a negative way, the actual content of legal rules, in order for them to be considered as compatible with the rule of law. As Hayek expressed it, in *The Road to Serfdom*:

> The Rule of Law implies limits on the scope of legislation, it restricts it to the kind of general rules known as formal law; and excludes legislation directly aimed at particular people.

Nor should law be aimed at particular goals. In other words, the Government has no place in usurping the authority of individuals by deciding their course of action for them. Within clearly defined and strictly controlled legal parameters, individuals should be left to act as they choose. The job of law is to set the boundaries of personal action, not to dictate the course of such action. Laws should not be particular in content or application, but should be general in nature, applying to all and benefiting no one in particular.

It is important to note that Hayek did not suggest that rules are not laws; they are legal, as long as they are enacted through the appropriate and proper mechanisms; they, simply, are not in accord with the rule of law. Hayek may very well have agreed with Karl Mannheim, whom he quoted, that the rule of law only operated during the classical liberal competitive phase of capitalism, but he certainly regretted and condemned the change that had taken place in the form and function of law. His regret and condemnation arose from two sources. First, from the economic perspective, as only the particular individual concerned can fully know all the circumstances of his or her situation, the State should, *as a matter of efficiency*, leave that individual to make his or her own decisions. Secondly, from the moral perspective, to the extent that the all-encompassing interventionist/welfare State leaves individuals less room to make decisions as to their actions, it reduces their freedom.

Other legal philosophers have recognised the need for, and have come to terms with, State intervention in the pursuit of substantive, as well as merely formal, justice and have provided new ways of understanding the rule of law as a means of controlling discretion without attempting to eradicate it completely. Joseph Raz, for example, took Hayek to task for disguising a socio-economic argument as a legal one, in order to strike at policies of which he did not approve as being contrary to the rule of law, and he suggested that such reasoning was in danger of identifying the 'rule of law' with the rule of 'good law', that is, law/policy of which Hayek approved.

If both Dicey and Hayek laid great emphasis on government by law, rather than by men, Raz recognises the need for the government of men as well as of laws and that the pursuit of social goals may require the enactment of both general *and particular* laws. Indeed, he suggests that it is actually inconceivable for law to consist solely of general rules. Raz claims that the basic requirement from which the wider idea of the rule of law emerges is the requirement that the law must be capable of guiding the individual's behaviour. On that basis, he lists some of the most important principles that may be derived from the general idea. These are as follows:

(a) laws should be prospective rather than retroactive, for the reason that people cannot be guided by and expected to obey laws which have not as yet been introduced. The laws should also be open and clear in order to enable people to understand/guide their actions in line with them;

(b) laws should be relatively stable and should not be changed too frequently, as this might lead to confusion as to what actually is covered by the law;

(c) there should be clear rules and procedures for making laws;

(d) the independence of the judiciary has to be guaranteed, to ensure that it is free to decide cases in line with the law and not in response to any external pressure;

(e) the principles of natural justice should be observed, requiring an open and fair hearing to be given to all parties to proceedings;

(f) the courts should have the power to review the way in which the other principles are implemented to ensure that they are being operated as demanded by the rule of law;

(g) the courts should be easily accessible, as they remain at the heart of the idea of making discretion subject to legal control;

(h) the discretion of the crime-preventing agencies should not be allowed to pervert the law.

Raz recognises the validity of, and the need to use, discretionary powers and particular goal oriented legislation in contemporary society and, to that extent, he differs from both Dicey and Hayek. Yet, he also sees the rule of law as essentially a negative value, acting to minimise the danger that can be consequent upon the exercise, in an arbitrary manner, of such discretionary power. In seeking to control the exercise of discretion, he shares common ground with Dicey and Hayek.

Question 46

To what extent do you agree with the claim that 'the rule of law is unqualified human good'?

Answer plan

This question is similar to the previous one, but relates to more abstract political considerations. The quotation is a very famous one and frequently forms the basis for questions; so candidates should be able to respond to it. As with the previous question, the following is only one approach:

- consider the lack of precision in the idea of the rule of law;
- explain AV Dicey's understanding of the rule of law;
- introduce an explanation of the continental *Rechsstaat* and compare it with Dicey's version of the rule of law;

- explain Friedrich von Hayek's market-oriented version of the rule of law;
- explain EP Thompson's equity based version of the rule of law;
- consider what links possibly can exist between Hayek and Thompson.

Answer

In modern Western societies, law is seen as the embodiment of many of society's values. Liberty, equality of treatment, the sanctity of private property, the protection of individual rights and the pursuit of individual interests; all of these are enshrined in the form of law and, at least in theory, are protected by it. Indeed, in liberal capitalist societies, such as the UK, law as embodied in the notion of 'the rule of law' assumes the status of a central value in its own right and one to which almost mythic properties are attributed. This can be seen in the frequent appeals made by judges and politicians of all parties to the idea of 'the rule of law' as the protective bulwark against which beat the destructive forces of anarchy. It is somewhat disconcerting, however, to note that the particular values supposedly enshrined in, and supported by, particular versions of 'the rule of law' tend to bear a direct relationship with the political views of its various proponents. In the words of the German writer on jurisprudence, Otto Kirchheimer, the rule of law can be seen as 'a mixture of implied promise and convenient vagueness', and it is this very vagueness that permits the idea of the rule of law to be appropriated by people with, apparently, irreconcilable political agenda in support of their particular political positions.

This phenomenon is highlighted in the cases of EP Thompson, a Marxist historian whose words form the basis for this essay title, and FA von Hayek, a proponent of a free market capitalist system; both of whom see the rule of law as a protection against, and under attack from, the encroaching power of the modern state.

The explanation of this apparent paradoxical convergence of opinion can be located in the unresolved tension that is evident in AV Dicey's *Law of the Constitution* first published in 1885. In that book, Dicey described the concept of the rule of law as one of the two fundamental elements of the English polity; the other being parliamentary sovereignty or, in other words, the effective undisputed supremacy of Government. The former was aimed at controlling arbitrary power but the latter could, within this constitutional structure, make provision for the granting of such arbitrary power by passing appropriate legislation. In a system in which Parliament is supreme, the political realities ensure that a Government with a majority in the House of Commons can enact such legislation as it wishes, irrespective of any supposed restrictions placed on it by reference to the rule of law. Indeed, where the rule of law has been reduced to a matter of procedure, to the mere requirement that legislation be passed in the prescribed manner, the most arbitrary of party political decisions are readily cloaked with legality.

Dicey did not resolve the conflict between the rule of law and the sovereignty of Parliament, but it has been suggested by Franz Neumann that, in any case, the lack of compatibility was more apparent than real. For, the reality was that those people who benefited from the enactment and implementation of general laws as required by the rule of law, the middle classes, also effectively controlled Parliament and could benefit just as well from its particular enactments. Thus, in terms of 19th century England, the doctrines of parliamentary sovereignty and the rule of law can be seen as complementary rather than antagonistic.

Hayek believed that the meaning of the rule of law, as it was currently understood in contemporary jurisprudence, represented a narrowing from its original meaning which had more in common with the German concept of the *Rechsstaat* than it presently did. The idea of the *Rechsstaat* was a much stronger version of the rule of law than that described by Dicey, in that it was not undermined to the same extent by a doctrine of parliamentary sovereignty. In the *Rechsstaat*, the State was limited by the need to produce general law and could not legitimately make laws aimed at particular people.

This strong version of the rule of law, however, had come under attack and had been replaced by a weaker version following Dicey's assertion as to the unlimited extent of the legislature's power. The ultimate conclusion of this weaker version was that, so long as the actions of the State were duly authorised by legislation, the claim as to the preservation of the rule of law could be maintained.

Hayek disapproved of this diminution in what was meant by the rule of law, but, it is clear from his writing, that what he really regretted was the suppression of a free market economy by a planned economy regulated by an interventionist State.

The contemporary State was no longer satisfied simply to provide a legal framework for the conduct of economic activity, but was, increasingly, becoming actively involved in the direct co-ordination and regulation of economic activity in the pursuit of its own goals. The replacement of the free market by a planned economy has major consequences for the form of law, as clearly stated, and fixed general laws are replaced by open textured discretionary legislation empowering State functionaries to take action as they consider necessary. Also, whereas the strong version of the rule of law had operated in terms of abstract formal rights and duties, formal equality and formal justice, the new version addressed concrete issues and endeavoured to provide real substantive equality and justice.

It always has to be borne in mind that Hayek was a protagonist of competitive market capitalism and that even his jurisprudential work has to be understood as a polemic in favour of that system and against the interventionist State. He saw the conditions of the competitive market as, not only economically, but morally superior to the modern system, but, it must be noted, he never claimed that the interventionist actions of contemporary Governments were not legal, just that they were not in accordance with the rule of law. According to Hayek, the rule of law as it had developed, as a means of constraining the activity of the State, represented the 'legal embodiment of freedom' for, as he expressed it:

> Nothing distinguishes more clearly conditions in a free country from those in a country under arbitrary government than the observance in the former of the great principle known as the Rule of Law [*The Road to Serfdom*, 1944].

EP Thompson shares Hayek's distrust of the encroachments of the modern State and he is equally critical of the extent to which the contemporary State has intervened, not to say interfered, in the day to day lives of its citizens. From Thompson's perspective, however, the problem arises, not so much from the fact that the State is undermining the operation of the market economy, which he would be in favour of, but from the way in which the State has used, and continues to use, its control over the legislative process to undercut civil liberties in the pursuit of its concept of public interest. Thompson is concerned primarily with the way in which the State, as he sees it, has progressively lopped branches off the 'liberty tree' by increasingly interfering with the civil liberties and rights of individual citizens. Examples of this process can be cited as not just increases in police powers, but the effective 'militarisation' of the police, limitations on rights to take positive action as being contrary to public order, the increased use of surveillance and information gathering techniques, the reduction and, in some cases, the withdrawal, of trade union rights, attempts by the State to control access to information and the criminalisation of the trespass laws. The point is that these are only examples of a general process in which the State and its functionaries centralise and increase their power and at the same time remove existing rights from individuals.

In *Whigs and Hunters* (1975), a study of the manipulation of law by the landed classes in the 18th century, Thompson devotes a substantial part of his final chapter to a consideration of the rule of law, essentially, in order to defend it against those on the political left who would dismiss it as no more than an ideological confidence trick. His historical analysis of the evolution of the doctrine of the rule of law leads him to conclude that it is not just a necessary means of limiting the potential abuse of power but that:

> ... the rule of law itself, the imposing of effective inhibitions upon power and the defence of the citizen from power's all-intrusive claims, seems to me an unqualified human good.

In reaching this conclusion, Thompson clearly concurs with Hayek's assertion that there is more to the rule of law than the requirement that law be processed through the appropriate legal institutions. He, too, argues that the core meaning of the rule of law has more connotations than this mere procedural propriety and suggests that the other essential element is the way and the extent to which it places limits on the exercise of power in the hands of the State, although it has to be stated that the exact legal basis for this protection remains unclear.

Thompson's work on the rule of law provides a timely warning to the effect that, where the rule of law has been reduced to a matter of mere parliamentary procedure, as arguably it has in the contemporary situation of the UK, it does not go far in protecting individual rights and general civil liberties from legislative encroachment. It is, perhaps, for this reason that there has been the substantial recent pressure for the UK to have either a written constitution or to incorporate the ECHR into its law as means of entrenching civil liberties and providing the safeguard that, arguably, the strict version of the rule of law used to provide. In conclusion, it may be said that the ambiguous nature of the concept of the rule of law prevents it from being accepted unquestionably as a unqualified human good, but that there remains a need for the limitation and control of State activity which, arguably, the rule of law provides, at least in certain formulations.

Question 47

What are the prerogative orders available under judicial review and what is the procedure for achieving such remedies?

Answer plan

This is a fairly straightforward question that looks to assess candidates' knowledge of not just the remedies available under judicial review, but also the impact of the Woolf reforms on the procedure for applying for judicial review. Candidates must be aware of the new Pt 54 of the Civil Procedure Rules (CPR) and must be prepared to explain them in detail. A suggested plan for dealing with the question is as follows:

- consider the three prerogative orders in turn explaining the effect of each of them;
- explain the genesis of the new CPR Pt 54 paying particular attention to the Bowman Report;

- consider the provisions of Pt 54 in some detail;
- pay particular attention to the changes introduced under Pt 54;
- in particular, consider permission, standing and pre-action protocols.

Answer

The remedies available against a public authority are the three prerogative orders: a quashing order, a prohibiting order and a mandatory order.

A *quashing order*, formerly known as *certiorari*, is the mechanism by means of which decisions of inferior courts, tribunals and other authoritative bodies are brought before the High Court to have their validity examined. Where any such decisions are found to be invalid, they may be set aside. An example of this can be seen in *Ridge v Baldwin* (1964). The Chief Constable of Brighton had been charged with conspiracy to obstruct the course of justice, but was acquitted. On the basis of criticisms made of him by the trial judge, he was subsequently dismissed from his post, by the local Watch Committee responsible for the supervision of the local police force, without a hearing. The House of Lords eventually held that the denial of a hearing was contrary to natural justice and, therefore, that his dismissal had been carried out in an improper manner. The House of Lords also rejected the argument that *certiorari* did not lie in this case as the Watch Committee was exercising an administrative rather than a judicial function: it was emphasised that the important issue was the *consequences* of the decision not whether it was administrative or judicial.

A *prohibiting order* is similar to a quashing order in that it relates to invalid acts of public authorities, but it is pre-emptive and prescriptive with regard to any such activity, and prevents the authority from taking invalid decisions in the first place. An example of the use of the prohibition order arose in *Telford JJ ex p Badham* (1991), in which committal proceedings in relation to a rape charge were discontinued on the grounds that the alleged offence had taken place some 15 years previously and the lapse of time could not but seriously prejudice the defendant in the preparation of his defence.

A *mandatory order*, previously referred to as *mandamus*, is an order issued by the Queen's Bench Division of the High Court, instructing an inferior court, or some other public authority, to carry out a duty laid upon them. Such an order is frequently issued in conjunction with an order of *certiorari*, to the effect that a public body is held to be using its powers improperly and is instructed to use them in a proper fashion. An example of how the order of *mandamus* operates and an example of the consequences of ignoring such an order arose in the famous (infamous?) cases involving the Poplar Borough Council in 1922 (*Poplar BC (Nos 1 and 2)* (1922)). When the council refused to comply with a statutory requirement to levy rates in order to make a payment to the county council, an order of *mandamus* was awarded against it which instructed it to make the payment and, if need be, to levy a rate for that purpose. When the Labour Party majority on the council refused to comply with the order, an action for contempt of court was taken against them and some of the recalcitrant councillors were actually imprisoned.

The prerogative orders are so called because they were originally the means whereby sovereigns controlled the operation of their officials. As a consequence, the prerogative orders cannot be used against the Crown, but this shortcoming is not of major concern as the prerogative orders can be used against individual ministers of State and it is to such people that powers are delegated.

In order to secure one of the above remedies, the procedure for judicial review as provided in CPR Pt 54 must be followed.

Alternatively, the non-prerogative remedies of declaration, injunction and damages are available against public authorities.

Until recently, the procedure for initiating an action for judicial review was made under Ord 53 of the Rules of the Supreme Court. Although in his report on the civil law system Lord Woolf made recommendations as to how judicial review procedure should be altered, these were not put into effect. Instead, the old rules set out in RSC Ord 53 were re-enacted, with minor amendments, in a schedule to the CPR.

However the ever increasing number of applications for judicial review, especially in the area of immigration, ensured that something had to be done about the system and in March 1999, the Lord Chancellor appointed a committee, under the chairmanship of Sir Jeffrey Bowman, to examine the procedures of the Crown Office List, which dealt with judicial review.

The Bowman Committee proposed two crucial amendments to the system. Firstly, the permission stage was to become an *inter partes* procedure rather than an *ex parte* one, with the defendant being given full notice of the application. Secondly, consideration of permission applications should be a paper-based exercise only. The Committee also considered that a pre-action protocol, which required communication between the parties even before the making of a claim to the court, would assist in bringing settlements forward by focussing the parties on the issues in dispute and allowing them to consider the merits of the claim before legal proceedings were started.

The Lord Chancellor's Department subsequently issued a consultation paper and new draft rules on the procedure for judicial review. The outcome of this is that Ord 53 has been abolished and replaced by the new r 54.1 of the CPR.

The new rules adopt many of the recommendations of the Bowman Report and bring judicial review procedure fully within the style and purposes of the CPR.

Permission

Access to the public law remedies has never been directly open to the public and the new Pt 54 retains the requirement that claimants seek permission from the Administrative Court before they can pursue their action. Under the old Ord 53 procedure the application for permission to proceed acted as a filtering mechanism essentially to weed out unsustainable claims, but under Pt 54, in the pursuit of more economic use of the courts, it has been turned into a form of *inter partes* proceeding. A claim must be started not later than three months after the grounds to make the claim arose (r 54.5) and now, in order to get permission, the claim form must comply with the requirements of CPR r 8.2

and Practice Direction 54. In particular it must include a detailed statement of the claimant's grounds for seeking judicial review, the remedy they are seeking, a statement of facts relied on, copies of any document on which the claimant proposes to rely and a list of essential documents for advance reading by the court. The claim form must be served on the defendant, and any person the claimant considers to be an interested party, within seven days of the date of issue. Any person served with the claim form who wishes to take part in the judicial review must file an acknowledgment of service not more than 21 days after service of the claim form. If the defendant wishes to contest the claim, they must set out a summary of their grounds for doing so in the acknowledgment. Failure to acknowledge service does not, however, exclude the defendant from subsequent participation in the proceedings, although it might affect the court's decision in deciding costs.

The question of permission will generally be decided on the documents submitted without a hearing. However, where the court refuses permission, or grants it subject to conditions, the claimant may request a hearing. There is also a right to apply to the Court of Appeal for permission to appeal against any refusal and the Court of Appeal can give permission for judicial review to proceed, in which circumstances the case will proceed to a hearing in the High Court.

Standing

In order to pursue a claim for judicial review the claimant must demonstrate that they have 'standing' (formerly referred to as *locus standi*). In other words they must show that they are not just some officious bystander with no recognisable interest in the matter in question. Whether a person has sufficient interest is for the courts to decide on as a matter of law and fact, as decided in *IRC v National Federation of Self-Employed and Small Businesses Ltd* (1981). Standing to seek judicial review was extended to pressure groups with a particular interest in the matter at issue and where it was unlikely that any other party would seek to raise the issue in *R v Inspector of Pollution ex p Greenpeace* (1994) and *R v Secretary of State for Foreign Affairs ex p World Development Movement* (1995).

The new rules say nothing about standing at all so presumably the previous rules as to standing will apply. However, the issue of public interest is recognised in r 54.17 which gives the court power to permit any person to file evidence or make representations at the hearing of the judicial review. This follows with recent practice, thus, for example, Amnesty was allowed to participate in the hearing of the *Pinochet* case.

Pre-action protocol

In line with other Civil Procedure Rules and the specific recommendation of the Bowman Committee, the Lord Chancellor's Department issued a Consultation Paper, March 2001, on the subject of a proposed pre-action protocol in relation to judicial review.

It proposes that, before making a claim, the claimant should send a letter to the defendant using a standard format letter which should contain the date and details of the decision, act or omission being challenged and a clear summary of the facts on which the claim is based. It should also contain the details of any relevant information that the claimant is seeking and an explanation of why this is considered relevant. A claim should not normally be made until the proposed reply date given in the letter before claim has passed, unless the circumstances of the case require more immediate action to be taken.

Defendants should normally reply within any reasonable time limit contained in the claimant's letter, once again using the standard format letter. Failure to comply with the pre-action protocol is to be taken into account by the court when making decisions on case management or costs.

Question 48

Consider the development of judicial review in the light of the judiciary's attempt to control the exercise of administrative discretion.

Answer plan

This is a much more subtle and searching question than the previous one. It requires a consideration of modern forms of law, the rule of law, the constitutional role of the judiciary, as well a knowledge of the procedure for judicial review. Consideration of the following will cover the above points well:

- the development of administrative law;
- the tension between the exercise of discretionary power and the rule of law;
- judicial review as the court's means of curtailing abuse of discretion;
- the grounds for judicial review;
- the possibility of the doctrine of 'proportionality' as the means of extending judicial review in the area of substantive administrative decisions;
- judges' competence to make policy decisions;
- the constitutional situation of the judiciary.

Answer

According to AV Dicey, in *Law of the Constitution*, published in 1885, the UK knew no such thing as administrative law as distinct from ordinary law. In Dicey's exposition, it was essential that all activities be open to the ordinary law of the land for the maintenance of the rule of law. Whether or not he was correct when he expressed this opinion, and there are substantial grounds for doubting the accuracy of his claim even at the time he made it, it can no longer be denied that there is now a large area of law that can be properly called administrative, that is, related to the pursuit and application of particular policies, usually within a framework of statutory powers, although the powers under question may be derived from the common law. The lack of a more precise definition reflects the extent to which the State and State-appointed bodies intervene in contemporary life and the multiplicity of areas in which they act. It is certainly true that the 20th century saw a large scale increase in the power of the State –

both central and local – and its various functionaries and appointed bodies to intervene in the day to day lives of its citizens. The question that arises is whether such activity is subject to judicial control and, if it is, how such control is to be exercised.

Dicey described the concept of the rule of law as one of the two fundamental elements of the English polity; the other being parliamentary sovereignty, or, in other words, the undisputed supremacy of central Government. The former was aimed at controlling arbitrary power, but the latter could, within this constitutional structure, make provision for the granting of such arbitrary power by passing appropriate legislation. The historical reality is that, in the course, of the 20th century, with the emergence and development of the interventionist welfare State, the government increasingly took over the regulation of many areas of social activity and delegated wide ranging discretionary powers to various people and bodies in order to implement its policies and to deal with particular problems as they arose. It has been suggested by some that, in fact, the rule of law has been reduced to a matter of procedure, to the mere requirement that legislation be passed in the prescribed manner and that the most arbitrary of party political decisions can, thus, be readily cloaked with legality.

Dicey did not resolve the potential conflict between the rule of law, as represented by the decisions of the ordinary courts of the land, and the sovereignty of Parliament, nor can it be claimed, as yet, that such tensions have been resolved. Indeed, it might be argued that the tension between the two principles has not only continued, but has intensified with the growth in State activity. There are significant indications that the higher judiciary may well be attempting to re-assert, at least a measure, of control over the executive, but, if this is the case, it is not, in itself, unproblematic and has important constitutional implications for the UK. The importance of this process was not lost on the former Master of the Rolls, Sir Thomas Bingham, who described it, in an interview ((1993) *The Observer*, 9 May), as follows:

> Slowly, the constitutional balance is tilting towards the judiciary. The courts have reacted to the increase in powers claimed by the Government by being more active themselves.

Judicial review may be seen as one of the ways in which the courts have attempted to maintain a measure of control over such activity in an endeavour to re-assert the dominance of the rule of law ideal. Of all areas of law, judicial review is the one in which most growth is apparent, as can be seen from the fact that, in 1980, there were only 525 applications for judicial review; and, in 1998, there were 5,201 such applications, a 10-fold increase in less than 30 years.

In the same *Observer* article, the now Lord Chief Justice, Lord Woolf was quoted as stating that:

> Judicial review is all about balance: between the rights of the individual and his need to be treated fairly, and the rights of government at local and national level to do what it has been elected to do. There is a very sensitive and political decision to be made.

In this, he shares the views of former Law Lord, Lord Browne-Wilkinson, who, as Sir Nicolas, had observed, on a BBC radio programme, that a great void was apparent in the political system deriving from the fact that no Government had a true popular majority and, yet, all Governments were able to carry Parliament in support of anything they wanted. He went on to express the view that Parliament was not a place where it was easy to get accountability for abuse or misuse of powers. As he stated:

> While judicial review could not overcome the will of Parliament, judges had a special role because *democracy was defective. Who else but the judges could ensure that executive action is taken in accordance with law, and not abused by growingly polarised political stances?*

Some, therefore, see judicial review as the means to curtail the power of the executive and as a counter to the use of discretionary forms of regulation. There are doubts, however, as to the effectiveness of such intervention, but, of perhaps even more importance, is the matter of its constitutional propriety. Before considering these matters, however, it is necessary to consider under which circumstances the procedure can be used.

The grounds of application can be considered under two traditional heads *procedural ultra vires* and *substantive ultra vires*. Procedural *ultra vires*, as its name suggests, relates to the failure of a person, or body provided with specific authority, to follow the procedure established for using that power, or to follow the requirements of natural law. Substantive *ultra vires* occurs where someone does something that is not, actually, authorised by the enabling legislation and its most interesting area of operation relates to areas where it is sought to challenge the substance of a decision.

In *Associated Provincial Picture House v Wednesbury Corp* (1947), which concerned a local authority's decision to impose a condition on a licensing of a cinema, Lord Greene MR established the possibility of discretionary decisions being challenged on the basis of it being unreasonable. As Lord Greene pointed out:

> ... the decision of the local authority can be upset if it is proved to be unreasonable in the sense that the court considers it to be a decision *that no reasonable body could have come to.*

Lord Greene's approach was endorsed and refined by Lord Diplock in *Council of Civil Service Unions v Minister for the Civil Service* (known as the *GCHQ* case) (1984), where he established the three grounds for judicial review to be:

(a) illegality;

(b) irrationality;

(c) procedural impropriety.

In delivering his judgment, however, Lord Diplock, intriguingly, introduced the possibility of a much wider ranging reason for challenging administrative decisions. The additional ground for applying for judicial review was based on the doctrine of 'proportionality'. This doctrine was considered by Jeffrey Jowell and Anthony Lester QC in a book entitled *New Directions in Judicial Review*, published in 1988, in which they stated that:

> As it has developed in European law and as it has been applied in English law, proportionality is a principle that requires a reasonable relation between a decision, its objectives and the circumstances of a given case. It requires the pursuit of legitimate ends by means that are not oppressively excessive. *It looks, therefore, largely to the substance of the decisions rather than the way in which they are reached, but it also requires the decision maker not manifestly to ignore significant alternatives or interests.*

Thus, it can be seen that, through the mechanism of judicial review implementing a principle of proportionality, the judiciary has, at its disposal, means for addressing the potential for abuse that has followed on from the growth of discretionary power in the hands of the modern State and that, apparently, such judicial control is not simply limited to matters of procedure, but equally extends to substantive issues. Even if a relatively newly appointed and apparently increasingly self-confident higher judiciary avails itself of the opportunity that such means provide to interfere in administrative matters, it does so at no little potential cost.

First, there is the question of the competency of the judiciary to overrule substantive decisions. Judges are experts in law; they are not expert in the questions of policy that come before them in the guise of legal cases. They may disagree with particular decisions, but it has to be, at least, doubted that they are qualified to take such policy decisions. A classic example of this arises from the infamous 'fares fair' case, *Bromley LBC v GLC* (1982), in which the courts held that a policy to subsidise transport within London was not legal. When an amended scheme came before the court in *London Transport Executive ex p GLC* (1983), it was decided that the Greater London Council could instruct the London Transport Authority to implement policies that would effectively reduce its revenues. Thus, the courts could reject schemes, but could not replace them with other ones.

There is also the wider question that, in interfering with substantive decisions, the judiciary involves itself in political matters and, therefore, exceeds its constitutional powers. It has to be remembered that judges are unelected and unaccountable. The question as to their suitability to take such, essentially political, decisions cannot but be brought into question. As Farquharson LJ commented in the *Observer* interview:

> We have to be very careful: the executive is elected. We have a role in the constitution, but if we go too far, there will be a reaction. The Constitution only works if the different organs trust each other. If the judges start getting too frisky, there would be retaliation, renewed attempts to curb the judiciary.

In conclusion, if judicial review has firmly placed the judiciary in the political arena, the introduction of the HRA 1998 can only increase that process of overt politicisation, in that it expressly gives judges the duty and power to protect individuals' rights from attack from public authorities. The question that remains to be answered, especially in the light of criticisms directed at the conservative nature of the judiciary, levelled by some commentators on the political left, is whether the judiciary are the right people to be given such power.

Question 49

Explain the background and content of the HRA 1998.

Answer plan

This question asks candidates to provide a brief consideration of the incorporation of the ECHR into UK law, through the mechanism of the HRA 1998. It requires a basic knowledge of the content and effect of the HRA 1998. The following points should be covered:

- explain what the ECHR is;
- explain the disadvantages of the UK's relationship to the Convention prior to the HRA 1998;
- list the various Articles that have been incorporated by the Act;
- consider the effect of the Act on public bodies;
- explain what is meant by a declaration of compatibility in relation to legislation;
- assess the role of the courts in relation to the Act;
- explain fast track remedial action for legislation that is found to be incompatible.

Answer

The UK was one of the initial signatories to the ECHR in 1950, which was created in post-war Europe as a means of establishing and enforcing essential human rights. In 1966, the UK recognised the power of the European Commission on Human Rights to hear complaints from individual UK citizens, and, at the same time, recognised the authority of the European Court of Human Rights (the Court) to adjudicate in such matters. It did not, however, at that time, incorporate the ECHR into UK law.

The consequences of non-incorporation was that the Convention could not be directly enforced in English courts. In *R v Secretary of State for the Home Department ex p Brind* (1991), the Court of Appeal decided that ministerial directives did not have to be construed in line with the ECHR, as that would be tantamount to introducing the Convention into English law without the necessary legislation. UK citizens were, therefore, in the position of having to pursue rights, which the State endorsed, in an external forum, rather than through their own court system; and, in addition, having to exhaust the domestic judicial procedure before they could gain access to that external forum. Such a situation was expensive, time consuming and extremely unsatisfactory and not just for complainants under the Convention. Many members of the judiciary, including the former Lord Chief Justice Lord Bingham, were in favour of incorporation, not merely on general moral grounds, but, equally, on the ground that they resented having to make decisions, in line with UK law, which they knew full well would be overturned on appeal to the European Court. Equally, there was some discontent that the decisions in the European Court were being taken, and its general jurisprudence was being developed without the direct input of the UK legal system.

The HRA 1998 corrected this anomalous situation, by incorporating the rights enshrined in the ECHR, together with the protocols to it, into UK law. The Act received Royal Assent on 9 November 1998, but was only brought fully into force on 2 October 2000. The reason for the delay was so that the courts, from the magistrates all the way up to the House of Lords, could be adequately trained in the consequences of the Act.

The rights incorporated are listed in Sched 1 of the Act and cover the following matters:

- a general commitment to human rights (Art 1);
- right to life (Art 2);
- freedom from torture and inhuman or degrading treatment or punishment (Art 3);
- freedom from slavery and forced or compulsory labour (Art 4);
- right to liberty and security of person (subject to a derogation applicable to Northern Ireland) (Art 5);
- right to a fair and public trial within a reasonable time (Art 6);
- freedom from retrospective criminal law and no punishment without law (Art 7);
- right to respect for private and family life, home and correspondence (Art 8);
- freedom of thought, conscience and religion (Art 9);
- freedom of expression (Art 10);
- freedom of assembly and association (Art 11);
- right to marry and found a family (Art 12);
- prohibition of discrimination in the enjoyment of the Convention rights (Art 14);
- right to peaceful enjoyment of possessions and protection of property (Art 1, Protocol 1);
- right to education (subject to a UK reservation) (Art 2, Protocol 1);
- right to free elections (Art 3, Protocol 1);
- right not to be subjected to the death penalty (Arts 1 and 2, Protocol 6).

The above rights can be relied on by any person, non-governmental organisation, or group of individuals. Importantly, as has been discovered in Canada, which has similar legislation, it also applies where appropriate to companies which are incorporated entities and, hence, legal persons and other bodies. It cannot be relied on by governmental organisations, such as local authorities.

The general list of rights are not all seen in the same way. Some are absolute and inalienable and cannot be interfered with by the State, or, at least, only to a limited and tightly circumscribed degree. Others are merely contingent and are subject to derogation, that is, signatory States can opt out of them in particular circumstances. The absolute rights are those provided for in Arts 2, 3, 4, 7 and 14. All the others are subject to potential limitations; and, in particular, the rights provided for under Arts 8, 9, 10 and 11 are subject to legal restrictions, such as are:

> ... necessary in a democratic society in the interests of national security or public safety, for the prevention of crime, for the protection of health or morals or the protection of the rights and freedoms of others [Art 11(2)].

In deciding the legality of any derogation, courts are required not just to be convinced that there is a need for the derogation, but they must also be sure that the State's action has been proportionate to that need. In other words, the State must not overreact to a perceived problem by removing more rights than is necessary to effect the solution. With further regard to the possibility of derogation, s 19 of the Act requires a minister, responsible for the passage of any Bill through Parliament, either to make a written declaration that it is compatible the Convention or, alternatively, to declare that, although it may not be compatible, it is still the government's wish to proceed with it.

The HRA 1998 has profound implications for the operation of the English legal system. Section 2 of the Act requires future courts to take into account any previous decision of the European Court. This provision impacts on the operation of the doctrine of precedent within the English legal system, as it, effectively, sanctions the overruling of any pervious English authority that was in conflict with a decision of the European Court. Also, s 3, requiring all legislation to be read so far as possible to give effect to the rights provided under the Convention, has the potential to invalidate previously accepted interpretations of statutes which were made, by necessity, without recourse to the Convention.

Section 6 declares it unlawful for any public authority to act in a way which is incompatible with the Convention and s 7 allows the 'victim of the unlawful act' to bring proceedings against the public authority in breach. Section 8 empowers the court to grant such relief or remedy against the public authority in breach of the

Act, as it considers just and appropriate. However, where a public authority is acting under the instructions of some primary legislation, which is itself incompatible with the Convention, the public authority will not be liable under s 6.

It can be seen that the Act reflects a move towards the entrenchment of rights recognised under the Convention, but the Act expressly states that the courts cannot invalidate any primary legislation, essentially Acts of Parliament, which are found to be incompatible with the Convention. The courts can only make a declaration of such incompatibility and leave it to the legislature to remedy the situation, through new legislation (s 4). The Act requires that the Crown be given notice of a case where a declaration might be given and the Crown is given a right to intervene in the case. This will enable the Crown to argue that the provision can be interpreted compatibly with the Convention rights. It also ensures that the Crown is in a position to respond quickly where a declaration of incompatibility is made. In this respect, the Act provides for the provision of remedial legislation through a fast track procedure. This fast track procedure enables a minister of the Crown the power to alter primary legislation by way of statutory instrument. This power is also available to implement judgments of the Strasbourg Court against the UK which are made after the coming into force of the HRA 1998. It is also available in urgent cases, where subordinate legislation has been quashed or declared invalid.

Question 50

Assess the likely impact of the HRA 1998 on the UK Constitution and the English legal system.

Answer plan

This question requires, not an analysis of the detailed provisions of the HRA 1998, but, rather, requires the candidate to consider the provision in its wider social and political context. Such a goal is achieved in the following structure:

- what the HRA 1998 is and where it came from;
- its impact on the UK Constitution and on the English legal system;
- changing role of the judiciary and its relationship to Parliament;
- possible difficulties in the present provision.

Answer

It was a commitment of the Labour Party's manifesto, for the general election in 1997, that they would introduce the ECHR into UK law. It had always been anomalous that, although the British were the force behind the Convention, had drawn it up, were signatories to it, and subject to the jurisdiction of the European Court, the Convention had no place in the UK legal system. Individuals could take their cases to the European Court and the UK Government was frequently subject to adverse rulings of the Court; but the same individuals could not apply to UK courts for a decision in line with the Convention and could only apply to the European Court when they had gone through all the legal proceedings within the domestic jurisdiction. The HRA 1998 seeks to make the ECHR an integral part of UK law and, in so doing, it is bound to have a major impact on the operation of the English legal system, as well as profoundly affecting the Constitution of the UK.

The new Act changes the whole philosophical approach required of the judiciary. In the past, it might have sought to protect individuals from the abuse of State powers by using judicial review to decide that particular decisions of the executive had been taken in excess of the authority granted to it, or in a way that was unreasonable, as decided in the *Wednesbury* case. Now, under the HRA 1998, judges are being asked to decide cases against public authorities on the basis of, and to protect, individual rights. The shift in focus, from abuse of power to protection of rights, required to achieve this new end marks a major change in direction and legal philosophy for UK judges. One of the reasons given for the repatriation of the Convention is that it will encourage the creation of a human rights based jurisprudence in the UK courts and, relatedly, it will allow UK judges to make an impact on the development of human rights jurisprudence in the wider European sphere. It has to be said that the validity of this argument is not a little undermined by the present composition of the House of Lords, which tends to be dominated by commercial lawyers who have not previously exhibited any great commitment to human rights, either in the abstract or the concrete (see *R v Brown* (1993) for evidence of the House of Lord's complete failure to understand what was truly beyond their ken). The recent appointments Sirs John Hobhouse and Peter Millet, both commercial law experts, do nothing to discourage this perception of the higher echelons of the judiciary; and, indeed, the fact that Sir Peter Millet has been appointed, raises the accusations of Professor Griffith (see Question 21, above), in that he was one of the judges who maintained the injunction against the newspapers involved in the *Spycatcher* case.

Another major change that flows from the new Act relates to the constitutional position of the judiciary. For the past 300 years, the judiciary has bowed before the doctrine of parliamentary sovereignty, which has always been understood to mean that Parliament can pass whatever laws it chooses to and that the judiciary's role is merely to interpret and to give effect to such law. Without going into the naiveté of the notion of judicial passivity in relation to the creation of law that underlies that approach, it may be the case that, as a consequence of the HRA 1998, that the situation may be about to change.

The Act provides that the courts cannot declare primary legislation invalid, but they can issue a declaration that it is incompatible with the provisions of the Convention as contained in the Act. On the issuing of such a declaration, the Government *may* make use of a 'fast track' legislative procedure to amend the existing law to bring into line with the provisions of the Act. In this way, the Act endeavours to introduce a compromise system in which the judiciary still, at least, pays lip service to the principle of parliamentary sovereignty and parliamentary democracy can assert its predominance over an unelected judiciary.

Related to the foregoing, is the difficulty that, although the Act faithfully introduces the ECHR, it has to be said, and past judgments of the European Court have shown, that the source document itself, the Convention, is by no means a straightforward statement of absolute, inalienable rights. Indeed, the Convention is written in such a way as to balance rights against the broad requirements of organising and maintaining a democratic society. Indeed, some of the provisions of the Convention are potentially contradictory. As a consequence, they have to be interpreted. This process of interpretation by necessity passes political power to those who have the authority to interpret its provisions; in this instance, the judges.

Some commentators have expressed concern that that the HRA 1998 will pass such power to an unelected, and unrepresentative, body of judges who are not accountable for the consequences of their decisions. These people tend to see the introduction of the Act as an extension of judicial review and a way for an apolitically conservative judiciary to forestall, or undermine, the decisions of a democratically elected Government. Others, alternatively, see the increase in judicial power as a necessary and welcome safeguard against, what they see as, the ever increasing dominance of an unaccountable, at least in the short term, executive. Indeed, some proponents of this view see the doctrine of parliamentary sovereignty as, itself, being no more than a common law principle that could, in the future, be relied upon in the achievement of a real and equal separation of the powers; with the judiciary exercising real power in relation to striking down what it considers to be invalid legislation.

This whole issue, necessarily, reintroduces a consideration of the representative nature of the judiciary and the way in which its members are selected for office. If they are going to act in the same way as the Justices of the US Supreme Court, then they must open themselves up to scrutiny, and approval, by elected representatives, as those judges do. It is maintained, certainly by the left, that the selection of the judiciary can no longer be left to the arcane workings of the Lord Chancellor's office.

It has been suggested that, as it stands, the Act will provide a means for the wealthy and, in particular, large business corporations, which are legal persons in the eyes of the law, to pursue their interests, whilst ordinary individuals will be left without remedies, on account of their lack of money to pursue satisfaction in the courts. The answer to this might be the establishment of a Human Rights Commission, with the job of advancing awareness and understanding of the Act and with the ability to finance cases which it considers to be in the public interest. Such a Commission would be similar to the present Commission for Race Discrimination, which has proven successful in raising the profile of the abuse that is race discrimination. Although it was the policy of the Labour Party, before the 1997 election, to institute such a Commission to support the incorporation of the ECHR, it has since resiled from that position and no longer sees the establishment of a Human Rights Commission as an immediate priority. As Lord Chancellor Irvine stated, in the House of Lords, and repeated, in the press:

> ... although we have given the proposal much thought, we have concluded that a human rights commission is not central to our main task today, which is to incorporate the Convention as promised in our election manifesto ... we would want to be sure that potential benefits of a human rights commission were sufficient to justify establishment and funding for a new non-governmental organisation.

In conclusion, the impact of the HRA 1998 is bound to be extremely significant, for the simple reason that it represents a signal and significant shift in the way in which the judiciary will be expected to deal with issues relating to the protection of civil liberties. Judges may not be handed power directly to strike down legislation as being unconstitutional; but their indirect power to declare legislation incompatible with the HRA 1998 may be tantamount to such a power, at least to the extent that it would be extremely difficult for any Government to sustain legislation in the face of such a declaration. In any event, however, such a possibility must lead the judiciary into the political arena and, in that space, the judges themselves will be open to the glare of the political spotlight; a scrutiny they have, in the past, made every endeavour to avoid, but one which they may now not be able to deny. From this, it would seem, once again, that the dictates of cost benefit analysis and economic stringency demand that the proper funding of a potentially advantageous system be undermined to a level which precludes its working effectively. Somewhat ironically/cynically, it is, perhaps, of passing interest to note that Lord Irvine himself was once a proponent of such a Commission. This was, of course, before he took on the burden of office. In place of a Commission, the Lord Chancellor has proposed the establishment of parliamentary committees with a specific remit to look after human rights issues; but, here again, some have questioned, not only the effectiveness, but the genuineness of such a proposal. As an example, the director of the reform group, Article 19, actually suggested that:

> The Government's lack of vision on this matter brings into question its commitment to successful implementation of important legislation.

INDEX